THE
BRIDGE HOUSE,
CANNING TOWN

THE
BRIDGE HOUSE,
CANNING TOWN

MEMORIES OF A LEGENDARY
ROCK & ROLL HANGOUT

TERENCE MURPHY

FOREWORD BY
GARRY BUSHELL

Pennant Books

First published in hardback in Great Britain 2007
By Pennant Books
A division of Pennant Publishing Ltd

Text copyright © Terence Murphy 2007
Edited by Brian Belton

The moral right of the author has been asserted.

British Library Cataloguing-in-Publication Data:
A catalogue record for this book is available from
The British Library

ISBN 978-1-906015-02-2

Design & Typeset by Envy Design Ltd

Printed and bound in Great Britain by Clays Ltd, St Ives plc

Pennant Books Ltd
PO Box 5676,
London W1A 3FB
info.pennantbooks@hotmail.co.uk

CONTENTS

ACKNOWLEDGEMENTS

This is my very large and wonderful family, who have made me what I am. And am not. With all the love and thanks I can offer: my dear wife Rita; children: Terence Jr, Glen, Lloyd, Darren, Vanessa; wives and partners: Ann, Linda, Michelle, Wendy, John; grandchildren: Glastra, Glen, Natalia, Lucy, Rachel, Emilio, Chantelle, Lloyd, Ethan, Mason, Ellis. Nikki, Glen Jr, wife and mother of my great-grandson Cassius Terence; partners: Sean (Glastra), Edward (Natalia).

My siblings and their families: John & Eileen, John Jr, Peter, Julia, Rosy. Michael & Jean, Michael Jr, Kerry. Marie & Fred, Suzanne, Tony, Sarah. Jimmy (ex Iris) & Leanne, Kerry, James, John. Ann & William, Melissa, William Jr. All the O'Neils, Murphys, Wrights, Lucys, Gaigers, Davies, Dixons, Lewis.

Rest in peace Mum and Dad; brother John; brothers-in-laws: Joe Lucy, Fred Hammond, Bill Carty; my son Terry's partner Ann and their daughter Rachel.

Congratulation to number-two son, Glen Murphy, who has been awarded an MBE, Member of the British Empire, by her Majesty the Queen. A few years earlier, he was awarded the Freedom of the City of London.

My kids never fail to amaze me. My daughter Vanessa earned her PhD and became a psychotherapist, and I am proud to say that Terry Jr, Lloyd and Darren are also all doing well in their chosen fields.

Thanks to all the bands and all their members who entertained us all for seven years.

Contributions by Chris Thompson, Steve Harris, Tom Robinson, Gary Fletcher, Dennis Stratton, Glen Murphy, Ray Winstone, Steve Fisher, Colin Barton, Laurie O'Leary, Brian Belton, Garry Bushell, Geoff Whitehorn.

Those who have passed on but have left their markers: Rory Gallagher, Ian Stewart, Steve Waller, Steve Marriott, Ronnie Lane, Lou Martin, Nicky Hopkins, John McGeady, All Bridge House regulars.

Photographs: Colin Rapp, John Squires, Jeff Ellis, Paul Bearfield, John McDonald and Brian Hanrahan; www.geoffreyyoung.co.uk

Great thanks to Jeff Ellis, Brian Belton, Cass Pennant.

I first met Jeff Ellis at the Bridge House 1978/79. He was one of those boys who were always there when you needed help. He would be the cashier at the door, barman, roadie, DJ, drummer, guitarist – need I say more? Yes, he became Wasted Youth's photographer and recorded their first video; he also completed all their artwork for the first two singles and the first album *Wild and Wandering*, even touring with them. He was the founder member, with Paul Ballance, of endless bands that included the Sperm Wails. He was the sort of boy you knew would be a success in life.

Fast forward 20 years and I started to write this book, searching through the pictures I had, and on the back of Wasted Youth pictures was Jeff Ellis's phone number. So I rang and got in contact with him; of course, he had moved on and was a university lecturer and computer expert. Every Monday he would come to my offices in Stratford, to teach me how to use my computer, which has made writing this book so much easier. He also designed and set up our website and forum. Oh, I almost forgot, he also digitally records all our CDs from the Bridge House Records days. Thank you, Jeff, you're a pal, forever.

Brian Belton made contact with me after getting in touch with my son Glen, when he wanted to do a book about all the East End professional boxers. During our first meeting, I told him I had almost finished this book; he was very interested and, in boxing terms, became my second in my corner, giving advice and more importantly encouragement to finish it. He also agreed to edit the book for me.

After I had a few refusals from publishers, he introduced me to Cass Pennant, who by now had become a seasoned publisher. He read the script and, I think because it was about Canning Town, and I was a West Ham supporter, he offered me a publishing deal. He and Brian have been very tolerant and helpful; I thank them wholeheartedly for that.

And, lastly, thanks to any relation and friends I may have forgotten to mention. Yes, you!

FOREWORD BY GARRY BUSHELL

The Bridge House in Canning Town was always my favourite venue. It was never glamorous, but it had a heart as big as the neighbouring flyover and it was as important in Britain's musical history as the Roxy was.

I knew it first as a pub Rock venue. Bands like Remus Down Boulevard, Zaine Griff's Screemer, Filthy McNasty and Jackie Lynton's Happy Days were regulars. But Guv'nor Terry Murphy was shrewd enough to run an open booking policy, which meant many major acts played early gigs at the Bridge, from Alison Moyet to Iron Maiden via Bad Manners.

The small atmospheric corner of London's East End was also to play midwife to some vitally exciting youth cults. The new Mod bands of 1979 incubated there, groups such as the Purple Hearts, Secret Affair, the Chords and (spit) the Merton Parkas. The Bridge was always chock-a-block for Mod nights. Many of the 2-Tone bands appeared too. It was a heady time to be young and alive.

When I managed the Cockney Rejects, from nearby Custom House, it seemed logical that they should play at the Bridge too and so the pub became the birthplace for the new exciting Street Punk of the Oi bands. Cock Sparrer, the Business, the Angelic Upstarts, the 4-Skins … these groups, who went on to inspire today's monster bands like Green Day and Rancid, cut their teeth at the Bridge House.

Many American Punk Rockers still make the pilgrimage to E16 to see the site of this temple of spiky dreams.

My association with the pub goes back to the mid-1970s. I first saw Chas & Dave there, and then, almost inevitably, the Tickets.

Canning Town was always a rough area, and many of the pubs were notorious for trouble, but not the Bridge. The Murphy family made sure of that. Bands and punters alike appreciated the good-time feel of the place. I loved it enough to have my 25th birthday party there. Cock Sparrer re-formed for it and Terry's wife Rita even baked me a cake! I enjoyed the evening far too much to remember much about it now. In fact, the many years I spent going to the Bridge have merged into a series of indistinct but happy memories. Stand-out gigs include performances by Steve Marriott, Judge Dread, Iron Maiden and Rory Gallagher. And, for every one of them, the place was more packed than a Toyko tube train.

At one stage, when the Purple Hearts were on stage, the cellar needed emergency building work because the sheer weight of people above was putting a severe strain on the ceiling.

I saw Depeche Mode at the Bridge; they played with their synthesisers mounted on beer crates! And Terry allowed me to put on two Prisoners Rights benefit gigs, which saw the Cockney Rejects at their brilliant blistering best.

[Them beer crates cost 50p each deposit and they used to nick them for their next gig – so they pinched the ones I had pinched; justice was done, ha ha! – Terry.]

Back then, Terry's son Glen, who was to go on to find TV stardom as George Green in the ITV smash-hit series *London's Burning*, was a humble barman. Another son, Darren, played bass in the legendary Wasted Youth, an early Goth, post-Punk outfit with echoes of Syd Barrett. They were better than I gave them credit for, but, hey, you can't be right about everything.

Terry formed his own Bridge House record label, another first, to bring out Wasted Youth's records and other seminal releases like the *Mods Mayday '79* compilation of 1979.

The Cockney Rejects' story is about to be made into a film, so somehow we'll have to recreate the look, sound and feel of the Bridge House. It's going to be tough. The place was a one-off.

I can never drive through Canning Town without looking over at where the venue used to stand and feel a warm glow of nostalgia. Today's charts are full of manufactured muppets and karaoke warblers. The Bridge House stood for something better: real music, raw music. The sounds of the street!

Garry Bushell, 2007

EDITOR'S INTRODUCTION

The Bridge House seems to me something eternal. I was born and brought up in the West Ham area (which would be subsumed into the London Borough of Newham), and the big old pub, the first pub in West Ham as you crossed the border marked by the Iron Bridge, is an image that will, for me and my generation of East Enders, be a location and a spirit perennially associated with the place that made me, London's Docklands, North of the River, East of the Tower.

My grandfather used the pub, after coming out of his shifts as a stoker in the Becton Gasworks in the 1930s. He would go into the Bridge with his mates to quench a thirst from hell; those men worked in Satanic conditions, stoking the great furnaces that made gas for East London, they were forced to labour naked, except for the iron boots that protected the soles of their feet from the blazing embers that fell from the fires. They would drink up to 10 pints of salted water a shift to rehydrate their gasping bodies. This was a breed of steel tough men, whose existence should embarrass those who in later generations would call themselves 'East End hard men.' The stokers of Beckton would have devoured them in seconds.

My dad and mum also frequented the Bridge, taking in pre-Rock'n'Roll entertainers of the late 1940s and early 1950s.

The first time I entered the Bridge House as an 'independent punter' was in 1970. I was 14 years old. I was a big lad for my age (alas, I seemed to stop growing about a year later) and was earning good money, working every hour sent by God when I wasn't at Burke Secondary Modern School, in my dad's timber business. As such, I tended to have much more 'disposable income' than my 'age peers', so was able to began my 'pub life' a fair bit earlier than my classmates. This is what opened the doors of the Bridge to me, going there with other blokes who worked with and for my old man, but little did I know what it would mean; I found that live music is something you catch and live Rock is addictive. I made contacts and friendships at the Bridge that took me right across London in search of the best sounds – the Talley Ho, Kentish Town; the Brecknock, N7, the Golden Lion, Fulham; the Fox and Hounds, North Finchley; the Dublin Castle, Camden Town; Dingwalls, Camden Lock; the Standard, Walthamstow. To the uninitiated, these names sound little more than the usual epithets of the ubiquitous 'local boozer', but to those 'in the know' these were 'venues' in the most colourful sense. They conjured up a sparkling panoply of interest, excitement, passion and plan old-fashioned fun, within a rock'n'rolling kaleidoscope of music cultures, from Mod to Punk, from Skin to New Romantic and everything in between.

But, amongst them all, standing out like a beacon on the banks of Bow Creek, facing the place where Thames Ironworks once roared like thunder day and night, the place that gave birth to West Ham United Football Club, was my base, my lodestone, my initial inspiration and the best of the lot … the Bridge House, Canning Town (or as we who knew it best pronounced it – the Bridge Aase, Kan-nin' Taan!).

This book is about that place, but it is also about the people who live and still reside there. It is about people who played and celebrated music, and the Murphy family who, in running the Bridge right through the 1970s to the 1980s, made this gala possible. That was a time that built on the wonder of the previous decade and resuscitated Rock, making it if anything a much more enduring force in the world. At the centre of all this was the writer of this book, Terry Murphy. Terry would never tell you this himself, but he was the gatekeeper to a complete realm of music in East London. He breathed life into more East London bands and individual performers than anyone else, living or dead.

Terry's lineage in Canning Town goes back generations. Like my own father's father, his grandfather John and his brother Bill were both stokers in the gasworks as were Terry's two elder brothers John and Mick. John built a boxing gymnasium there and, as a youngster, Terry would go and spar with the men who used the facility John had supplied.

Again, like my own family, Terry's grandfather's family lived in Bidder and Woulden Streets, E16. His father Michael was a stoker in the Merchant Navy from the early 1920s until 1944 – four hours on and four hours off. Terry told me, 'All they did was cough up black phlegm.'

Terry's endeavour at the Bridge invigorated and played a big part in creating modern music culture right across the region, stretching from Southend to Aldgate, from the south-eastern banks of the Thames to Hertfordshire and the borders of East

Anglia. The influence of the Bridge House was massive not only in terms of British music, but it also had its impact in both America and Europe. Some people play in bands, some people manage bands, but Terry gave bands the one thing that all bands need to survive: a chance, and often even a second chance, and from this gift so many who played under the broad rafters of the Bridge grew, flourished and enlivened the musical universe. At the same time, in doing this, Terry brought huge joy to a whole generation of Cockneys, of whom I am an appreciative representative.

So please, as you read this book, don't just see it as a chronicle or a record relating to a music pub in East London; it is much more than that. It is not an epitaph, nor does it seek to make the Bridge House a kind of metaphoric monument. It is a social history that shows a clear path to the present and beyond; above all it says, 'the Bridge House rocks on', because that place *was* the music, and the music never dies – Let's rock!

Brian Belton

DR BRIAN BELTON was born and bred in the West Ham/Canning Town area. His father was a stall holder (costermonger) based in Queens Road, E13 and Rathbone Street, E16, just down the Barking Road from where the Bridge House stood. He later owned a timber yard. After finishing his initial education at Burke Secondary Modern School in Plaistow, Brian started his working life alongside his father. He went on to take up professional training in youth and community work and then attended City University to gain his BSc. He completed his Masters degree at Essex University and was awarded his Doctorate by the University of Kent in 2000.

Brian is now an academic by profession, but he is also an

experienced author and social historian. He has taught all over the world and has written more than 20 books (many focusing on his beloved Hammers). He is a senior lecturer at the YMCA George Williams College in Canning Town.

TO THE **B.D.** CLINIC
ALMOST LIVE AT
THE BRIDGE HOUSE
CANNING TOWN

1st SEPT.

BLIND
DRUNK

·FEATURING·
STEVE MARRIOTT · JOE BROWN
RONNIE LANE · ZOOT MONEY
SPUD · PUMP · AND THE BARON

AND TOSSERS GALORE
COME!

PREFACE: BRIDGE HOUSE DAWN

What a day, every single phone call seems like bad news. Two bands have pulled out of next week's gigs with the advert already in the *Melody Maker*; if I can get a decent band I may be able to get it in the *New Musical Express*, or *The Face* magazine. Where's my list of local bands? There's this band that have been asking me for a gig – where's that number? They live just down the road in Poplar, Steve something.

I called the number; yes, they would be delighted to do it.

'What's the name of the band? Oh yes, Iron Maiden. All right, you got Thursday. Two 45-minute sets with a 15-minute break. No, you can't do one set. When the punters are watching the band, they're not buying any beer. Start at 8.45. Yes, we close at 10.30 in the week; soppy licensing laws. I know in Poplar they stay open until 11pm. I see them run from the Bridge House in Canning Town the 150 yards or so over the bridge and "over the border" to the Iron Bridge Tavern for the extra half-an-hour's drinking. You should have named your band Iron Bridge! Ha ha. See you Thursday. Yes, you can have your own PA. We open at 7pm. Sound check over by 8.15. You get £20 but if you bring a crowd with you I will give you more, another £5 or £10. How much is our beer? It's 20p for a pint of bitter, 26p lager. Yes, the band can have a pint when they arrive and one when they finish. I'll get that … See yer.'

Now what about this other night? Whoever rings next gets the gig – it's 6pm and Rita has got my dinner ready.

Glen answers the phone and calls me: 'Dad, there's the IRA on the phone and if they don't get a gig they will blow you up.'

Glen is smiling so I know he's joking. But there was major concern around this time, so you couldn't be too sure. I pick the phone up.

'Is that Terence Murphy?'

'Yes, it is.'

'Er, what a great name, you don't sound Irish.'

'No, I was born and bred in London.'

'My name is McGuinness, I'm managing this band and we are planning to get a tour together and try for a better record deal.'

'I wish you luck.'

'Can you give us a gig?'

'Are you in London at the moment?'

'We are, yes.'

'You can play next Wednesday then. What's the name of the band? What? You Too? No? Spell it. Oh, U2! OK, we open at 7pm. Don't be late. Silly name, though, who thought of that?'

'Oh, you know what these boys are like.'

Good job I asked him how to spell it.

The printers phone to say there has been a big mistake on the new album cover, it's on the artwork, and they have started printing it, but stopped when they noticed it.

I ask who proofread it. They tell me, 'We never did the artwork.'
'OK,' I reply, 'who did? I'll have to find out.'

I tell them to scrap what they have printed and let me know how much it'll cost me for new plates. I will get back to them later.

Wasted Youth have broken down on the way to Coventry in a hired van. The place they hired it from is closed till the morning. I'll phone the promoter, the band will ring back in 10 minutes.

The promoter said they can use the support band's drums. The PA is laid on. When they call back, I tell them to jump in a cab. 'Take the guitars with you, and leave a roadie with the van. I've rung the RAC and said it's got to be towed to a garage.'

None of the roadies can drive, nor can the band. John will have to stay with the van. They need two cabs and that will come to £30 each. They haven't got any money; they've spent last night's money. Where are they? Near Birmingham. I get them to stay there and I'll be there in about an hour-and-a-half. This is lovely! It's the middle of winter – snow and ice everywhere!

It's a Friday and Slowbone are playing so we will be very busy.
The intercom rings. Two bar staff have phoned in. Both their

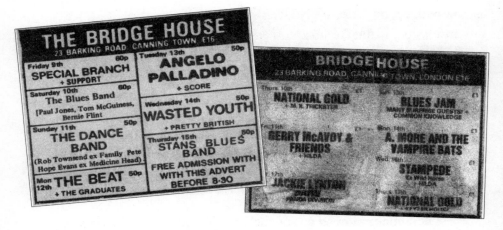

mothers are sick and they cannot leave them. And they're mates as well, what a coincidence! Glen rings round to get replacements, but no luck.

We ring Lindsey, and her mate Lyn, they will help us out.

'Stop Lloyd going to the table-tennis tournament. Terry will be home from his menswear shop by eight o'clock. I have got to go. I'll ring when I am on my way home.'

'We won't be able to hear you. We'll all be in the bar.'

'All right, all right!'

I was back by 11pm to get the crowd off the premises by 11.10pm, as the law at the time required. Wasted had a great gig. The van was repaired the next morning, and they carried on with the tour. I sacked the two bar staff, and got the artwork for the sleeve done (free of charge), only a back plate needed for the album.

Perhaps tomorrow will be a better day …

I've done something I never did before: booked two unknown bands. I hope they can play or my reputation will be down the drain. I should have auditioned the bands first or got a demo tape from Iron Maiden, a Heavy Rock band. But I thought, 'Well, you've got to take chances sometimes.' Won't help if there's no crowd. Might help the bands if they get some record companies interested. If they're lucky, an A&R man might see them.

What a good band Iron Maiden is. A really good well-behaved crowd too: very Heavy Metal. I'll book them again.

U2, a nice band, worked really hard. No chance of making it, not different enough. I might be wrong though, have to wait and see. Yes I would give them another gig.

The bell rings, it's 7am, the brewery are here with our delivery.

'Glen, make sure to count the empties, you know what them drayman are like.'

PART 1

THE BRIDGE HOUSE

THE EARLY YEARS

Well, I am much too old to give you a full description of my whole life, so I will just give you a synopsis. I was born in 1934 and I had three brothers, John, Mick and Jim, and two sisters, Marie and Ann. With our parents, Mick and Marie, we lived in Canning Town, where they had both been brought up by their parents, John and Bridget Murphy, and Joseph and Elena O'Neil. Granddad Murphy worked most of his life in the Beckton gasworks and Granddad O'Neil was, as my father became, a merchant seamen.

My early years were devoted to boxing; at 13, I won the Schoolboy Championship of Great Britain. Then I won two London titles and the ABA Junior Championship of Great Britain. At this time I was working as a fish porter in Billingsgate Fish Market. I then turned professional. I fought twice for British titles and was featured fighting on the opening night of Independent Television; so I was the first ever boxer on ITV in 1955.

A year prior to this in 1954, I had met and married Rita Ann Wright, and at the time of this boxing match Rita was five months pregnant with our first child Terence who was born on 1 January 1956; Glen, Lloyd, Darren and Vanessa were to follow.

Rita's brothers George and Eddie were both professional boxers, Rita's sister Stella was married to the British lightweight champion Joe Lucy, So I had married into a well-known boxing family.

When I retired from boxing, I bought a greengrocery business. I then moved on to other businesses, before getting my first pub – the Rose of Denmark in Canning Town, in 1970 – where I first started to become involved in music. It was a small pub so we could only have duets and solo singers. After three years, I took over a disco pub, the White Hart in Bethnal Green, E2.

In 1975, I moved to the Bridge House in Canning Town, E16. My brother John had run the Bridge House for a few years from 1973 to 1975. Courage the brewery had just made John the new manager of the Royal Oak in Canning Town, where he started the gymnasium above the bar; he even managed to get Terry Lawless to train his boxers there, including world champions such as John H Stracey, Maurice Hope and Frank Bruno.

Courage, the brewery, had put in a holding manager at the Bridge House after John left, but they wanted to change it to a tenancy instead of a management and they offered it to Teddy Haynes, an old boxing friend of mine, who already had two Courage pubs in South London. At the time, I was doing a relief for my brother Mick at the Cock Tavern in East Ham High Street, E6, when in walked Teddy with my best friend Olympic and British boxing title holder Terry Spinks. Teddy wanted to know if I would be interested in taking on the tenancy of the Bridge House. After talking to him for a while, I said that I would like to check it out with my brother first and I would let him know.

In those days, you were tied to one brewery, and pubs were

really hard to get, unless you had proved yourself. So John said, 'Grab it!' and I did.

Teddy and I worked out a deal and we started off at the Bridge House on 22 August 1975.

THE BIRTH OF PUB ROCK

To set the scene for you a bit, after the Second World War, most pubs had a piano in the bar and anyone who could play would have a go and often the 'pianist' or someone else would sing a number. Some of these ensembles were really terrible, but there was an obvious demand for music to accompany the social activity and drinking that pubs offered. So landlords started to find proper musicians and singers, particularly for the weekends. They were often paid for their trouble (although some did it for love) and the guv'nor hoped that the punters attracted by the prospect of a bit of 'quality' entertainment would boost bar takings enough to pay for the performers, who usually supplemented their fee by passing the hat around as well.

This was relatively popular, but in the main it was restricted to Saturdays and Sundays, leaving the pubs few entertainment opportunities for the rest of the week. The small pubs were OK; a few customers made it look busy and produced some atmosphere; in the winter it was a welcoming, warm retreat from the biting cold of the British weather, providing something of a homely ambiance. But the bigger hostelries needed to have a lot of people in to generate anything like this good feeling. And, as, during the austere post-war years, the working-class pub clientele had little in the way of disposable income, weekday drinking was not really an option for most, perhaps restricted to the odd pint after work. This being the case, those who looked to the pub for distraction and socialising made the weekend the time for this.

During the late 1950s, pubs began to provide piped music and juke boxes. With the 1960s came the disco dancers and strippers, which were OK for the smaller pubs. But, from the mid-1960s into the early 1970s, bands really boomed. As the band scene began to grow and the youngsters started imitating their idols, the proliferation of groups looking to push themselves forward meant that there was little opportunity to use the relatively few rehearsal rooms that existed at the time. Of course, the dictates of supply and demand caused the cost of such spaces to soar. But one place that was often available to a struggling band with a little bit of talent and determination was the local pub; this is how the pub Rock started.

I had my first pub, the Rose of Denmark, from 1970 to 1973. It was in Shirley Street, Canning Town, less than a mile from the Bridge House (down Silvertown Way, left before the flyover, opposite the Essex Arms, on the corner of the road that leads to the famous Peacock Gym). Like the Bridge House, it has also been razed to the ground.

While we were there, my son Glen decided to form a band and asked me if he could rehearse in the bar when the pub was closed in the afternoon between 3 pm and 5.30 pm. As always, I said of course.

After about a month, the band came to me to see if I could get them a gig. Glen was 14, the others 15 or 16, not even old enough to go into pubs! They played a couple of times for me, and they were good. So I phoned a few publican pals and got them some Sunday mornings playing for £5 a session. This went well until they wanted more money. We asked for £10 and lost the work. Their big moment came when they appeared at the Barking Assembly Hall supporting a fully fledged orchestra. They won over the audience, but as I was to find out later the adult band got the hump with them and gave them a hard time.

But at this time Glen was really busy with football, boxing and

DJing at the pub, and so the band folded. A few of the other guys later formed a new band and called themselves Toad.

When we moved to the Bridge House pub in 1975, I remembered those rehearsal days at the Rose of Denmark and gave them a few gigs. There seemed to be acres of space to fill at the Bridge House and the costs were much higher – rent, electric, gas, etc.

My first meeting was with the band Remus Down Boulevard (RDB) who had played for my brother John and I had seen them at the Royal Oak. We had big discussions as they had been getting £15 a night and now wanted £20. After a few drinks, I gave in and said they could play Sundays and Mondays. The next band in were Slowbone, who had previously played the Bridge but had left after a row about money and had taken up a residency at the Cart and Horses, Stratford. But I had heard they were good and pulled a big crowd, so I gave them Friday nights. And, when I gave Saturday night to Scarecrow, my first weekend was up and running!

And my first flier was for the month of November 1975:

Sun	Remus Down Boulevard
Mon	Remus Down Boulevard
Wed	Satisfaction
Thurs	Bone Idol
Fri	Slowbone
Sat	Scarecrow

I said I would keep them all on as long as the bar takings did not drop and I kept my word. We went on for a few months, but then Scarecrow had to go. They were a good band with a good singer, and they made a nice album later, but they were Heavy Rock which I was beginning to faze out. It was too much the same, long solos, head bangers and dope smokers. I wanted to change our image and stamp my own signature on the Bridge. But we remained friendly and they came back from time to time to do a gig for us.

During the afternoons in the week at the Bridge House, we would let bands rehearse in the pub and some of their friends would turn up and have a few pints each, so we took a few bob over the counter. As the bands got better, they would ask me for a chance to play their set. All the family, mates and a few onlookers would come along and enjoy the night. They'd tell their mates, people at work and so on, and the next week there'd be a lot more punters. As word spread, more bands would ask for nights and, so, slowly, almost unintentionally, the Bridge House was becoming something of a 'venue'. It was a good start for me, as all the time I was learning about the bands and the music.

After a year or so the rehearsals got out of hand. It wasn't the new bands any more; we had moved on to gigs every night, two bands a night. One afternoon we had Manfred Mann's Earth Band on the stage; Paul Young's Q-Tips on the first floor and Remus Down Boulevard in the cellar. None of the bands was using a PA, so it wasn't that loud, but, when the evening band turned up, they couldn't get in.

Before I took over the Bridge, the set-up had been to have the same band playing Friday, Saturday and Sunday and maybe a band in the week, all heavy hippie bands. I changed this, and got Rock bands in every night except my night off on Tuesdays. We had auditions on Sunday lunchtimes, when between four and six bands would show us what they could do, playing four songs

8

each. If I thought they had potential, I would give them a support slot in the week, with a band that was compatible with them.

We moved through the Heavy Rock, Funk, American West Coast music, to Blues, Punk, New Wave, Gothic and Psychedelic. I was always looking for new sounds, especially after we started our own record company, Bridge House Records, in 1978.

As it turned out, 1979 was a really big year for the Bridge House. We had followed the *Week at the Bridge* album in 1978 with the *Mods Mayday '79* album and released four singles. U2 made their debut for us on 11 December 1979 and Wasted Youth emerged from their nest.

Sadly, this great year was spoiled with some really bad news for my family when my eldest brother John was taken from us in a nasty way at the tender age of 50. He's gone but will never ever be forgotten.

THE STAGE

When we first arrived at the Bridge, the stage was in the upstairs bar. It was around 6ft long, by 7ft deep, and the front was only 6ft from the bar.

I used to ask the regular bands what they thought of the gig, and how I could improve it. It was unanimous: they needed more room on stage. So the old Murphy in me came out! Down the cellar we went, fetched up 20 empty crates, sent George Mears (our resident chippie) to get two 6 x 4 plywood sheets; 4 x 2 crates each end, 6 x 4 over the top and this added 6ft in length at each end of the stage. Bands were then able to set up their PAs at each end.

This worked great until the end of the gig. There was always a visiting guest of the band who wanted to jam, which meant reorganising, and some of them had to go behind the speaker on each end. The crates and plywood were a bit lower than the actual stage. For us, it was quite funny, because the first time they got up there they would trip up the step between the crates and the stage, especially at the end of the night, when they had had a lot of beers. This always got loads of laughs. When Rory Gallagher first came to the Bridge to jam, we warned him about this. He said, 'Ah, not to worry.' So, when he decided to give a few numbers, he ran up to the stage and jumped on it. The only trouble was the ceiling was low and of course Rory bashed his head on the ceiling. This did not stop him though. He went straight into the song. What a performer!

Afterwards, he lifted his long hair up and showed me the big lump on his forehead. As in the old saying, 'It was as big as an egg!' I went and got some ice in a pack. He said, 'Ice is no good without brandy! Get me a double.' So I took a bottle back to the dressing room. He said, 'Aye, that's the way to get rid of the pain.'

When the plywood started to wear out, we got George Mears to build an extension at each end, making it even longer: 40ft long, compared with the 16ft when we first arrived.

At last, the artists were happy. But now the customers started to complain! They couldn't see the bands because of the PAs and they could only hear what was coming out of whatever end they were standing, and, of course, it was so loud now the bar staff couldn't hear what the customers were ordering.

The house PA I had was 1,000 watts and the bands used to add to that. So we started to have lip-reading sessions, with me as the teacher. All we had to do was repeat what we thought they had said and they would nod yes or no.

We got all the little problems sorted out, although we still had a few difficulties. One night, we were really busy; the place was packed, and of course everyone wants serving first. And, of course, we wanted to take their money, didn't we? That's what we were there for. Well, this big bloke at the bar started shouting at my son Lloyd because he thought he should have been served first. Lloyd, who was a young man at the time, had a big temper, and, as this fellow kept on, Lloyd leaned over the bar and walloped him with a great right-hand punch. He was knocked out, but, with the pub being so packed, he just remained standing because all the customers round him propped him up, but were still trying to get drinks at the bar, not realising this bloke was unconscious.

After about 10 minutes, the band were back on stage so the bar was not so busy. This fellow, still in an upright position, came to. Lloyd went up to him, and asked, 'What do you want?'

The now conscious loudmouth answered, 'A glass of orange juice please.'

Well, at the end of the night, this caused a big discussion in the family. I said he swallowed it.

Glen said he thought he was out and didn't remember what happened.

Lloyd said, 'I don't care. I was ready to give him a bit more if he had started.'

Rita said, 'I hope the poor man's all right.'

Terry Jr said, 'Well, I was watching all night and he was with some other blokes, and they ran out the door when the gig ended.'

So we don't know the real answer, but we reprimanded Lloyd, who never took the fellow's money for the orange juice, and fined him a fiver for losing us four customers!

After a couple of years I decided to make the Bridge like a real gig, with dressing rooms, and a nice big stage facing the audience.

In the front of the pub we had the poolroom which was about 60ft x 40ft. We got rid of the wall between the downstairs bar (which was about 90ft x 40ft) and the poolroom. We also took out all the leaded light windows that were behind the bar dividing the upstairs and downstairs.

Now we had a real gig where the audience could position themselves where they preferred to watch. It looked good and was ideal for sound. Everyone could see and hear the bands. Perfect.

But do you now what? The atmosphere was never the same. Even the bands agreed and said they preferred the old stage, which we had left in the upstairs bar. One or two of the bands continued to use the old stage, but, although it was good for the bands, it was no good for the audience, or the bar staff, who did not have to lip read with the new stage.

We kept on and had some really great gigs, but within a few years it was all over, we were out of there. This is the story of some great times and some great bands.

MEMORIES OF THE BRIDGE

Glen Murphy, MBE, Terry and Rita's son and actor, *London's Burning* 1987–2002

My transition from the gentlemanly art (of boxing) to the theatrical art (of acting) took lots of twists and turns, none more so than being a publican's son. My school friends were immensely jealous when I was just 13 and able to glimpse a part of the adult world which was in the main shut off from kids; where mums and dads went in the evening to drink and to listen to music. The drink didn't interest me much at 13. I was in training to become the light-heavyweight champion of the world, just like my dad who was a boxing champion, and the first ever sportsman on

ITV. But the music did capture my imagination, especially live music. Back then my interest was aroused by a guitar-playing duo who did the Saturday-night gigs around the East End. I could not believe you could make the sort of sound from something made of wood and wires, so I started to practise with a broom.

When the family moved pubs to the famous Bridge House, there were proper professional guitarists playing in bands complete with drums. This really did get my interest going. I even bought a real guitar and the broom returned to its former employment.

I started to let it go, as I began mimicking the guitarists I'd observed gigging at the Bridge. I made some noises, that didn't sound primeval so I thought I was really good after the first week. Some school friends asked me to join their band. 'WOW' and I was on the way to becoming not only the world boxing champ, but also the next big thing in music.

However, it wasn't long before I realised that the only reason I was asked was because I had access to a large room and free electricity. But I had read somewhere that you had to suffer for your art. I didn't dwell on it too much, and even learned to play more than one string!

Soon I was really being inspired by some of the bands who had even appeared on the telly.

All sizes and quality of bands came and went at the Bridge House, and you will read all about it, in the following pages, none more so than the greatest guitarist of them all, Rory Gallagher. This really impressed my band-member mates, Ferguson and Steve Mathews, who were about to throw me out of the band for being crap.

Shortly after, the Bridge booked the Blues Band with lead vocalist Paul Jones, who was also appearing in Andrew Lloyd Webber's West End musical *Joseph and His Amazing Technicolor Dreamcoat*. We managed to blag a couple of tickets to see the show, which was great, not only because of the music, but also being in a real West End theatre, WOW!

That was the moment it hit me that I would like to do theatre, and many years later I managed to get on stage (albeit a film stage) and I did have something in my arms but, of course, it wasn't a guitar, it was a fireman's hose.

But it really all started at the Bridge, the acting and the music. Like so many East Enders, the Bridge House was one of my most powerful inspirations and it is the product of the collective achievements of all those that were motivated by what went on in the place, together with the fun and fulfilment people remember having there, that makes the place live on in the hearts of tens of thousands of people.

EAST END FRIENDS

Many people we knew in our early days from the East End have happily gone on to great success, not just the bands, but people who were family friends have done well in different fields. Ray Winstone, a family friend, who was a member of the same boxing club as my sons, and a very promising boxer, has gone on to great success as an actor. Another friend of ours, Bill Curbishley, entered the music business as well and went on to manage the Who and Led Zeppelin and his brother Alan is now West Ham United manager, having managed Charlton for many years.

We really got to know the Curbishleys when Bill met my younger brother Jim when they were 14 years old and they became – and still are – the best of friends. They have had some great times together, and unfortunately a few bad times too. Bill used to love to visit our parents' house in Ravenscroft Road, Canning Town E16. He used to say, 'If I ever get rich, I am going to buy this house.' He was about 16 years old at this time. Well, he is very rich now but he has not bought the house, as he prefers to live in North London.

As a teenager, Bill would go home with Jimmy after a night out, usually with a couple of girls, and creep in, so as not to wake our mum and dad, who were in bed. Bill slept over many a night. He got barred a few times when my father came down for breakfast and all the egg and bacon had been eaten, as Jimmy had to blame Bill to get out of trouble himself.

By this time, I had moved to my own home with my dear wife Rita, in Braemer Road, Plaistow, and Jimmy and Bill would be regular visitors. They were young, handsome and broke most of the time. So round they would come to big brother Terry. I had retired from my boxing career and, like the boys, wanted to make a buck or two. I had many connections on the 'what have we got to sell today sir?'. This was in the early 60s and there were loads of 'long firms' operating, so you could get some really good deals when the time came to wind up the companies. Being reasonably well off, I had the cash to buy big parcels of clothing, hardware, fancy goods and all types of watches. Me and my dear old pal Dave Sammons, who sadly passed away a few years ago, had our own wholesale shop in Barking Road, East Ham E6.

Bill and Jimmy would sort out what they could carry, mainly watches and other small items, in their pockets and go round the pubs and spielers selling the stuff to make a few quid. They were then supposed to come and pay me for the goods, which I don't think they ever did. Jimmy would blame Bill and Billy would blame Jim but they always had plenty of other excuses. When they were broke again and looking for something to sell, they would come out with the old story, 'we will give you our profit on this to pay for the last lot', and I knew they were kidding me.

They were young and learning about life and I knew I would never get paid anyway.

But Bill has paid me back in full. Now, whenever we go out with him, to golf clubs or dinners, the bills are not even mentioned; they are always taken care of and he has made some really big donations to West Ham Boxing Club where Jimmy is the competition secretary.

So thanks, Bill, you're a pal. And do not forget that game at Wentworth you promised us.

A few years later, when the children were growing up and playing football for the schools (I had Terry, Glen and Lloyd playing most Saturdays or Sundays), I would meet Alf Curbishley who was there keeping an eye on his younger brother Alan and my sons Terry and Lloyd, who were both goalkeepers. They would dread giving away a penalty against Alan's team, as Alan was so good at taking the pens. In fact, he was way beyond his years as a footballer, a real born player, who went on to have a great career in the game, even if he did (in his own words) 'underachieve' at West Ham as a footballer, before going into management. He even came close to being England manager.

Alan was a schoolboy with West Ham but, like all East End boys, got himself a job for his pocket money. My brother Jim gave him employment bottling up in his pub in Stepney, and Alan carried on doing this until he signed as a professional for West Ham.

Alf always managed to get a good living on 'what's on offer today sir?' after running a few companies. He became a publican in Plaistow with his wife Pat and brought up her two sons as his own. We had many a nice drink with all his family when Bill came to visit. Perhaps this is where Alf got the flavour, as they say, in the booze game, and sadly he died a few years ago in his early fifties, a terrible tragic death. However, his name lives on. Alf's sister-in-law, West Ham-born actress Carol Harrison, had a son with actor Jamie Foreman and called him Alfie. He was a lovely man and his death was devastating.

The Curbishley family home was just a couple of hundred yards from the Bridge House, so young Paul (Alan, Bill and Alf's brother), who was aware of the family connection, became a regular. His mate, Mickey Harris, played drums for Remus Down Boulevard. Paul, following in his big brother's career footsteps as a footballer, played for West Ham's reserve team with Alvin Martin (now a radio presenter, but he's a former England international and West Ham skipper). Paul would arrive with Alvin and boogie many a night away. They would get in free of charge, as they were on the guest list, and Alan would also come along. Bill and Alf were always pleased about this because they knew I would keep an extra eye on them and keep them away from any bad influences.

We never saw a lot of the Curbishleys' sister Laura around this time. We had become friends with her when her parents used to send her round to Braemer Road looking for Bill when he'd stayed out all night with Jimmy. Laura lives in New Zealand now, and Alan went to visit her for the first time in years when the Charlton supporters bought him plane tickets as a leaving present when he resigned as manager of the club, having been one of the longest-serving managers in professional football. I also got friendly with their father, who was a regular customer at my first pub, the Rose of Denmark (in Silvertown Way, E16). The dear mother of the family I only met a few times, and she would never leave her house.

Well, happily, the Curbs are now doing great. You never get

used to losing a brother, but you have to get on with life. Paul is now training the juniors at Charlton, his sister Laura is with another old pal called Peter and big brother Bill has gone on to be a great success, managing top bands like the Who, Led Zeppelin and others; he is also a successful film producer and has been involved with many major films.

NO TROUBLE HERE

One of the most amazing things at the Bridge was the good behaviour of the clientele. Sometimes we had crowds of Punk Rockers, Skins, Mods, Hells Angels, Hippies and Bikers all in the pub together with hardly any trouble. Our rule was anyone causing trouble was banned forever. I believe the crowds we drew really liked the gigs so they behaved themselves.

We were an East End pub and trouble was always round the corner, but I was an ex-professional boxer, born and bred in Canning Town, and this was a big help to me, as were my four sons, Terry Jr, Glen, Lloyd and Darren. We were good at stopping potential trouble. Any signs and we would be over there before it started; a little chat, no trouble. All the local customers knew my sons and their fathers knew me, so pretty much everyone behaved and we could handle those that didn't. If any of them started, I would tell them, 'Behave or I will tell your father.' I didn't have to wallop many people at all, only a few when there was no other way to get them to leave the pub. We never needed the police.

But we did try to keep the different 'tribes' apart. We would have the same type of music on the same night of the week, for example, Friday, Saturday, Sunday – Rock; Monday – Mods; Tuesday – Punk; Wednesday and Thursday – West Coast Rock. We knew that Punks followed Punk bands and Hippies and Hells Angels wanted Heavy Rock. But Mods used to come to Punk nights and Skinheads would come to Mod and Punk nights, so you would get a small overflow sometimes. The Bridge was a big pub, so generally it wasn't a problem, although on some weeks we would have 2,000 customers in through the door. Our record for one night was officially 950 on the Friday night that the Roll-Ups had advertised that they were disbanding, although the pub was so packed I think even more may have squeezed in.

We were only licensed for 560 customers but Steve Marriott's Blind Drunk pulled 840 on a Wednesday night. Wasted Youth came close and, if we had counted all the liggers, they probably would have held the record. They had gigs all over the place nearly every night, usually in London at places like the Lyceum, the Venue and the Marquee, so the fans didn't have to travel very far.

But overall the best bands were the regular Rockers – RDB, Chris Thompson, Gerry McAvoy, the Roll-Ups, Jackie Lynton, etc. They pulled big crowds regularly on a weekly basis with no troublemakers. So, over the year, they worked out a better average. The younger bands were more exciting and noisier and, although they weren't as good musicians as more experienced bands, we all hoped they would be the stars of the future. I'm glad to say some of them were.

We had started to have the 'battle of the band' nights in 1982 (and they turned out to be just that) with four bands playing nightly once a week, and it was going well. After a couple of weeks, this band turned up from South London with two coachloads of fans. The band went on stage and they were struggling with their sound – out of tune, they were terrible. The crowd started to get on their back, even their own fans.

The vocalist started shouting abuse, kicking out at the fans in front of the stage. I told him to behave himself, but he then threw a glass into the crowd. That was it. He had to go. I pulled the plug on them and fronted them on stage. I told them to get out. They jumped into the audience and started fighting. In we go! We threw them and their fans out. We were battling with them; our policy was never to call the police and we never had minders, so me and my boys, Terry Jr, Glen, Lloyd and Darren, were on our own. Well, three loyal customers helped us out, Mick O'Brien, Dermot and Andy Rowland. We locked the doors when we got them out. They started kicking the doors, throwing bricks through the windows. We got in a group together. I opened the door and we ran at them. We stayed together as a group and, as they came at us, we picked them off. It was a real battle. As we were fighting, I threw a punch and my watch came off. Like an idiot I bent down to pick it up and got a kick full in the face! Mind you, the watch was a rare collector's item, a Gold Omega Constellation. To get it back was worth a kick in the face – only a black eye and busted nose, no problem. We carried on fighting. After about 10 minutes we started to get the better of them. We ended up chasing them, at least 40 people, down the road. They jumped on their coaches, drivers revving up, and were gone.

Quite funny really, seeing seven or eight people chasing 40 or 50 down the road. Our policy at the Bridge was that we were there to stop trouble not start it. Sometimes you have to show your authority and this can start trouble, but you can't let liberty-takers get away with it. We got a call the next day from someone who said they were from an equipment-hire company. They told us they had to pick up the band's equipment that had been left. Well, if this was a hire company, they were the hardest-working men ever; they were in and out in minutes. They were in no danger, though, as we never carried grudges. But we were well prepared in case they fancied a return. Lloyd had got a few of the West Ham United Snipers ready – they all used to come to the pub and my son Lloyd was the best fighter of the lot (says his father).

Still, I should have known when I booked them; the old South Londoners love a fight. Earlier in my life I had done a lot of business 'South of the River' and I believe they are very similar to us West Ham boys.

The only time we ever felt in real danger was when we were invaded by Hells Angels. Once we were really established as a Rock venue, because we needed a break, me and Rita decided to stop having bands on a Tuesday night and have a day and night off. Bill Curbishley knew a married couple who wanted to learn the pub business. He asked me if I would train them so they could learn the trade, and he would then buy them a pub. So I got them to do our relief on Tuesdays. My sons, Terry, Glen and Lloyd, all under 20 at the time, knew everything anyway, but you are never comfortable leaving your children in charge when you are not on the premises.

Things went along fine, they were doing a good job and their takings were on the increase. Then they phoned me to ask for the next Tuesday off. Bill had invited them to a night out with the Eagles who were touring Britain at the time. I said, of course, and my son Terry said he would do the relief that night so me and Rita still went out.

The next day, Terry told me that the pub had about 40 Hells Angels in. As Tuesday was usually a quiet night, we used to block off the downstairs bar to make that evening a bit easier for the bar staff. Young Terry, who was on his own that night, had to go and tell over three dozen Hells Angels that they were not allowed in that bar, and he asked them to leave. He was shocked when they agreed to go into the other bar; brownie points for the Hells Angels and Terry. Nevertheless, I wasn't happy; I had nothing against the Angels, but they had the reputation of being trouble and there is no doubt that customers would stay away in fear of them.

So, no more Tuesday nights off. I didn't blame the relief couple; they stayed on with me and eventually ended up with their own pub.

The next Tuesday, I went down to the pub and there they all were, round the pool table area. As I said, there was no band but we always played our music very loud. There were these two guys dancing, which is not allowed, as, although we had music and a dancing licence, it only covered the stage area. So I went over and told these guys that they couldn't dance because of the licence, and they did stop … until the next record started.

When the record stopped, I said, 'I've told you − no dancing.'

If looks could kill, I'd have dropped dead there and then. I noticed one of them had a sheath knife in his back belt, as many of them did at that time. I had made my mind up that if they danced again they'd have got to go. I was being stupid, but it was one of those things you have to do. My sons were with me, so I was also endangering them. However, I had my rules. I was being challenged and my pride was at stake.

The next record came on, and off they went again, that

shoulder-turning dance, left, right, etc. So, in the middle I went and grabbed both of them.

I heard a voice behind me saying, 'All right, governor, it won't happen again.'

He then told the two Angel dancers to leave the premises, which they did.

He asked me to have a drink with him. He was a bit older than the rest and over the next few weeks we became friendly, passing the time of day. However, I still did not want them in the pub.

I knew that the Hells Angels liked Heavy Rock music, so the next Tuesday I put on the Punk bands. I thought that would make them leave but it didn't. The Punks were very rowdy and on one of these Tuesdays a fight broke out. This Hells Angel asked me if I wanted any help, but I said, 'No. I will handle it.' And I did, thinking, 'Oh, yes, the old moody … help you out for a bit of protection.' But I was completely wrong; he was the nicest man you could ever have wished to meet.

He said to me, 'You don't want us in your pub, do you?'

I answered, 'No, I don't.'

I felt my authority was being threatened. But he shook my hand and told me that he would find somewhere else for Tuesdays. He said they would be back at the Bridge the following week for their once-a-year convention that had already been arranged. This was when all the American and European chapter heads came over, and, as it turned out, it was a great night. He shook my hand at the end of the evening and told me he respected me as he did all brave men. I have never seen him since.

Later on, I asked my brother-in-law Joe Lucy, who had the Ruskin Arms in East Ham (the Hells Angels were there every Friday), if he knew the mystery Angel. He thought the bloke must have been 'The Doctor', and if it was the Doctor, Joe said, he had passed on. I was sorry to hear that; he was a nice guy. It seems his title was more than a mere nickname; apparently, he was a real doctor!

The only man to be barred from the Bridge and who is now a lifelong pal, step up Mickey Boyton, a mate of my son Darren. Mickey had a row with his girlfriend and put his fist through the door window, the old leaded type. He paid for the window, and, although he was still barred, I used to see him lurking around thinking he was keeping out of sight.

We did have trouble with some Greasers; these were the worst of the lot. Not to be confused with Bikers who are also a nice crowd, Greasers are motorbike riders, but greasier and dirty. My old friend Terry Spinks, who had bought a pub in the Brighton area, came to see me at the Bridge with his new bride, his second wife. It was the first time I had seen him for a few years, and we had a couple of drinks and a chat.

As we were talking, in walked these Greasers, and, if Terry and his wife had not been there, I would have got them out straight away. They were on the old stage standing with empty glasses in their hands, and one was holding a broken glass. I ignored them but also kept an eye out. Terry said they had to go to see his dad and they left, but he was back on his own within eight minutes. He knew there was going to be trouble so he got his wife out before coming back to help his old mate out. Loyalty!

I'm glad he came back because we had a nice drink together, but, as soon as Terry had taken his wife out, I went up to these five Greasers, took their glasses out of their hands and slung them out. Little did I know that they had smashed up the toilets in the downstairs bar. Gutless people doing damage when nobody can see them. I'm glad I never knew what they had done or else I would have liked to have had Terry's help. And guess who mended the toilets for me. The up-and-coming apprentice plumber Mick Boyton ... Ban lifted!

So, the Bridge House was what my brother John said to me when I was offered the pub – 'An island in the sky'. There were other small fights, but overall it was a place of peace.

BRIDGE HOUSE RECORDS

The Bridge House became more than a gig when we started the record company in early 1979, and the Bridge had the distinction of being the first pub in the world with its own record company. We were making records to promote the bands, not to make hit records. We hoped they would get some airplay to promote the pub and the company, but we did it mainly for the bands. It was working perfectly – we were having major established bands playing that would pull in the crowds so we could make our living selling beer, and not much spirit. Rock fans just love a pint of beer and a spliff.

And, by making a living, we could help the new bands who were just starting out. This was my buzz, seeing these bands arrive, driven by their parents in dads' cars because they never had any transport. It was tough when after the gig I had to tell them the truth, which I always did, but I would not say, 'Forget music, get a proper job' or things like that. The really new bands generally did cover versions of their favourite songs so I would say, 'Work harder. Start writing your own songs. Rehearse and rehearse some more. Give me a ring in a month or two.'

We would get all the music papers so we would see if they were getting any gigs. Most bands only got one chance, unless they were locals who used the pub or those who were prepared to work at it. We were getting tapes by the dozen every week and, as our reputation grew, we got main bands that were on the circuit who were guaranteed to pull in a crowd. The agencies with reputations were ringing and all the up-and-coming managers were coming to the Bridge. But we still had to sell beer for a living! And, blimey, did we sell some beer at that time! So we made a good living.

The record label actually started over a few drinks at the end of a gig in 1978. The A&R people from the major record companies would listen to the tapes that were sent to their record companies. The bands would keep hustling on the phone to find out if they liked the demo tape. If they did, the A&R would say, 'Where are you playing? I'll come and see you.' They probably said this 20 times a day to different bands, so, if they watched two bands, there were 18 disappointed. The band may have paid for rehearsal rooms for a week, hired a light show, a 1K PA (1000 watts) and got themselves new clothes. All their friends and family would turn up and, of course, no show from the companies. This was happening at least three to four nights a week at the Bridge to many different bands.

There were a lot of bands out there and not that many gigs that the A&R men would come to. It could be months before a band got another gig. So, over those drinks one night with Colin Barton, Chris Thompson's road manager, we started talking about live recordings. He said, 'How about doing a live album?'

He had already spoken to Chris about it and I said, rather than one band, 'Let's do a *week* at the Bridge with a different band each night. We could leave all the equipment up and ready for the next night.'

We sorted out the costs of doing this and we went ahead. The big problem was what bands were going to be on the album. We settled on Filthy McNasty, RDB, Gerry McAvoy Jam, Jackie Lynton, the Roll-Ups, Salt and the Sprinklers. We called it *Live – A Week At The Bridge E16*. We had told the audience well in advance that we would be taking pictures of all of them to go on the inside cover of the album and that we would be accepting orders for the album for a £1 deposit. This, of course, was my devious way of paying for it. My thinking was that they would buy the album with their picture on it, even if they did not like the album.

We needed to make sure that all the bands were compatible with a similar audience. We had a really great week and the Bridge was packed every night. A live recording for an album in a pub was a very rare occurrence in the 70s. In fact, it may have been a first!

'Watch the gig and take it home with you' was my motto. In the first week, we had deposits for a 1,000 records and £1,000 in the bank. We had worked out the cost of the recordings, which was fine, and the cost of the album cover, which was expensive and complicated. We got a major company in, Derek Rubbing Associates, and we asked them to superimpose the pylons on top of the Bridge House. This was to be both our logo and on the front cover. It worked wonderfully but it was costly. Another blow was that there was too much material for one album so the Sprinklers were dropped. We made a gate-fold cover (which was twice the cost of a conventional cover) and put out a 12" album and 12" EP. Jackie Lynton covered one side of the EP. He's a great entertainer. He said at the time of the recording that he was doing one long song so we did not cut him out. This one song was three times as long as those of the other players. He is a great man.

So the six unsigned bands were on vinyl and we were showing the record companies that we could do it. Now we had to prove we could market and distribute the album. The press was good to us; all the major companies were asking for meetings and copies of the album. This was a completely new game for me. I quickly got the knack of playing one against the other in much the same way as they were doing with me.

Brian Sheppard of EMI made the best offer. They didn't want us to sell the records as they were going to repackage the whole thing but they were willing to give us and the Bridge House a credit on the album sleeve. Remember, the album wasn't even out yet. It would mean giving back all the deposits as there would be no pictures of our audience on the cover (which I had promised there would be), although the photos had already been taken. So, should I have taken the money and run or stayed faithful to my family, friends and customers, and carried on running a successful pub? Well, when they found me a year later in the Bahamas, I had spent the £50,000 advance. That didn't matter. They needed me to get back to the pub and start running it again …

Perhaps that's what I should have done, but instead I turned EMI down. My family and friends are worth more to me than money. But if he had offered £75,000!

Another nice offer came in from Freddie Cannon and Pete Hinton at Carrere Records. (Freddy 'Boom Boom' Cannon, was a 'teen idol' and hit-record-making singer/guitar player in the 60s. We still hear his hit songs on the radio to this day.) This deal didn't offer much money upfront but they were going to promote the pub as well the album. At the time they were really strong in Europe. They said we could sell the first 2,000 with our own original presentation. They also wanted to change some of the artwork and promote the venue as the best gig in London. They were going to overlay a picture of the Bridge House on an image of Tower Bridge and the Tower of London; the Europeans would love it. The Tower Bridge in Canning Town, London E16!

But all these meetings were taking a lot of time. By now, Trident had cut the album and the artwork was finished. The orders kept coming in, every shop in London wanted copies. So I decided to go with the flow and do it myself. It was a great time, loading the boot up with records, going round the shops, putting the posters up, being interviewed and still selling them every night in the Bridge.

With the buzz of the album, we were busier than ever in the pub. More bands were calling for gigs, so me, Chris Thompson and Colin Barton formed Bridge House Records Ltd. and Bridge House Music Ltd.

It was around this time that I phoned the *Guinness Book of Records* to find out if we were the first public house in the world to have its own record company. They entered our request and said they would get back to me. Well, the reply was disappointing. They said, yes, we *were* the first pub to have its own record label, but until another pub had one it was not a record. I am sure within the last 20 years another pub must have had a label, I must check it out. But at least we were the first.

Things were good, the pub was busy selling records, bands were hustling, not only for gigs, but also wanting to sign to the record company.

When Chris, Colin and I first formed the record company, instead of continuously hiring mobile recorders, I decided to buy my own. We found a really good van that had been sound-proofed with proper floors and ceiling. It was great. It was like a big room in a house, carpeted out and complete with a kitchen. It was nearly new and cost me £3,500. This van stayed outside the Bridge for the first six months waiting to be equipped by Colin. Chris took it round to some studios and I never saw it for a year. I was waiting for Colin to buy the mobile recording units. This never happened. The van got plenty of work, but of the wrong kind. I wonder why they called it the mobile nest! It was a good job there were no tape recorders available.

I later sold the van for £2,000 and put Wasted Youth in the studio to make an album. With cash upfront, we got a better deal.

When Chris Thompson was touring in Germany with the Manfreds in 1978, a distribution company contacted him and placed an order with him for 5,000 copies of the *Live – A Week At The Bridge E16* album. We had to negotiate a new deal regarding the costs. It was a large order so we came down to their figures (about £1.60 each), but we still made a profit at that price. We had just pressed 2,000, so we sent them straight away; they had to wait for the rest. It worked out better for us because we got the money for the first consignment before sending the next. They were a big distribution company but they were strangers to me so better safe than sorry, but it turned out fine anyway. We did a lot more business later with the Wasted Youth albums.

Chris Thompson had by now almost got the sound he was looking for, so, after a tour with Manfred to promote their new album, Chris took time off to tour the States with his new band Night. What a great band, a Top-20 single in America with their first try. They had signed to Richard Perry's label Electra.

When Colin Barton also went with him, the record company became a one-man show. I called in John McGeady to help in the office, booking the bands. He was in a band called the Tickets, so he became Johnny Tickets. He and Ken and Andy Scott were Punks. They had their first release on the Roxy album from the club of the same name. It wasn't long before he started helping with the label. He was young, played guitar and had a good ear for the younger bands coming through. Needless to say, our third single was 'I'll Be Your Pin-up', by the Tickets. This single made up their minds that they all had to move on. The Punk thing had started to run out. Andy joined the Cockney Rejects, John became full time in the office. Ken was on the loose ...

THE BRIDGE HOUSE PYLONS

When we formed Bridge House Records, we decided to make the logo, as if the pylons were coming out of the Bridge House roof and the power from those pylons was needed, because of the power the bands were using. The first logo read 'The Bridge House Blast' – it was all about power.

They had pulled down really big chimneys at the gas works where all the coal was burned to give off energy, but over the whole of that part of Canning Town where the Bridge House stood there were many pylons. When we first went to the Bridge, the council put in double glazing and air conditioning. While we were chatting, the fitter told me, 'You know this is to keep the fumes out, not because of the noise.'

I thought they had put the double glazing in to keep the racket of the flyover traffic down (Canning Town flyover was almost on the front doorstep of the pub). This started me thinking, Why? Of course! The Big C! It use to be consumption (TB) in the 1930s, then it was cancer. My father, a Canning Town working man born and bred, had died from cancer in 1967, at the tender age of 60. He also lost two brothers to this terrible disease.

And here I was being told that the council are trying to keep the fumes that could possibly cause this terrible disease out of my home. So is it safe to walk the street? I had my wife Rita, sons Terry, Glen, Lloyd and Darren and daughter Vanessa, Glen's wife Linda, my grandchildren Glastra and Glen Jr to think about. I thought, 'I am out of here!' And this is the very real reason why we left the Bridge House. I think I was right. Almost 20 years later, I read an article by Sir Richard Doll, in the *Sunday Times* under the headline: 'PYLONS ARE CANCER RISK OFFICIAL'. High-voltage cables have been officially linked to cancer for the first time. A study shows that children living near them run a small but significant increased risk of falling victim to leukaemia. Charged particles emitted from the power cables, called 'ions', may be inhaled – Sir Richard thinks there could be a link.

The electricity association, which represents many of Britain's power generators, said there is no concrete evidence that the electric and magnetic field generated by power lines cause cancer. However, health risks, no matter how small, need to be taken seriously.

MANAGEMENT AND PUBLISHING

Tom Watkins had a really good band called Grand Hotel – I think around 1976/77. He would turn out to be the master of management and went on to be very successful with the Pet Shop Boys, Bros and many more. I learned a lot from him. He would make sure the bands looked very smart and were well behaved. Grand Hotel's line-up was Colin Campsie (vocals) (who was to be part of the Quick and Giant Steps and be closely involved with, but was not a member of, Pop band Go West),

Rob Green (guitar), George McFarlane (bass), Junior Woolway (drummer) and Ivan Penfold (keyboards). It just didn't happen for Grand Hotel. Colin got a couple of hit numbers later and he married a great singer called Beverley Craven and became her manager. Rob Green joined the Roll-Ups.

Tom Watkins would get the bands to sign management and publishing contracts with him and would then get them a publishing deal. This gave him the money to promote the band, which he did admirably. But I know publishers don't give anything away, and they would hook you by saying, 'We believe you have got something, we will give you a three-year deal, worth £160,000. If and when you get a record deal, sign here and we will help you to get a deal.'

After signing, you read the contract – 'For the first album in the first year we will give you £4,000; for the second £6,000 and £10,000 for the third. The second year, £20,000 for each album. The third year we will give you £40,000 an album for two albums.'

Of course, you come out delighted. But you still haven't got a penny in your pocket. Remember, if your manager or the publisher doesn't get you a record deal, it is all null and void. If you get the record deal and the first album fails, they don't take up the option in the contract so you owe them the advance plus any money they have spent on your behalf. Generally, you don't have to pay it back, as they have got the publishing rights on all the songs on the album and they can try to get other bands to cover your songs. If you get a hit, they will take their money back first, before you will get a split of the royalties.

It might sound as if I am anti-publishers, but I'm not at all. A writer needs a good publisher or else you don't get paid for your songs. There is the PRS (Performing Rights Society) who do a good job, collecting your money. The trouble with this company is, when you stop writing songs, they discontinue the contract.

The three-year deal I had with Martin and Coulter was perfect. I never earned any money but I got a great education. We published in the region of 200 songs, and we're hoping to revive some of them when we got the Bridge House revival project going. My son Darren is getting back into the swing of music once again and we have our own website, www.thebridgehouseE16.com, and Forum to keep in touch with everyone. Perhaps, for old time's sake, Bono or Dave Gahan will cover some of our numbers. Well, we can hope, can't we?

Jazz Summers was another manager I became friendly with. He would regularly visit the Bridge looking for new talented bands. He also looked for pubs that had a nice room with plenty of space and would promote his own gigs. This way he could get the bands at the venue to play and, if he liked them, he would sign them to his management. The hard work he put in paid off in the end when he discovered a band called the Young Executives. Whether it was Jazz or his partner Simon Napier Bell who discovered them I don't know, but they ended up being the band's joint managers and renamed the band Wham: George Michael and Andrew Ridgeley.

While sorting through some old demo tapes that were sent to me at the Bridge House, I recently found one with the name Young Executives on it. I wonder if it is George and Andrew. I will have to get an expert on the case to find out. I have in the region of 1,000–2,000 tapes that were sent to me. It would be interesting to find how many and who amongst all those who made those recordings broke through. I might attempt it one day but it'll be a lot of work because a tape we have by a particular band may not be the name the band that laid down the recording.

Jazz Summers went on to manage Lisa Stansfield and Yazz (Yasmin Evans) who he made into a star and then married her. They were later to divorce.

Jazz had a bet with Dave Edwards that Dave couldn't form a new band and perform new songs in two weeks. He did and Jazz knocked him for the fifty quid.

Ex-CIA investigator and FBI (Frontier Booking International) agent Miles Copeland, father of the Police drummer Stewart Copeland, also came to the Bridge looking for new recruits for his management company. One of the bands I remember was the Beat, who I think were from Birmingham, and were one of the new 2-Tone Ska bands. They had a new sound that seems to have started in that area when UB40 started a modern version of the old black Reggae of the early 60s. They were a good upbeat, exciting band and it didn't surprise me when they went on to be hit makers. I don't know if Miles ended up signing the band. His interest in them certainly helped their cause. There was a lot of media interest at the time, and all the music press were around the pub. Miles did not stay very long. The drink I bought him was the only one he had. A wave of the hand and he was gone. He missed Public Enemy No 1 that night. On his toes Skully!

John Bassett was another regular at the Bridge. He played guitar, wrote songs and managed bands. He also had his own recording studio in Selbert Road, Forest Gate. We used his studio a lot. Depeche Mode did their first recordings at John's studio and Stevo, from Some Bizarre, recorded there as well. Chris Thompson produced some great demos for Wasted Youth at John's place. In fact, we used some of them as masters and released them. Chris captured their sound beautifully.

MARTIN AND COULTER, MEWS MUSIC, BILL MARTIN, PHIL COULTER, RICHARD GILLINSON, BERNARD BROWN

After we formed the record company, it made sense to have a publishing company. This is where the money is made in the music business. Bill Martin and Phil Coulter were hit writers going back to the 60s when they wrote 'Puppet on a String' for Sandie Shaw, a Eurovision Song Contest winner. They also wrote 'Congratulations' for Cliff Richard. These two alone sold 10 million copies throughout the world. Dana's 'All Kinds of Everything' was another Euro winner for them. They also wrote 'My Boy', a hit for Elvis Presley, as well as hits for Bay City Rollers, the Dubliners and many others.

Richard Gillinson was the dynamo in the office. He did not miss a trick. He was later to get an Oscar for some film music. As soon as he heard about the Bridge House recording live albums, he became, at my invitation, a regular. We had missed getting the publishing on the *Live – A Week At The Bridge E16* (BHLP.001). Chris Thompson, as producer of the album, originally told all the artists to use the songs they played best. But, as most of these were cover versions of already published songs, Chris then told them to keep their best songs for when they signed a major record deal. At around this time, original songs were wanted, so, if you got record company interest, you would also get publishing companies after you. There's big money if you are successful. The public were fed up with cover versions and wanted to hear new original songs, written by the new bands.

Remus Down Boulevard, the Roll-Ups and Jackie Lynton all played original songs. For me, on this album, this was the sensible thing to do; get your own song heard. They would soon get their own record deals. If we'd had some publishing for the first album, they would have got us more radio play, which was difficult for us because, being live, you also had the noise of the audience on the recording and, as the radio presenters say, they are not very radio friendly. If it's a good song, it will get played by someone. When a writer finishes a new song, they own all the rights to that song. When – if they're lucky – it is played on the radio, the writer would be paid £30 or more every time it was played. When the record company released it, the writer would get Mechanical Rights (MCPS), say 5 per cent of the price of the record sale, for being the writer. They would then get their percentage of the sales of the record from the record company generally about 16 per cent. If the writer is in a band, this is split between them. If it's a solo act the writer would get it all.

It's extremely hard to get radio play, so you get a good music publisher to do the hard work for you. For that you would get approximately 60 per cent of what the publisher gets. They are professionals and know their job, so there are two different entities here: the record company, who record and make the records, and the music publishing company who push the songs, and sometimes get other artists to cover them. When a record is covered, they do not get any publishing money, the original writer gets it. As an example, on an 11-track album, Bridge House Publishers had nine tracks, the other two being published by another company. If only Bridge House music songs were played on the radio the company with the two tracks would get nothing and the MCPS 5 per cent would be split; let's say £11 royalties came in, Bridge House would get £9 and the other company £2.

With our second album, *Penfriend*, by Dogwatch (BHLP.002), we had six songs out of eight published. Paul Ballance, the singer in this band before leaving to form the Warm Jets, had the other two songs published. The next album, *Mods Mayday '79* (BHLP.003), we had 12 out of the 15 songs published, Secret

Affair having the other three. With *Low Dives for High Balls* by the Roll-Ups (BHLP.004), we had two tracks (the single 'Blackmail' and 'Cover Girl') of the 10 tracks on the album published. With Gerry McAvoy's *Bassics* (BHLP 005), we had nine songs out of 11 published. Wasted Youth had all original songs which were published by us. The only cover they performed was 'Real Good Time Together', a Lou Reed song. Wasted made four albums for us: *Wild and Wondering* (BHLP.006), *Beginning of the End* (BHLP.007), *Inner Depths* (BHLP.008) and a *Live* album (BH.100). We also released 15 singles and an EP called *Arrods Don't Sell 'Em*, by Zorro (BHEP 1a) (the song was about Harrods not selling condoms!).

We arranged for the band to play this tune outside Harrods on a Saturday morning, and we got all the press and TV cameras there. The band was due to turn up on the back of a lorry and play. But they never turned up! Can you believe it? Things like that make the job hard work. The band who had sent the finished tape down were from the Midlands and, as I made the record, I thought, 'It's a gimmick, yes, but let's give it a try.' It never worked. I wonder if Harrods sell them now … condoms, I mean, not the record.

There were more recordings. The Governors were a good band. They were to be produced by Phil Coulter. This was a major step forward, with him being such a well-known producer. We had signed them to a full record and publishing deal. Phil came to the Bridge House to see the Governors live. He liked them and asked me to give them a few more gigs before taking them into the studio so that they could work on some ideas he had given them. Phil produced a really good single, using strings, brass, backing vocals. The song's title was 'You Give Me No Choice'. I wanted to release it straight away but I was overruled. They would get a major label's deal with a big advance to cover costs, etc. I couldn't argue, it's what we all wanted. They never got the deal. The single never got released, and the band split up a month later. That's the trouble with major companies; they never tell you what's happening. Why? Because they don't know. Big meetings, 'we will do this', 'you do that', 'ring me next week', 'we'll have lunch', and so on.

Anyway, I'll release it soon on the Bridge House singles collection. Jeff Ellis is soon to start digitally remastering them. So that's something to look forward to for all our loyal customers.

The deal we had with Martin and Coulter was, on reflection, the right deal for us. We were new to the song-publishing game. Bridge House Music Ltd. signed to Mews Music Ltd., a subsidiary of Martin and Coulter, with a 50 per cent share of the publishing. We had a three-year deal. When this finished, we were demanding, and getting, a 70/30 per cent split our way. We had learned the game. When we first started publishing, I would just ring Bernard Brown who would do all the paperwork involving the Mechanical Copyright Protection Society and the Performing Rights Society. I would get the forms the next day, get the bands to sign and it was over. We also signed life deals with other bands. At the start of a contract, you say to a client, customer, stranger, best friend, 'We're mates. We will have an even 50/50 split.'

But 50 per cent of our 50/50 with Mews Music, when we passed on the 50/50 to our songwriters, meant they were getting 50 per cent of our 50 per cent, i.e. 25 per cent. I am still giving them a 50/50 deal from my percentage but we both end up with 25 per cent each. When I signed the contract, this was not pointed out to me, and we just didn't read the small print. I'm not suggesting in any way that this was sharp practice; this was the normal first-time contract which I had gladly signed.

Bridge House Music enjoyed three years of a good

relationship with all at Martin and Coulter. Bernard Brown was a very fair, astute and wonderful man. I still speak to Richard Gillinson when I have a problem. I would have liked to get to know Irishman Phil Coulter better. Scot Bill Martin was certainly the hard man of the business. He gave me £5,000 for a live album, saying to me, 'You know this is a piece of shit.'

I just took the cheque and said, 'At this price there's a lot more where that came from!'

He had a deal with a major company where he had to give them an album every six months. He would have been getting around £30,000 – although I'm only guessing – and it would have already been banked. His deal had come to an end and one more album was needed to fulfil it. We had almost all the publishing on the album but, alas, the album never got its major release. It probably cost around £2,000 to make so at least I got my outlay back. We also split the balance, £1,500 each, with the band. We released the album and made some more money. For that type of music, it was a good album, a true sound of the band, whatever Bill says. We all made some money, so thank God for all that shit!

Bill used to organise the Bob Hope Golf Classic tournament every year. He gave me a signed copy of Jack Nicklaus's book of golf instruction with audio cassettes. I still have it, read it every week and play golf three times a week. Thanks, Bill!

Phil Coulter left the company in 1984 when they sold the building; they were in on the south side of the embankment. We had moved on and we all lost touch until I called Richard, when my daughter Vanessa was producing a musical with some great tunes, and we got Richard down to have a listen. Richard's own company is called Lion Heart Music.

We have in the region of 200 songs published. We are having another listen. There must be a hit song in there somewhere (he prayed!).

SOUNDS INSANE THEATRE COMPANY

My son Glen showed early signs of the determination that would set him on the path to his successful acting career. He had been involved helping out on a few of the record productions, and he came home from boxing training one night and said, 'I have spoken to Tony Burns, my trainer, and we would like to make a record.'

I said, 'OK. Who is going to pay for it?'

'You are,' Glen replied.

'Thanks!' I said. 'What song are you going to sing?'

Glen told me, 'I am writing a song.'

That's confidence for you. Well, he did write the lyrics with a lot of help from his wife Linda. He called in Lea Hart from the Roll-Ups who arranged and produced the song with him. The song was called 'Jab and Move' and was credited to the Repton Boxing Club. It was a radio hit, and they got two 10-minute slots on the BBC *Nationwide* TV programmes, interviews on Radio

London and plenty more airplay. It was a great example of Glen's determination to start a project and, more importantly, finish it. Of course, he had his bit of luck by inviting me to be on the record. It was my recording debut and he let me pay for all the recording and presentation. Was this the sign of a young man who would go far and maybe become a star?

Later on, Glen asked me to form a theatre company at the Bridge and kindly made me a director and the secretary no less ... which meant all the paperwork was down to me. Well, as all fathers know, you must help your kids to achieve their goals in life. This had all started while his future was almost assured. He was at the time an international boxer with the Repton Boxing Club and was sparring with all the world champions at the next pub along from us, the Royal Oak, managed by my brother John and his lovely wife Eileen and their family, John, Peter, Julia and Rosy. We had to bar Rosy for fighting at the Bridge!

Having made sure there was no opposition from the brewery, John had persuaded Terry Lawless, the fight promoter and manager, to build a boxing gym in the upstairs bar. Terry Lawless was a classroom companion of mine at the age of 11 at St Bonaventure School in Forest Gate, and he had built a great stable of boxers ably assisted by Frank Black. Glen was training and sparring here with the likes of John H Stracey, Maurice Hope, Kirkland Laing and many more then current and future world champions. At that time amateurs were not allowed to spar with professionals, so we had to keep it quiet, but Glen was more than holding his own with these boxers and he was offered good contracts to turn professional by all the managers who saw him sparring. I thought our plan was for Glen to stay amateur and win some titles, then go to the Olympics before turning pro. We talked boxing all the time.

Glen was training at Repton one night when a director of a theatre group walked in and asked Tony Burns, the trainer, if any of the guys would like to help him in a play he was putting on in Aldgate at the Old Half Moon Theatre. Just shadow boxing in a make-believe gym. All the guys were up for it, but, to quote Glen, 'They chose me first because I was the best looking.'

He stayed for one year and was hooked. When the play finished, he came home and said, 'I'm not boxing any more. I am going to be an actor.'

I was shocked, but he had done this before. He had been a brilliant footballer, playing for West Ham, Chelsea and Charlton as a junior. One day he came home and said, 'I'm going to be a boxer. I'm not playing football.' So I just thought, 'Here we go again.'

Later, Glen and his wife Linda were invited by one of our regular performers Paul Jones to see him in a big musical in the West End, *Joseph and the Amazing Technicolor Dreamcoat*, I think. Of course, that made him even more determined to make it in the acting game.

The first request by Glen was to put a play on Sunday mornings. We had stopped the auditions by then, so I said, 'Sure.' The first Sunday he had the MP for Newham and the Mayor sitting in the front row of seats. Where he got the seats from I will never know. He had about 60 and about two-thirds were full. And there he was on stage learning his new trade. This play ran for four weeks. Then he came into my office and said, 'Can I have your Tuesday nights? It is your night off. I think I can make it work.'

The Sunday lunchtimes had taken more money than we did with the bands, but at first I said, 'No, Glen, this is a Rock venue.'

He came back at me, as persuasive as ever: 'We have got a really good part that we would like you to play. It's a really tough part.

We were thinking of asking Bob Hoskins if you won't do it.'

Well, flattery will get you everywhere. 'Oh all right, Glen,' I said. 'But I am not wearing make-up.'

So there I was in the play, which was playing to a packed house, including family and friends, etc. From behind the stage, my part was to kick the door in and punch and kick our friend Frank Scinto while shouting and hollering. Well, I hadn't told anyone that I had a part in the play, and my two sisters, Maria and Ann, who were in the audience, thought I was serious! Ann, my baby sister, even started to cry, thinking I was going mad and perhaps that I had too much to drink. But we had a good laugh about it afterwards. Ann's husband, Bill Carty, said to her, 'Stop crying. It wasn't that bad a performance.'

Glen went on and built the quiet night up with different plays every four weeks, producing and acting in them. He performed in a musical called *Jailhouse Rock* in which he played the lead role and I believe (being his father) that he was better than the original singer. I can't remember the bloke's name ... Elvis something?

Managers and agents started to come to the Bridge, and needless to say Glen was offered a major part in a play in Stratford. No, not the home of Shakespeare, but Stratford in London E15. At first he said he would refuse it and carry on with the Tuesdays at the pub, but he knew I wouldn't hear of this. It was a chance for him to go forward. All I said was: 'Is there a part in it for me?'

When that play finished, he was booked to appear in another play at the Soho Polytechnic, in London's West End. He has since gone on to make a good career for himself in film and television playing many different roles. He was in *London's Burning*, a very successful show, for 15 years playing George Green. He has also produced and acted in *Peter Pan*, where, of course, he was Captain Hook.

PART 2

THE BANDS

ROCK BANDS AND
EAST END SOUNDS

The story of the Bridge House is bound up with the story of the bands, the bands made the music, but the Bridge House made the bands.

REMUS DOWN BOULEVARD (RDB)

RDB were the first band to play for us when we took over the Bridge. They were a really great Rock band and always packed their home gigs at the Bridge, but, unfortunately for them, they appeared at a time when everyone was looking at the New Wave of music.

We put on a special gig for RDB on a weekday afternoon in 1978 so that Jonathan King, head of record company UK Records, and his brother could see the band live. There was no audience at all. Jonathan King left his Rolls-Royce outside and someone broke into it and stole some documents, radio and tapes, but we made some enquiries for him and got the documents back. He loved the band and booked the Marquee Club for a live recording and signed them to his record label. We packed the place out, coachloads of us.

At this time, the record deal that King had with EMI was coming to an end, so unfortunately RDB's album was never released, but they signed a management deal with Colin Johnson, Status Quo's manager, and they toured all over Europe and Britain with Quo.

As with all management companies, Johnson wanted to change things. Ron Berg was brought in on drums and Gerry Cunningham on bass and these two excellent musicians are on our live album. But the real line-up for Remus Down Boulevard was: Dave Edwards and Dennis Stratton (vocals, guitars), Mickey Harris (drums) and Steve Gough (bass). This was the original band that played for me on my opening night and re-formed to perform on the last night, seven years later, when we closed the pub.

Steve had a very lucky escape one night; when playing, he got electrocuted when he plugged his guitar into the wrong amp. We rushed him to hospital, and thank God he survived. Linda Lewis was a regular at the pub who always sang a few songs for us when she came in, and her brother Keith became the bass player with RDB while Steve was recovering from his accident. Linda's husband Jim Cregan also used to play for us when he was off the road with Rod Stewart's band.

Dennis Stratton ended up joining Iron Maiden and toured the world with them as their guitarist. Dave Edwards and Dennis are still playing and in big demand locally. Dave has toured America with a recently formed Country band. He had a sensational voice and should have made it big time.

RDB's management would not let them play at the Bridge House because they were promoting them as a headline band. They were doing big gigs and I understood their motives, so, for the next few months, on Sunday and Monday, we had the DD Band, alias Dave Edwards and Dennis Stratton! They had their own crowd so it didn't make any difference to us and the band would rather play a gig than have to go to a rehearsal studio. This was one of the bands who did actually put me first. The only time they let me down was when my family put on a surprise birthday party for my 60th, as they already had a gig that night. They did phone the party at one o'clock in the morning and that was 12 years after they closed the Bridge. Good guys.

While I was writing this book, Dennis sent me some of his recollections about the Bridge House.

MEMORIES OF THE BRIDGE
Dennis Stratton, RDB

The Bridge House played a really big part in my musical life. This is where I had watched Snafu, Freedom, Power Pack and many other bands when I was a young lad, hoping one day to be in a band. From about 12 years old, I had been mucking about with the guitar, singing and writing songs. As we progressed, my first serious band was called Harvest; we had two guitars, bass and drums. We got a gig at the Coach and Horses in Stratford. Me and my college mate Steve Gough got the band together. This is where I first met Barry Hart, the lead vocalist and guitarist in his band Slowbone, who played at the C&H regularly. At this time we were doing covers of other songs, like 'In the Summertime' (Mungo Jerry) and the Beatles' 'Hey Jude'. Things were not working out, so we formed a new band, me and Steve that is, called Wedgewood. We had Roger

Diamond on drums and Jeff Terry on keyboards. We started to do better songs like Elton John's 'Love Lies Bleeding', dramatic songs. We lasted a couple of years. We then heard of Dave Edwards, who was a great singer/guitarist, with his band the March Hares, so me, Steve Gough and Dave Edwards formed the band Remus Down Boulevard. We got a great drummer called Johnny Richardson, who had been doing well with a band called Blockade. We persuaded him to play with us. We rehearsed for a couple of weeks, and got our first gig at the Bridge House, Canning Town E16, and we went down a storm, packing the pub out! It was great! This is where we had been longing to play, all of us being Canning Town people. We were playing raunchy Rock with a lot of harmonies and big guitar riffs. We were lucky that Terry Murphy had seen us playing at his brother John's pub, the Royal Oak, also in Canning Town. Terry gave us the Sunday and Monday nights, at the Bridge House. Word got round that we were a good band who pulled a crowed every time they played, so we were on the circuit – the Greyhound and the Golden Lion, in Fulham, etc.

The head of UK Records, Jonathan King, arranged to see us at a special audition one Monday afternoon. Him and his brother arrived in a big white Rolls-Royce, which impressed us. He quickly signed us up and booked a gig at the Marquee, in Wardour Street, in the West End, to record a live album. The place was packed and there were many fans from the Bridge House who had come in coaches to see us. It was a great night. The recordings came out and they were (as we were told) brilliant! This great night was spoiled when Jonathan's distribution deal finished and the album never got released. Jonathan went into production and it was shelved. Terry Murphy later called their office to try to get permission to release the album on his Bridge House record label, but was refused. They said they might release it themselves at a later date.

In the meantime, we had signed a management deal with Colin Johnson and Quarry, a big company that managed Status Quo, Rory Gallagher, Jackie Lynton, Snafu, Nutz and Kokomo. We toured Europe with Quo for three months non-stop! It was great. We also played with the other bands, most of whom we had met at the Bridge House: Bobby Harrison, Mick Moody, Snafu, Jackie Lynton, Steve Waller and Kokomo.

We asked to play on the live recording of *Live – A Week At The Bridge E16*, a compilation album of all the favourite bands that played there. A lot of the bands did covers to save their original material, but our two songs were our own. I wrote 'Only For You' and Dave Edwards and I co-wrote 'Gun Runner'. It is a great album. The last time I was in Japan at a record signing, a fan came up and asked me to sign this album. I was amazed. This was 20 years after it had been recorded! They tell me it has become a rare collector's item and they are worth hundreds of pounds now. Jackie Lynton, Chris Thompson, Manfred Mann's lead singer Steve Waller, Kokomo, Lea Hart's Roll-Ups and Rory Gallagher player Gerry McAvoy.

The Bridge House was good to me over the years. Steve Harris had first seen me playing there and asked his manager, Rod Smallwood, to get me to join Iron Maiden, which I did!

GERRY MCAVOY'S JAM

I met Gerry McAvoy for the first time when he started to come down on RDB nights in 1976, and we soon got him up on stage and jamming. A great friendship was soon to develop and we had some great nights with Gerry McAvoy's Jam.

Gerry was a Belfast-born Irishman who started off in the music business playing in a band called Deep Joy. They did many gigs supporting Taste, Rory Gallagher's first band. Both Taste and Deep Joy decided to finish around the same time and have a think about their future. Gerry got a call a while later asking him if he wanted to come to London and have a blow with Rory. Gerry was on the next plane. He started to rehearse with Rory and went on to play with him for the next 12 years without ever being asked to join the band or sign a contract.

Gerry, Rod De'Ath and Lou Martin made up the Rory Gallagher Band. When Rory wasn't gigging, they often used to play for me at the Bridge House as the Gerry McAvoy Jam, and, in fact, it was at the Bridge House that Gerry first introduced me to Rory. The Gerry McAvoy Jam included Steve Waller (vocals), Stevie Smith, Dave Edwards, Sam Sampson, Andy 'Snake Hips' Johnson: on brass, Mick Eves, Ron Carthey, Brendan O'Neill, Ted McKenna (drums), Mark Feltham (harmonica), Lea Hart (guitar). There were always plenty of other guests as well – Chris Thompson, Dennis Stratton, Paul Jones, any known artist was welcome for a blow.

Gerry McAvoy was one of the best bass players around, and he also used to do backing vocals with Rory. He started to write and sing, and he released a single and an album, *Bassics*, with Bridge House Records. He then went into producing, and all the up–and–coming Irish bands would contact him for gigs at the Bridge; the Bank Robbers and the Kids were two he produced. This was possibly how U2 heard about us.

RORY GALLAGHER

When Rory got to hear about us, down he came, but he kept us waiting. 'Is he or isn't he going to do a song?' The last song of the night, up he went, and never came off the stage for two hours, continuing until 1am; and we were meant to close at 11pm! But Rory overruled any laws; if the police had come in, I don't think they could have stopped him. He was so good, they wouldn't have wanted to anyway.

Before their next tour, in 1981, Rory Gallagher and his band appeared on stage Live at the Bridge; what a great night! Rory's brother Donal, his manager, allowed us to advertise the gig and before 8pm the pub was packed with fans from all over Britain and Europe. Donal made a video of the gig at the Bridge. I wonder if he has still got a copy of it. I must try to contact him, as I would love to see it.

Rory was born in Ballyshannon in Donegal in 1948, but lived in Cork where his family had a pub. Rory loved it there. Here we had the ordinary fellow at home not the Rock star he was in all parts of the rest of the world. Well, that was *his* feeling, but to the community, while at home, people would just stand and watch every move he made. There is no other expression for it but 'hero worship'. In his adopted home town, he was a king.

When he was 15, he left home and joined a show band. He later lived in Belfast where he formed a new band, and so as not to leave a bad taste he called the band Taste. This was the band my good friend Gerry McAvoy was to join. Another friend who was in Taste was Wilgar Campbell, who played drums. He would later form his own band and play at the Bridge House in a three-piece with Gary Fletcher (guitar) and Dave Kelly as front man, when not working with Paul Jones in his Blues Band.

After Gerry McAvoy introduced me to Rory at the Bridge

House, we became good friends. He invited me to all his gigs and I went to most of them, being offered the VIP treatment, with limos, backstage passes, etc. I even got to ride in his helicopter when we got lost at the Gallagher Macroom Festival in Cork.

The Macroom Festival was the very first open-air Rock gig in Ireland. It was held in the grounds of Macroom Castle in the summer of 1977 and what a day/night and day it was.

Gerry and Tom Driscoll had popped into the Bridge House for a quiet pint before going on their travels. Gerry had said, 'You've got to come to the festival. Rory would love to see you.'

'Great!' I replied. 'Where is it? Hammersmith Odeon?'

Gerry in his soft Irish voice answered my question saying, 'Aw, no, no. It's at Macroom.'

'Is that outside London?' I asked.

'Just a little,' said Gerry.

Tom cut in: 'Jesus! It's in Cork, in southern Ireland!'

We all had a drink and I asked my son Lloyd, who was serving us, 'Do you fancy going to Ireland to see Gerry and Rory play?'

I knew he was a big fan of their music so he jumped at the chance. Gerry gave me his hotel number and told me to ring him once we got to Cork.

We arrived in Cork the day before the gig and booked a nice room in a hotel. We met up with Gerry in his hotel and went straight to the bar. The Murphy's stout was going down a treat so we had a very pleasant evening.

The next morning, we had a tour of Cork in the limo that Rory provided for us. Then we went off to the gig. These cars had special passes to get into the backstage car park, which was kept a secret. The route had been made known only to promoters, the artists and management. If the fans had found out, we wouldn't have been able to get through the crowds. I

58

believe there were something like 50,000 fans, so there had to be a clandestine entrance.

When we arrived, we went straight to the band's dressing room. Gerry, Rod De'Ath and Lou Martin were waiting there. Gerry said that Rory would like to see me, and he took me into Rory's dressing room. Rory was all alone and, when I went in, Gerry left. This surprised me, but this was Rory, a quiet unassuming man, completely different from other Rock stars I have met.

He gave me a drink, I thanked him and said, 'God bless you, Rory.'

He looked me right in the eye and asked, 'Do you mean that?'

'Of course I do!'

'Let's prove it.'

So we sat down. I looked at him and said the Lord's Prayer. After I had finished, he smiled and said, 'And God bless you, Terry Murphy.'

He asked me where my ancestors had come from and I told him Cork. 'Ay,' he said thoughtfully, 'that's the reason; we may be related.'

I don't know what the reason was, I never asked, but it did seem as if he had been thinking about me. Perhaps being older than him, I was the father figure he was looking for.

Gerry came back, so we wished them all good luck and said we would see them after the gig.

There was a special place set up in front of the stage for the guests of the artists. There were other great bands on the show including Status Quo. But everyone was waiting for Rory. Earlier, back in his adopted home town, the crowds had gathered to watch and cheer as he arrived in his helicopter.

Quo at last finished their set. Now, they awaited their 'god of Rock' to arrive on stage.

We watched as Tom Driscoll did all the last-minute checks to the onstage equipment. He winked and raised his splayed right hand; five more minutes to wait. The DJ finished his last record and it went deathly quiet. Then there was a screeching of car tyres and seconds later Rory ran on stage.

'Welcome, Mr Rory Gallagher,' shouted the announcer, but nobody heard it.

Rory was straight into 'Bullfrog Blues', the perfect start. The gig just went into full throttle, getting better and better, and the fans were going mad.

Standing in front of us was one Johnny Rotten aka John Lydon (of Sex Pistols fame), along with Bob Geldof of the Boomtown Rats and a publicist I was to meet later, as well as a few other friends of theirs. Lydon had come in with this bucket of urine, and his friend had another one, and they threw it at the band. Me and Lloyd rushed over to stop the second bucket being thrown. The security was quickly there and they were thrown out. Yes, Sir Bob included! Rory was raving, although none of the urine reached him. If it had gone on his guitar or the amps, they could have been electrocuted or set alight.

There was a reception after the gig and the newly formed *Hot Press* was handing out awards to the bands. It was a nice reception. Gerry, Lloyd and me were standing at the bar, when who walks in but Johnny Rotten. As he came bowling up to the bar, Gerry, remembering the earlier incident, said, 'I'm going to kill him.'

Gerry threw the best right-hander he had ever thrown, but Lloyd blocked it and I grabbed Gerry. I told him, 'That's what he wants, cheap publicity. Don't let it show.'

By this time, Rotten had run away. This whole incident was filmed by a German film crew, and Gerry has a copy of it, which will be nice to see one day.

Gerry's management had come to his aid and ushered them

all out the door, and then they were gone. There was me and Lloyd left in the hall with no idea where the band were. They had left the hotel where they were staying and there was another reception that we had all been invited to.

While we were standing there wondering what to do, an official came over and told me that Rory was on the phone. He told me not to worry and that he would send someone down to pick us up in about half an hour. We waited for well over an hour, and then all of a sudden there was a terrible loud noise over the hall. What a surprise! Rory had sent a helicopter to pick us up and take us the 10 miles back to Cork. A lovely time was had by all.

Gerry and Tom came back to London with us and who's sitting next to us on the plane? Bob Geldof! During the flight, we downed a couple of bottles of champagne and Tom looked like he was going to give Bob a wallop. A good job my son Lloyd was there to stop him. We managed to get to London without any serious incident and I dropped Tom off at his home before we hurried back to the Bridge House where we had a busy gig to promote.

We were to see a lot more of Rory, Gerry, Rod and Lou as they continued to play for us at the Bridge. Rory was to change his drummer on a couple of occasions, first to Ted McKenna and then Brendan O'Neill; they both became regulars at the Bridge, thanks to Gerry McAvoy.

Gerry and Brendan now play with another band that started at the Bridge, Nine Below Zero. They had started with us as the Stan Smith Blues Band, and their harp player, Mark Feltham, had joined Rory's band with Gerry and Brendan. Now they're altogether in this band fronted by founder member Dennis Greaves on vocals and doing very well indeed as one of the busiest bands on the circuit.

The last time I saw Rory was down the Kings Road, Fulham, in 1994. My daughter Vanessa had put on a musical play down there. Rory, seeing the name Murphy on the promotional material, had come down to support us. He was living locally and he looked fine. It was lovely to see him. He didn't stay to see the musical but we had a drink together. I remember saying to him, 'See you at the next gig,' and he replied, 'I will not be playing any more.'

I turned to him and said, 'What about Gerry and the guys?'

He looked me in the eye, and his eyes were sad as he said, 'Oh, they've got a new band together. They're looking after themselves.'

This was not the Rory I knew. He had put on a bit of weight, which all musos do when they're not on the road, and he seemed very sad. Little did I know that at that time his liver had packed up and he was waiting for a transplant. Sadly, he died on the operating table at the age of 47. It was a really big loss to the whole world.

On the day of Rory's funeral, the hearse left O'Conner's Funeral Parlour with Rory's Stratocaster guitar laid alongside the coffin. Crowds of people lined the streets, and traffic was at a standstill. Nobody cared; they were all in deep mourning. As the hearse pulled up at the church, the rear door was opened so Donal could lift the Strat away from the coffin. He handed it to Tom O'Driscoll, who had been with Rory for 18 years. As Tom took the guitar, his eyes met Donal's. It was the very same action as when Rory left the stage, always handing the Stratocaster to Tom. The tears were never far away.

Then a strange thing happened. The very quiet deep-in-sympathy crowd began to cheer and applaud, a very rare occurrence at a funeral. This showed us that this was not just an ordinary funeral. We had come to bury Rory Gallagher, our god of Rock. Everyone was pleased. Donal glanced at his wife, Cecelia, and his children and at last there was a smile in his eyes instead of the tears of the last week. Even the sun shone brighter at that moment. Was that the moment Rory was passing through the gates of heaven? We like to think so.

The untimely death of Rory Gallagher on 14 May 1995 shocked the world of music. Here are some tributes to the man:

Bono, U2
'He was one of the Top-10 guitarists of all time, but, more important than that he was also one of the Top-10 nice guys. When I saw Taste [Rory's first band] play, this was my first experience of seeing a real Rock band. That memory lives with me to this day and that day was the day I wanted to be a Rock star. At the time, just a dream, but now a dream fulfilled. Thank you, Rory.'

David 'The Edge' Howell Evans, U2
'A beautiful man and an amazing guitarist. I was there in Macroom, aged 15 in 1977, and he was what I wanted to be. He will be sadly missed. He was great. His Blues and acoustic playing I will always remember. Rest in peace, Rory.'

Larry Mullen Jr, U2
'We were utterly devastated on hearing this sad news.'

Adam Clayton, U2
'The first show I ever went to was the Carton in 1975 and Rory Gallagher was playing. It was with the greatest sadness that I learned of the death of Rory Gallagher. He was one of the most underrated Irish talents of all times.'

Paul McGuinness, U2 manager
'He was the first international Rock star from Ireland and he set a great example for all the younger players to follow. I know we did.'

Donal Gallagher
'It's hard for me to find words that could show or give insight into my brother, a very sensitive person. He wanted to make music that was timeless. He has certainly left his mark.'

When asked how he would like to be remembered, Rory Gallagher replied, 'In song and story, with a pint of Murphy's, not in my hand, but in my stomach.'

He said his dying words would be: 'There is an after life, isn't there?'

We had a Bridge House Reunion in July 2001. RDB, another of our regular bands, were doing the honours. Gerry and Brendan came along. Dave Edwards from RDB brought along a friend who plays in a tribute band called the Rory Gallagher Band. He looks and sings just like Rory and the idea was for Brendan and Gerry to play a few songs with him. Alas, it never happened, as we just ran out of time. But it was a real pity. However, it was great to see Gerry and Brendan again. Gerry and I both agreed that we looked fitter in 2001 than we did all those years ago at the Bridge House. Now, I wonder why that is?

SAM APPLE PIE

Sam Sampson, Andy 'Snake Hips' Johnson, Jim Mitchell, Bob Renny, Josh Brown, Jeff Brown, Jimmy Busy, 'Nosferatu' (the sax player Rex Morris) – all these guys almost made it big time in their first band Sam Apple Pie. This band, even today, has taken on a legendary stature. They moved on to be the Vipers which also featured Gary Fletcher who later joined the Blues Band. Andy played with Stevie Marriott in Fast Exit Mechanics and Blind Drunk. At this time, most of them had been professional musicians for almost 20 years, so they certainly knew how to play, and you can bet your life they are still playing now.

Ric Lee (drums), Stan Webb, John Martin and Mick Smith (guitar) were other members.

OLD MAN GOING DOWN HILL BLUES BAND AND JIMMY RIDDLE AND THE PISSPOTS

In 1979, we had been introduced to Jimmy Riddle and the Pisspots, Rhythm and Blues specialists. Gary Fletcher, who went on to be the Blues Band's bass player, used to play with the Pisspots. These same guys played for us many times under the name Old Man Going Down Hill Blues Band. If you booked them, you knew you would have in the region of 20 band members turning up. They wanted a keg of ale, Guinness, lagers, etc. 'Give us all we can drink and we don't want any money for the gig.'

Well, I thought, 'That's a cheap deal. I'll go for that.' But it only happened once! They nearly cleared me out the first time they played so after that a big percentage of the door was taken, and they still spent it over the bar.

PAUL JONES, THE BLUES BAND AND GARY FLETCHER

At one of Gerry McAvoy's Jams, with the newly named band the Old Man Going Down Hill Blues Band, I was behind the bar and we were very busy after the first set. The bands used to do two sets of 45 minutes each. This guy asked me if he could get up and play some harp in the next set. I knew his face but could not put a name to him. He told me that Billy Tarrant sent his regards. Billy was a fellow publican who was running the Southwark Park Tavern in South London; he was also a Canning Town man and a former professional boxer, and we knew his mother and father. It seemed Billy had been on the road with Paul Jones when he had been in Manfred Mann's band, which was how he knew him, and Paul had asked Billy if it was OK to come over. I told Paul to see Gerry McAvoy, who introduced him and he got a wonderful reception.

Paul told me later that he had seen the name Old Man Going Down Hill Blues Band advertised in the *Melody Maker* and he'd just had to come down to the gig. So it seemed the ads helped get artists into the pub as well as audiences!

Paul would turn up at all the Blues sessions in the next few months and so I got talking to him. He would never sing, only play the harp, but, of course, he was a singer and everyone wanted him to sing. He just said it wasn't his gig. So in I go: 'Why don't you get your own guys together and I will give you a gig.'

Paul wasn't sure, but he said he would think about it. I could see that Paul wanted to get back into music, but I don't think his wife at this time, who was a very successful author, wanted him to, although she did come to the gigs with him. But I am only guessing. (They later divorced, and Paul is now married to a very good actress, Fiona Hendley.)

Anyway, a week or so later, Paul came back to the Bridge and introduced Tom McGuinness, the guitarist who he was in Manfred's band with. Tom had previously formed McGuinness Flint and they'd had a number of hit singles. Paul said he'd got a band together for a definite one-off gig. Tom was adamant: *one only*. Well, the gig turned out to be sensational; the Bridge was packed and buzzing with excitement. Paul, Tom, Hughie Flint, Dave Kelly and Gary Fletcher – the Blues Band was born!

Paul was worried about whether they could live up to the name of the band, but they most certainly did. On the Saturday night, after they had finished their set plus three encores, I went over to congratulate them, and to ask them if they could do me a really big favour. The band I'd booked for the next Saturday had pulled out, but the ads had to be in the music papers before noon on Monday morning. It would not have been possible to get a good band organised as a replacement at such short notice and meet the advertising deadline. Paul looked at Tom and you could almost hear their thoughts: 'Here we go again!'

Paul seemed up for it but Tom didn't seem too keen. They said they'd have a chat and let me know within a quarter of an hour. Forty-five minutes later, they came back and said they'd do it.

I was pleased, of course, but I then had the horrible task of having to sack the bands I had booked for the coming week. Of course, every band wants a Saturday night, the best of the week. I tried to reschedule and had murders with one of the bands, but it had to be worth it; the Blues Band were just made for the Bridge. They played the next four weeks and were then regulars at least once a month.

They went on to record a live album at the Bridge and I was hoping to get it on our label, but they had good management who put it out on their own label through Arista Records. The next time I saw them was in 1981 in Cannes, when they were playing at the Midem Music Festival. They were one of the guest bands and insisted I come to the gig, which I did and a great time was had by all.

But it wasn't all plain sailing for the band. Hughie Flint, who is one of the nicest people you could wish to meet, left after a year or so, to be replaced by Rob Townsend, another great drummer. Dave Kelly got his own band together, and we gave him a lot of gigs with the Dave Kelly Band. He got himself a deal and managed to release some albums, but he always went back to the Blues Band when he was needed.

Dave's sister also played a few times for us with the Jo Ann Kelly Band. It was a good band and she was a great singer. Sadly, Jo Ann passed away in October 1990. She was only 44 but her 'delta' sound records are still being played, and I heard one recently.

When the Blues Band weren't playing, Paul would still come down to the Bridge for the jams and he had some great ones of his own. He was playing on the band's first birthday at the Bridge and just about all his old friends turned up, and, of course, they all wanted to play. Alexis Korner, one of the pioneers of the Blues in Britain, used his son's guitar that night. When he left, I went to the door with him; he complimented me and thanked me for the gig. We shook hands and he was gone. Forty-five minutes later, he rang back in sheer panic; while we were talking, he had put the guitar down on the floor and forgot to take it with him. I went outside expecting the worst, but there it was between the two cars we had been talking next to. What a relieved man he was when I told him. But then I thought I best check inside just in case ... It was there!

It is now more than 25 years since that first night at the Bridge and the Blues Band are still playing almost every week. If I had let them get away with the one-off gig, Blues fans would have been robbed of many a great night.

The following was written by Gary Fletcher for and on behalf of the Blues Band. Paul Jones, who is now a presenter on BBC Radio 2 every Thursday, playing the Blues, passed the request on to Gary, who was a founding member of the Blues Band and, I am pleased to say, played a lot of gigs for me.

MEMORIES OF THE BRIDGE
Gary Fletcher

This is what I recall of the first gig at the Bridge for the Blues Band and one or two other things.

Early in 1979 Paul Jones rang fellow ex-Manfred and Blues enthusiast Tom McGuinness to suggest forming an occasional Blues/R&B band to play the London pub scene on his days off from the theatre, where he was now earning his living acting. Tom was interested and called his old mate from McGuinness Flint, Hughie Flint. He made a few more calls and the line-up of what was to become the Blues Band was completed by Dave Kelly who brought me in, following a period playing together in an occasional band called the Wild Cats, run by Tom Nolan, which included several gigs at the Bridge House, Canning Town.

Always insistent that, even if we were only to do 'a couple of gigs', the band would not be a purely jamming 12-bar Blues band of the kind that would become so common in that era, the band rehearsed and got a pretty tight set together and started looking around for gigs. First to step forward and offer work was Terry at the Bridge.

I think it was 21 April 1979 when we all met at the Bridge, set up our amps and drums, etc. and then went to Tom's house, which was on the other side of the Blackwall Tunnel, in Greenwich, around 5pm for some food and a few drinks. The first-set start time was around 9pm so we set off to get back to the Bridge for about 8.30pm.

I distinctly remember us all being a bit miffed that, when we arrived back at the Bridge, there was nowhere to park for what seemed like miles and how rotten it was of Terry to put us on for our first gig the same night as what must have been a wedding party or something. We had, of course, hoped for an audience of some sort but genuinely didn't expect more than a small crowd of anorakish Blues buffs.

Of course, Terry hadn't double-booked us with a wedding do or anything else. In a classic example of 'right place, right time', the Blues Band had arrived on the scene at a point when the gig-going public were well up for what we were doing. Initially, I guess because of the previous form of most of the band members, and the Bridge was absolutely roofed out! It turned out to be a fantastic night, full of all the right ingredients, i.e. hot, sweaty, beer-soaked atmosphere, jam-packed crowd, pretty decent band and above all one of the great London (or anywhere else come to that) real music venues.

The Blues Band never looked back from that night and the ensuing annual birthday parties for the band brought us back to the venue even when we were enjoying our 15 minutes of fame in the spotlight.

Personally, I'd played the Bridge with various bands prior to the Blues Band, notably Sam Apple Pie (SAP). When I was with SAP, for some of the time, we were known as the Vipers, which was a vehicle for Sam Sampson and Andy 'Snake Hips' Johnson to try to revitalise the bookability of their long-running creation during the Punk years of 1976–78.

Actually, while writing this, I'd like to straighten out a mistake which appeared in Roy Bainton's book about the Blues Band called *Talk to Me Baby*. Roy quotes me as saying, 'With Jimmy Knox from Panama Scandal we formed Sam Apple Pie.' This is completely erroneous and was never claimed or stated by me. It was always Sam and Andy's band; I was just a passing member and I've always been embarrassed at the thought of either of them coming across this incorrectly attributed statement.

Much as the first gig of the Blues Band was a really important moment in what has gone on to be a pretty good career for the band and its members, the most memorable night for me at the Bridge was a gig I was lucky enough to do as part of the legendary (!) Jimmy Riddle and the Pisspots incarnation, put together, I think, by Sam and Andy in 1977–78 or thereabouts. To say 'memorable' is perhaps inaccurate, as, along with anyone else who was in this huge line-up of mainly East End/E17 musos, I can't really remember much of the evening at all, as we all got absolutely arseholed on the beer that Terry provided – I think in lieu of a fee. But it's one of those events that people tell you they were at and what a great night it was and you just trust them that it happened! Hopefully, someone else contributing to this book will have a clearer recollection than me!

The thing about the Pisspots' gig was that, in some ways, it distilled (pardon the pun) the essence of the Bridge more profoundly than the nights with the 'star' names, in so far as the line between the band and the audience disappeared completely, as did, for all intents and purposes, the line between landlord and punters. Everyone, absolutely *everyone*, was up for having a good time and, accordingly, a very, very good time was had by all. No moodies about borrowed equipment, no daft riders for the band, no dogmatic jobsworths, no star trips, no miserable whinging promoters, etc., etc.

Terry and, of course, Glen ran the sort of gaff that didn't invite bullshit of any sort and whenever anyone tried to inflict it on the Bridge it seemed to reject it automatically.

It was a terrible thing that the road builders did to flatten the Bridge.

STEVE WALLER AND STEVIE SMITH

When Steve Waller and Stevie Smith, whose band Salt played regularly at the Bridge, got together, which was almost every Jam, they would lift the roof off the pub. It was pure Blues. Steve Waller does all the vocals on the Gerry McAvoy Jam. And Salt are also featured on the *Live – A Week At The Bridge E16* album. Mick Clark, the guitarist in Salt, is one of the greatest Blues guitarists ever. Even the American producer Richard Perry was quoted as saying this. Little Stevie is a great front man; he was ruthless when on stage. I remember at the jam on Paul Jones band's birthday, Paul invited Stevie up to play some harmonica, which Paul always played as well. Stevie did his solo, and then Paul came in. It was time for Stevie to leave. But, as Paul finished, in dived Stevie, knocking Paul sideways. Steve carried on playing harp and singing all the vocals right up to the end of the song. Paul Jones had the right hump but, like a true professional, kept his temper. When these two were on stage together, it was war. I would not like to say who was the best harmonica player, they were both so good.

I recently heard that little Stevie Smith is still in a Blues band called the Ruthless Blues Band. Quite apt. Stevie wanted me to record and release his version of 'House of the Rising Sun', which he used to perform in his gigs. I am sure it was as good as the original release and would have been a big seller but we never got round to do it – I wish I had.

Steve Waller was a great front man. With his long beard, he really looked the part of the Blues man. He would experiment with different instruments to get unusual sounds and was always there when a Blues jam was on. He's on the *Live – A Week At The Bridge E16* album fronting the Gerry McAvoy Jam. They sang me a tribute, during the song 'Walking the Dog', which goes:

> *At the Bridge House Terry's mighty, mighty, lets it all hang out, he lets the bands play what they want to play, at the Bridge House. He sets out nights so we can jam this way, etc.*

In fact, Steve was discovered at the Bridge House by none other than Manfred Mann. He joined his band, toured and appeared on Manfred's albums. And, when that ended, he continued with his own Steve Waller Blues Band.

Sadly, Steve Waller left us in 2000 to play in the great Blues jam in the sky. He was just 49. He will, of course, be missed; however, we do have his vocals on the live album so he will never be forgotten.

MANFRED MANN'S EARTH BAND AND CHRIS THOMPSON

To be a top hit-record maker in the 1960s, battling it out with the Beatles and the Stones, etc. and then to continue through until now, you have got to be considered an all-time great. That is what Manfred Mann is: an all-time great musician and band leader.

I have not seen Manfred for over 10 years, but you can bet he has not changed one little bit; well, like all of us, he might look just a little older.

I met Manfred for the first time in the 1970s at the Bridge. He became a regular especially when he was looking for new faces for his band. He discovered Steve Waller, Willy Finlayson, Matt Irving, Stevie Lange, Dave Edwards, Allan Coates, Robbie McIntosh and many more, who would play for him. And for this he and I have to thank Chris Thompson.

One day in 1977, I was in my office above the pub when the phone rang.

'Hi, this is Manfred Mann's agent, Neil Warnock. Chris Thompson, the lead vocalist in the band, would like to play some gigs at the Bridge House.'

I thought, 'This has got to be a wind-up. Stars like him do not play pub gigs in the East End of London.' But I went along with it. 'Oh, yeah. I'm a little busy at the moment. Can you give me your number? I'll ring you back. OK?'

But now I was thinking, 'Could it be true?' I had spoken to a Chris Thompson a few weeks earlier. He had come down to sing a few songs with a band that were playing for us called Screemer. That Chris had said that he would be playing at the Bridge soon. Now, was this really Manfred's vocalist or someone with the same name?

We had become very friendly with Screemer – Matt Irving, Bernie Clark, Mark Pinner, Steve Bolton, the guitarist Dave Flett and Allan Coates – and their manager Terry Blackman, and they were a regular band of ours at the time. Glenn Mikkelson, the vocalist, later changed his name to Zaine Griff and relaunched the band as the Zaine Griff Band. When Zaine went solo, the rest of the guys played in the Sprinklers, then Special Branch and they also backed Kate Robbins when she formed a band. Some also ended up playing in Paul Young's band. One of them, Steve Stroud, married Cheryl Baker from Eurovision Song Contest winners Bucks Fizz. The last time I saw them all was on TV in the Jools Holland Band.

Anyway, at the time, Screemer had just changed their name and, after playing the circuit for a while, were a very good professional band, and I had given them a residency. One evening, I thought that they were playing well and sounded really good. Terry agreed and told me that they had been rehearsing quite a lot recently. As I was watching, the bass player, Matt Irving, nearly knocked this new guy I had not seen before off the stage and his glasses came flying off. At the break, I had a chat with the new guy and told him where he could get his glasses mended.

He thanked me and said, 'I'm going to be playing down here soon.'

I said, 'Who with?'

He replied, 'I'm getting a band together.'

This was news to me at this time, and I thought, 'Who does he think he is?'

I introduced myself and he said his name was Chris Thompson. I still did not get it. I just thought he must have the same name. So, a few weeks later, when Neil the agent called, I still didn't realise that I had been chatting to *the* Chris Thompson.

I'd expected a superstar, and I got one. But this was how Chris was off stage: down-to-earth, practical, hard-working and one hell of a nice guy. He knew some of the guys and was keeping his voice in trim. That's Chris, he just has to sing and play guitar.

So, still not sure, I rang back, and it *was* Manfred's agent. He told me that Chris wanted to keep his voice in tune while he was off the road with Manfred. As I was talking, I kept thinking, 'Great! But I won't be able to pay the fee he wants.'

I said, 'Well, he can have every Wednesday [this was the quietest night of the week]. What about his fee?'

Neil Warnock replied, 'I'll get Chris to call you. Sort it out with him.'

I thought to myself, 'Agents! Feeling you out to see how much you will pay.'

Anyway, Chris rang the next day. I told him how pleased I was that he wanted to play at our pub and that we did not charge on the door, so I would not be able to pay very much.

He just said, 'That's OK. I don't want any money.'

I couldn't believe it! Here was a guy who had a hit with 'Blinded by the Light', which had been the number-one record in America and number five in the UK in the charts, who wanted to play for no fee! At this time, I was paying £20 a gig, so I was expecting him to ask for at least £100. (Remember this was 1977 and a pint of lager would cost you 30p; today the average is £2.50, so the 30p is eight times dearer.) I said, 'I will give you £30 a gig [£240 today's rate],' but he said, 'Give it to the band.' He was probably paying them as well.

He even added that, rather than use rehearsal studios, he would rather *pay me* to play a live gig! Now this really did sound like a wind-up. But I went along with it.

We made all the arrangements; time of arrival, two 45-minute sets, 15 minutes' rest in between the two sets. And I wanted to do something, so I said, 'Well, I will pay for the PA.'

But Chris said, 'No, I'll fetch my own.'

Neil Warnock said that we could not advertise using Manfred's name. I was not even allowed to say Manfred Mann's lead vocalist and we could only use Chris Thompson's name on posters in the pub. So there was no advertising for the gig, apart from word of mouth.

Anyway, the big day arrived. I was introduced to Colin

Barton, the PA and sound man, who was first to arrive with his crew.

Chris and the band arrived early, set up and had a rehearsal and a sound check. I had employed a few more extra staff, expecting a very busy night, and I opened up the pub at 7pm, waiting for the crowds to pour in. No such luck! I could not believe it when only around 40 people turned up that night and it didn't get much better over the coming weeks. But I didn't mind, I had Chris Thompson, singing in *my* pub.

The band Chris had formed had its own lead singer who shared the songs with Chris and a lot of the songs were new and being tried out for the first time. He would not sing any of Manfred's stuff, and I still joke with Chris about it when I see him. They were terrible and it ended up a disaster of a night! And they didn't get any better.

One of the songs was called 'Dig Your Garden', which had been written by the co-singer in this first line-up, whose name I cannot remember, but perhaps Chris was trying to help him get a band together. Anyway, Chris, being the man he is, tried it out to see how it sounded. It was awful! I still have a copy of the recording we did that night. I have only just found it, so Chris doesn't even know that I have it, and I will be able to blackmail him for the rest of his life. 'Dig your garden, fill it full of weeds.' Need I say more?

Chris would have different musicians most weeks, as he was experimenting to get the players he wanted and it was going to take time. But Wednesday was the quietest night of the week, so I just let him get on with it.

However, four weeks later, Chris got his friends in and took over all the vocals. We never saw the original singer again. Chris had brought over his mates Billy Kristian (bass) and Mike Walker (keyboards) who he used to play with in New Zealand, so he had the basis for the band. One of the first guitarists he brought in was Geoff Whitehorn, a really great musician, who only played on the Filthy McNasty nights at the Bridge. (Geoff was also a member of Crawler which was another great band that played for us on their UK tour.) The duels between Geoff and Chris were great; it was our high noon with guitars, and the sound was immaculate.

Chris was almost there with the sound he was looking for, except for the drummer. We had Ron Telemacque, Clive Edwards, American Jimmy Johnson and Rick Marotta (who later played on the album *Night* with Chris). When he got Ron Telemacque, from Eddie Grant's band the Equals, on drums, he called the band Filthy McNasty, with a line-up that lasted for around a year.

Around this time, Stevie Lange joined him on vocals, and they changed their set around. Stevie, who was from South Africa, had come to England and married Mutt Lange, who went on to become one of the top producers in the world. Stevie, who had done plenty of sessions with many top bands, met Chris while she was doing backing vocals for Manfred Mann's Earth Band, and they'd become friends. Chris invited her down to the Bridge to sing with Filthy McNasty, and she was a huge hit; she had a really great voice and quickly won over the audience. Chris, who loved to play the guitar, was pleased to share the vocals with Stevie, as it allowed him to focus on his playing. When Chris said he needed another night, I gave him Thursdays as well.

The Bridge had been half full, but a month later it was almost packed. This proved to me that it's not the venue that pulls the crowds but the artists. The venue is very important because the customers check out who is playing and, if they like what they see, they come down to watch them. That's what pubs like the Bridge House did best. Charlie Watts did the same. When he was off the road with the Rolling Stones, he played the Bridge House with his band, Rocket 88, and he built the crowd up, as did Paul Jones's Blues Band who also had an old Manfred favourite Tom McGuinness on guitar. Paul and Tom formed this band after a jam session at the Bridge. They also played their first gig at the pub with the Blues Band. New bands like Depeche Mode, Cafe Racers (now Dire Straits), Iron Maiden, the Look and even our own Wasted Youth, and Punk bands like the Damned and Cockney Rejects, always had to build the audience up.

Within the year, Chris Thompson was an all-time favourite, bringing other star names in; Huey Lewis was always in the pub to play harp and sing, as were members of the Eagles; the Doobie Brothers, Tah Mahal and Crawler were others who came along. The Bridge became the place to be and there is no doubt that Chris was a major influence on the credibility of the Bridge. Chris had opened the door to pub Rock and others followed.

One night, for the first and only time, Chris was late (he always started at 8.30 and would have a 15-minute break between his two 45-minute sets). He got to the Bridge at nine o'clock, and, as the pub used to close at 10.30, he apologised and said they would play right through and not have a break.

The following day, I'm watching the regular Thursday-evening *Top of the Pops*, and there's Chris with Manfred Mann singing their latest hit, 'Davy's on the Road Again', which I think went to number one in the charts. That's why he was late; he had been recording *Top of the Pops* on the Wednesday! This was Chris; he just would not let anyone down.

The Thursday was back to normal and the line-up was doing mostly covers for the next year. This was a great time for the Bridge, with Stevie singing Aretha Franklin and Janis Joplin songs. It was a learning process in terms of both the arrangements and getting the feel of how a hit song should be played, but the band was acclimatising to playing together.

The next big surprise was when Colin Barton came up with the idea of recording the band live. He had spoken to Chris, who said, if I was up for it, he would produce the album. I said, 'Rather than record one band, let's do a week of bands.'

And, so, *Live – A Week At The Bridge E16* was born. We recorded six bands: Chris's band Filthy McNasty, Remus Down Boulevard, Gerry McAvoy Jam, Jackie Lynton, the Roll-Ups and the Sprinklers, who we dropped, as they had won a TV show called *New Faces*, and were too busy to mix the tracks.

Chris did a wonderful job producing the album, and his recordings of Filthy McNasty are the only tracks he released under that name, so they are rarities.

As the year went on, Chris was getting serious. He never said anything but I believe he really wanted his own band. However, he would not leave Manfred until he had found a replacement for himself. Manfred used to come down to see and hear different vocalists. I had recommended Dave Edwards, who went to his studio, the Workhouse, in the Old Kent Road and did some demos for him. Steve Waller and Willy Finlayson were next. I don't know what happened with Dave Edwards, but the next album and tour Manfred did, when he couldn't replace Chris, he used Chris, Steve and Willy with Stevie Lange on backing vocals. It was good for the old pub, three of our regular singers on a hit album and Chris with a number one.

Chris's new band was called Night and they got a deal in the States, which included a tour with the Doobie Brothers right across America. They released an album, *Night*, and a single from it, 'Hot Summer Nights', with vocals by Stevie Lange. Chris was to tell me later that, on the American tour, he got the crew to check out the shops for the album and not one stocked it. This is the record companies for you; they pay loads of money to the headline band so you can support them, then don't get the distribution set up for the release of the album. The band in the end has to pay these costs from their percentage of the sales. Regardless of this, 'Hot Summer Nights' went to number 18 in the American charts. The album did OK, but, with no major promotion, there was not much chance of a hit.

The complete line-up for *Night* was Chris Thompson (vocals, guitar), Stevie Lange (vocals), Nicky Hopkins (piano) (Nick also played on the Rolling Stones' albums), Robbie McIntosh (guitar), Billy Kristian (bass) and Rick Marotta (drums).

Night (Cat no. K52200; a 1979 Planet Recording and Warner Records release) has become a collector's piece, and, if you can find it, it's worth a lot of money. They also released 'Long Distance' in 1980 (Planet K52251).

Sad for Night was glad for me, when Chris came home and, with a new line-up and new name, started again. Two nights a week at the Bridge – Chris Thompson and the Islands. Chris recorded with this band and I recently asked him about the tapes. He said he would check it out, so keep your eyes open, maybe a live recording of Chris Thompson on Bridge House Records is on the way.

Chris Thompson lives in America these days and is still very busy. He comes over to Europe a couple of times a year to sing with the SAS Band. His son Daniel is a keen rugby player but he's inherited his dad's tonsils and has performed a few gigs with his father – so look out for Daniel Thompson in the future.

We have kept in touch all this time, and, if Chris is around when West Ham are playing Manchester United, he usually gives us a ring and we have been to a few matches together. Chris was born in London and it was his home until he was 15 when he moved to New Zealand, where he became a teacher and musician, before coming back to England. How can he possibly support Manchester United?! I suppose it proves nobody's perfect.

We have a link to Chris's website on ours (www.theBridgehouseE16.com). Have a look at his CV; it's remarkable. Chris Thompson is not only a great Rock star; he is also a great man. Last Christmas (2006), he sent me a pile of CDs, including his very latest release, *Time Line* (Rediscovery), from New Zealand where he was visiting his friends and family. Chris never forgets anyone, a true sign of greatness.

Chris wrote to me about his recollections of the Bridge House a little while ago, and it was good to read about his memories.

MEMORIES OF THE BRIDGE
Chris Thompson

Hi Terry,
I was in England for a couple of days, but spent as much time as I could with Daniel and the rest rehearsing, sorry I just never seem to have enough time … but I just started writing and this is what came out …
Love Chris

The Bridge House
The Bridge House in Canning Town was like a second home for myself and a bunch of my friends and musicians collectively know as Filthy McNasty, from 1979 to 1982. I had actually begun playing at the Bridge with another band. The owner, and now a great friend, Terry Murphy and his family were more than happy for me to come and play on

---

one of their off nights. If I remember rightly, there were 15 people on that first night. But Terry paid us £30 regardless and asked us back the next week. (I can't think why, as we were far from exciting and only lasted a couple more weeks.)

I told Terry I was going to put a band together with Stevie Lange and a bunch of musicians from New Zealand – Billy Kristian (bass) and Mike Walker (keyboards) and a variety of drummers.

We set up a regular Wednesday night. I can't remember how long it was, but shortly after that we started playing regularly on Wednesdays and Thursdays.

I think those nights were probably some of the best fun and most enjoyable musically I have ever had. The Bridge used to throb to our own brand of Rock and people seemed to come out of nowhere regular as clockwork. I remember one New Year's Eve when there were nearly 700 people in the pub and we had to stop playing for a while as even the building began to rock!!! The atmosphere at the Bridge became legendary.

As we were all involved in other projects, it was always a race to get there on time to play and Colin Barton, our trusted friend and sound man (and everything else), would keep us guessing to the last minute with the PA he had assembled for that evening. I remember playing one night after I had hurt my back and could hardly stand up. I think Terry and I must have walked a couple of miles before the gig trying to take my mind off the pain. But once the gig started the adrenalin took over.

We had a variety of regular guests including Geoff Whitehorn (really the sixth member of Filthy!) and the

Clover Band featuring Huey Lewis and John McFee. Billy
Kristian would regularly blow the audience to bits with his
motorbike bass solo, and Mike Walker would amuse us all,
and himself, with a fantastic array of keyboard sounds and
technical ability that sets him apart.

The music was always exciting with Stevie (one of the
greatest female vocalists in the world) always ready to entice
and excite the males in the crowd with her version of
'Move Over'; she always gave everything she had. And I
think that's what made that time so special, we were playing
for our lives really every Wednesday and Thursday, because
the people loved it so much and came back month after
month and gave us the feedback that is only found in clubs
like the Bridge House.

I remember Stevie and I holding the long note in
harmony at the end of 'Fire Down Below', both of us
refusing to give up first!

I think we all wish we could go back and recapture those
days (I know I do). But times have changed and those times
can only live in our memories. The best times for all of us,
I think. We used to sit for hours after the gigs chatting about
our hopes and dreams for the future, over sandwiches and
drinks from Rita.

I still bump into Bridge House fans all over England and
via the email. We all agree those gigs were something special
that the band and the audience took part in together. That
probably sounds far-fetched, but, if you look at *Live – A
Week At The Bridge E16*, you will see from the cover how
important the people were. I know that Terry and I shared
a dream or two and still do during our too infrequent

meetings and phone calls. I think at the Bridge House we were living the Rock'n'Roll dream and didn't realise it. Great musicians, great songs, great audience and a great venue; all one can ask for really. The Bridge House, thanks to all the Murphys for those times we will never forget. Long live Rock'n'Roll and sweat!

Stevie and Mutt Lange eventually got a divorce, and Stevie married Alan Bradshaw, Chris Thompson's recording engineer, who had his own company, Shape Systems. Mutt married Canadian Country/Pop star Shania Twain in 1993. They fell in love discussing song lyrics over the phone before they even met each other.

Mutt started off with many of the Heavy Metal bands in the 70s and 80s and he also produced Tina Turner. His latest productions have been Britney Spears and Celine Dion. Mutt went from Heavy Rock to Country music and had enormous success, but good producers have got the ear for music.

I am sure that he came down to the Bridge House just to listen to my vocals at the end of the night: 'Time, gentlemen, please, you're way past time. Let's have them glasses (empty ones).'

You can hear this on the *Live – A Week At The Bridge E16* album, after the Roll-Ups' second song. I do have it copyrighted, so no downloading please … unless I'm paid handsomely!

GEOFF WHITEHORN AND CRAWLER

The first time I met Geoff was when he came to the Bridge as a guest with a band called Rebel. Geoff was the best musician in Gravesend and would help all his fellow artists from that area. Rebel mentioned Geoff's name to help them get the gig, telling me he would come and play with them, so he had to turn up when I gave them a gig, whether he wanted to or not. His main band at the time was Crawler. The original name was Back Street Crawler. This was Paul Kossoff's band. Paul, who was the son of the great Jewish actor David, helped create 'All Right Now' with Free, one of the most enduring hits of the late 20th century.

Back Street Crawler were big in America but, tragically, Paul died of a drug overdose. The band and the record company wanted to carry on playing so they just called themselves Crawler. A big successful tour of America followed by a British tour was arranged through Geoff and Terry Wilson-Slessor, the vocalist in the band, and the Bridge House was included in the tour list as one of the London dates. This was really good for us because the posters were all over the country and, although we were detailed just as the Bridge House, Canning Town, we were the only pub on the list, and they were playing big venues on the rest of their tour. The Crawler night went off sensationally, with the line-up of John 'Rabbit' Bundrick (keyboards), Geoff (guitar) and Terry (vocals).

By this time, Geoff had become a regular with Chris Thompson and he became a good friend. Geoff and Rabbit recently played on a Who tour, so they are still going strong. Geoff's another musician who is down to earth; no airs and graces with him. Not long ago, I bought Geoff's CD, *Geoff Whitehorn in Gravesend*, and I have to say it's really worth the money, but it should have said, 'Geoff Whitehorn of the Who, and many more big names'. Elkie Brooks always had him in her band.

I've got some good pictures of Geoff and Crawler playing at the Bridge House. Terry Wilson-Slessor started coming down to the jams after the Crawler gig. I have a good picture of him,

Chris, Stevie and Huey Lewis jamming together at the end of a Chris Thompson gig.

REBEL

Rebel continued to play for us in their own right, and I liked their songs. Their line-up was Les Burgess (vocals), Schmeely (Yiddish street slag for 'goodnight') (bass, vocals), Pete Goodey (guitar, vocals) and John Smith (drums, vocals). As you can see, it was certainly a harmony band!

They once played at a car-racing tournament with a band called Wild Wily Barrett. The race was for small 2CV Citroen cars and took place at the Quarry Farm, Wiltshire. It was called '2 CV Cross Citroen', and Total Oil were supposed to be the sponsors. They withdrew their sponsorship so the band had a music and motors gig to raise some cash to keep them going. John Waggle, the British champion in 2CVs, was the main man. Tim Purcell interviewed him and the band on the live radio show after the races had finished.

We recorded Rebel for a single release and signed them to Bridge House Records and Music Ltd. 'Drift Away' and 'Rocka Shocka' were their two titles. 'Rocka Shocka' (BHS.2), which was our second single, was produced by Colin Barton and arranged by Rebel and it became the theme tune broadcast on Capital Radio on Saturday nights for Nicky Horne's 'Mummy's Weekly' show.

GRAHAM FOSTER AND ROBBIE MCINTOSH

This band was the second regular band of ours to appear on *Top of the Pops* (the first being the Leyton Buzzards). The Graham Foster Band had started out as Blitz and played for us for over a year in 1976. The line-up was: Graham (guitar and vocals), Eddie Williams (drums) and, from Sutton in Surrey, Robbie

McIntosh (guitar). Graham's brother Malcolm Foster, the roadie, ended up being the bass player with Chrissie Hynde's band the Pretenders.

Robbie, who started playing guitar at the age of 10, picking out things from any records he listened to at the time, was only 16 when he first came to the Bridge House to play with Blitz.

Having two older sisters, Robbie couldn't help but pick up on their record collections and was thus impressed by the Beatles, the Stones, the Kinks, the Spencer Davis Group and Jimi Hendrix, amongst others. His dad loved jazz, so Rob was also influenced by the likes of Fats Waller, Django Rheinhardt and Louis Armstrong. Oh, yeah, and his mum plays the piano.

Rob's first band was 70% Proof, which also included Paul Eager, Russell Ayles and Graham Mincher (who were all still at school). The band rehearsed on Sunday afternoon at the local dump, in the canteen. They played original material and covers of bands such as Humble Pie, the Who, Free and Stevie Wonder.

After taking A-levels at school, Robbie had ambitions to study biology at university but, when this didn't work out, he joined up with Graham and Malcolm Foster (who were a few years ahead of Robbie at the same school he attended in Raynes Park). Rob toured and recorded with the Foster brothers as Blitz right through 1977, before the band broke up at the start of 1978.

Following six months working as a lorry driver, Chris Thompson asked Rob to join Filthy McNasty as lead guitar late in 1978. The band went to Los Angeles to record with Richard Perry for his Planet Records label. Somewhere along the way, the name of the band was changed to Night and toured in America for most of 1979 supporting the Doobie Brothers.

Night split up during 1980, and Chris and Robbie formed

Chris Thompson and the Islands with Malcolm Foster, Wix and Mick Clews. They played a lot of gigs and did some recording but they never got a deal.

Robbie left in 1981 and put a band together, playing local pubs. Dean Martin's Dog (this moniker won band name of the year in *Time Out* magazine) was made up of Malcolm Foster, Mick Clews, Jez Wire, Rupert Black and Mike Dudley.

Around 1977–78, Robbie met Jimmy Scott (James Honeyman-Scott), and they had become pals but it wasn't until 1982 that Jimmy contacted Robbie asking him to join the Pretenders. Sadly, Jimmy passed away in June of that same year.

Rob toured and recorded two albums with the Pretenders (*Learning to Crawl* and *Get Close*). He left the band in September 1987 but continued session work in 1988, including some sessions for Paul McCartney after being recommended by Chrissie Hynde. Rob joined the former Beatle's band and was with McCartney up to 1993, undertaking a couple of world tours and working on two studio albums (*Flowers in the Dirt* and *Off the Ground*). Robbie also did three live albums with McCartney (*Tripping the Live Fantastic, Unplugged* and *Paul is Live*).

Douglas Adams, a good friend of Robbie's, pressed him to put together an album of instrumentals, compositions and arrangements he just played for fun at home, which became the *Unsung* album.

Rob was doing session work in 1998 when he created a band of his own. He brought together some of my favourite players and friends, Paul Beavis, Pino Palladino, Mark Feltham and Melvin Duffy, to generate the Robbie McIntosh Band. They did some gigs and recorded *Emotional Bends*, as their debut album.

Another Robbie McIntosh Band album, *Wide Screen*, was released in June 2001, but then the band gradually fell apart.

Mark now plays with Nine Below Zero, and Robbie

sometimes plays with this band. Melvin is still part of Los Pacaminos and works with Robbie Williams. Robbie still does sessions and gigs with Paul and Pino.

Robbie has now become one of the top guitarists in the UK and has played with many artists in the studio as a session man, for example Talk Talk, Paul Young, Tears for Fears, Joe Cocker, Cher, Kirsty MacColl, Boyzone, Roger Daltrey and Mike and the Mechanics.

He is now nearly 50, and to keep in tune Robbie is doing a few gigs. He has a Blues band the Steamer Ducks, made up of himself, Chris Lonergan, Andy Milward, Clive Ashley, Nick Gomer, Steve Mutter and Paddy Milner. Rob also plays with Beavis McWilson along with Paul Beavis, Steve Wilson and Holly McIntosh (Rob's bass-playing daughter), and Barry the Fireman recently gave me a CD of his set. He really is a great guitarist.

Rob has also been involved with the Polygenes, a progressive instrumental Rock band, led by cellist Chas Dickie, with Chris Lonergan (bass) and Chris Page (drums), and he made an album with them a few years ago. Recently, he's been doing sessions, short tours and one-nighters with Gordon Haskell, and has put half the Robbie McIntosh Band back together (Pino and Paul) along with renowned singer, piano and accordion player Geraint Watkins, who Rob made friends with when they both worked backing Mark Knopfler.

Occasional gigs with Los Pacaminos and regular trips to France to play as half of a duo with French star Diane Tell take up the rest of Rob's time.

THE ROLL-UPS AKA SLOWBONE (THE BAND'S FIRST NAME)

Lea Hart and Jeff Peters were to give so much pleasure but also some heartache. These were real professional guys, who had signed to Motown in the 60s as young men but they never got off the ground because the label were more interested in someone called Stevie Wonder (they supported Stevie at the Rainbow Theatre) and Martha and the Vandellas. Jeff ended up with Joe Brown and the Bruvvers.

After a while, Jeff and Lea got back together and formed Slowbone, a real Heavy Rock band. They used to pack the pub every Friday night, playing great Rock mixed with some comedy songs. They are on the *Live – A Week At The Bridge E16* album as the Roll-Ups, which they'd changed their name to by then. With new songs and a better stage presence, they set out to get that elusive record deal.

After the *Live – A Week At The Bridge E16* album came out, we made the *Mods Mayday '79* album which we signed to Arista Records. We had also released a single by Wasted Youth that became a radio hit, a great song called 'Jealousy'. Polydor Records were trying to sign them and all the record companies were interested in our label.

What we had all been waiting for finally happened after we made an album with the Roll-Ups and a single called 'Blackmail' to promote the album. I was in talks with Robin Blanchflower from Ariola Records and, after much discussion, we got a labels deal. The agreement involved producing five albums a year, at £20,000 advance per album, and eight singles per year, £3,000 per single. They had also offered £20,000 for the Roll-Ups album and single. Robin told me that the whole office believed 'Blackmail' would be a hit single which would also sell the album. I was delighted to ring Lea Hart to tell him the great news, and, of course, they were overjoyed. We had been hoping for an advance of £3,000 to £5,000, as, between us, we had laid out £5,000 but we had a major record deal.

I had made arrangements with Robin to meet the following

day to go over the contract. However, that day I got a call from an Australian informing me that he was the new manager of the Roll-Ups. He said he could get them much more money for the album and, thus, they would not sign the contract with Ariola. He also said I was using them to get a labels deal. I put him straight and told him that they could sign their own deal with Ariola that included options on their future work. I also told him what I thought of him!

Immediately after, I called the band, and you can imagine my state of mind at that point. I told them to fetch all the tapes back to the pub immediately, and they had them delivered to me within the hour. This was a band that had been waiting for 10 years to sign a record deal. If I had said, 'I have got a £1,000 advance, we will split it between us' (our deal was to be a 50/50 split), they would have been happy to sign (the word always goes round when a deal is about to be struck).

This Australian manager gave them the old soft soap: 'I will make you major Rock stars,' etc. He ended up being offered $800 for Germany and $1,500 for Japan and I lost the labels deal with Ariola. Punch line – we were all mates together and I never signed an option contract. I didn't want to stop them becoming the success they were striving for, but they should have trusted me.

An advance from a record company basically means that they give you a sum of money prior to any sales, but out of this you pay all the cost to make the record or album. If the record/album is successful, the advance is deducted from the royalties (profit) that the records make. This is a non-returnable advance.

I believe with the talent that was coming through the pub at that time we would have been a major label within a year. However, in business, as in life, it is better to move forward; it's no good looking back and not very productive.

★ ★ ★

The Friday night that the Roll-Ups had advertised that they were disbanding was a scary night, firstly because it was their last night and secondly because we had arranged to have the gig videotaped. We set up in the afternoon and rehearsed the band. The video operator, Ralph Meade, set up all his equipment and we prepared for a great performance.

When we went to open the pub, we found that Ralph had gone home with the keys. He said he would be back at 9pm when the band was due to start. We opened at 7pm and I managed to get one door open to let the early arrivals in. There were big crowds of fans. By eight o'clock the pub was packed. All the rest of the doors were firmly shut, secured with locks and chains. We were beginning to panic – what if a fire started?

I jumped in my car and drove to East Ham where Ralph lived. I didn't know the number or even his surname at the time, I only knew the road he lived in. I was banging on doors for at least half-an-hour but had no luck. I tore back to the pub, which was jam-packed. Although we had counted 950 inside, when Ralph finally came back with the keys we opened all the doors and people were fainting. They could hardly breathe, so we think there were more than 1,200 people in the Bridge that night. The Roll-Ups had done a really good job of publicising their last ever gig. For all that, after they disappeared for a couple of weeks, they were back, as usual, every Friday, having changed their name to La Rox!

I can't remember how many times La Rox played for us and usually we were packed with non-paying customers. They recruited Ian Mitchell, an ex-Bay City Roller; he later went on to form the Ian Mitchell Band and played a few times for us. Lea always got good media coverage whatever he did, and he certainly was talented when it came to promoting his band and himself. The new band folded, but Lea Hart got a record deal with RCA, and released a single called 'It's New to Me', backed with 'Your Love Affair is Over', produced by Lea Hart and Jeff Peters.

Jeff is now living in America and Lea is managing bands and promoting gigs and having a lot of success with Paul Di'Anno, the ex-Iron Maiden front man.

JACKIE LYNTON

The clown prince of Rock'n'Roll, Jackie has got it all: a great voice and a great comical outlook. A rude, uncouth, blasphemous man while on stage, but off stage a really great guy. It was a pleasure to be in his company and he has always managed to engage good musicians in his band, whose sound and style stalked the realm of Heavy Rock'n'Roll. I last saw Jackie in 1983. He was a major recording artist in the 1960s with hit songs in the Top 10 of the charts. He became a regular at the Bridge House playing for us every few weeks. He was a top songwriter, producing hits for Status Quo along with his good friend Rick Parfitt, who would often come down to support him.

We recorded Jackie on the *Live – A Week At The Bridge E16* album, but his song was so long we had to make a 12-inch EP to go with the album. We had arranged for all the bands on the album to have two tracks each, both around eight minutes. Not Jackie! One song lasted around a quarter of an hour! This was one of Jack's outrageous moves. He told us, 'I am going to keep playing, so you can't take me off the album.' But it was worth it to have a legend on the album.

His band on the album were: Jackie (vocals), Kirk Loader Riddle (bass), Graham Cupcake Cooper (guitar), Alan Clint Watkins (drums) and Greg Squeak (sax, harp). This was Jack – even his band all had to have nicknames.

In the early days, when he was not working, Jack used to like painting. Not the arts, painting houses! At this time, his manager got him a job painting a big house. He was up the ladder painting the windows on the first floor, when he heard a voice saying to him, 'Are you Jackie Lynton?'

He said, 'Yes I am, and who are you?'

The fellow said, 'I'm John Lennon, I own the house.'

Jackie said, 'Tell me, do you want two or three coats of paint on these window frames?'

Lennon walked away shaking his head. What he had heard about Jack was true. He got the job painting the other three Beatles' houses. But he was unable do the work because he was at number eight in the charts with 'Teddy Bears' Picnic' and had to go on the road to promote the song.

Jackie was playing the Bridge one night in 1978 and one of the barmaids said, 'I don't believe it! I've got a record at home called "Teddy Bears' Picnic" by Jackie Lynton; my mum bought it for me when I was a child.'

I told her not to say anything and to pass the record on to me the next time she was working. When she brought it in, I recorded it on to tape and waited for Jackie's next appearance.

Jack was prone to having a go at me and the staff for a laugh. He would come out with some pretty crude sexual references, but of course it was all good fun. If I came down a little late, he would say over the mike, 'Hello, Tel, where you been? Up the massage parlour? You will have to sell the place now the pub's busy.'

He was a real macho man so it was nice to have the chance to get our own back on him. Halfway through his set, the band would have a rest and Jackie would tell a story or two. When the band went off, it went quiet; we had a really loud PA system of our own and at full blast we put on 'Teddy Bears' Picnic'. Well, Jack was so shocked he could not talk. The audience were wondering what was happening so we started shouting out, 'Confess! Confess!' At this time he had a Heavy Metal band and that was in stark contrast with it being 'picnic time for teddy bears'. He just kept saying, 'I don't believe it.'

For the first time in his life I believe he was embarrassed (and shocked).

I made the announcement that this was one of Jackie's hit records in the 60s. We got the audience to keep shouting for him to play it. He quickly got his band back on to play some Rock'n'Roll. We got our own back at last!

We had the Bridge House reunion in July 2001. Jack turned up, sang a few songs and told a few stories. It was great to see him again. He is still gigging and is a regular actor on TV, mainly on *EastEnders*. Long live Jack! He wrote to me recently under the heading 'The Thoughts of Jackie Lynton'!

MEMORIES OF THE BRIDGE
The Thoughts of Jackie Lynton

The Bridge House, Canning Town, what a great gig and how I remember it, like yesterday. It must have been 1944 as we rocked and rolled, the bombs were dropping all round. Hitler certainly had it in for our Terry Murphy. Apparently, when Terry was a boxer, he had beaten a German called 'Englebert Fluck'! Hold on, was it 1954? No, 1974, that's it. Brain's gone.

What I do know is that the Bridge was where I made so many friends who became fans, as I became friends of theirs. And the great thing is they still come to my gigs, even now! Nearly 30 years on!

The Bridge was one of the first major Rock gigs in

Britain. I remember bands used to come from as far away as Sheffield, Oxford, Birmingham, Australia, oh yes, and Southampton, just to play there.

The stage was right in front of the bar. Terry had built it himself. Mick Avory, the Kinks drummer, joined me on stage one night and fell off the kit. Dave Bidwell and Savoy Brown also fell off the kit.

Alby Watkins, Greg Terry-Short and even Keith Moon all jumped up at one time or another and all fell off the drum kit. I mentioned this to Terry and wondered whether the stage was a little uneven, but he said they were probably all pissed. In retrospect, I suspect he was right.

If the gig was a dodgy night, Terry would give us £80 but if it was a good night, as it nearly always was, he would pay us £60. I never quite got the hang of that, still he was the management and he was fucking hard ... but we all loved him.

I met my dear wife Vanessa at the Bridge House and have been with her ever since, so some good came out of it.

The Bridge House was also the place to spot the stars. Regulars included Rick Parfitt of Quo, Jim Davidson, Ritchie Blackmore of Deep Purple, RDB and Chas & Dave, just to name a few. It was also the first to record live bands. I recorded my very first track at the Bridge. I saw some of the best live bands of all times there, but nothing lasts forever. Shame!

Terry always made you feel welcome, with a few beers, sandwiches and good chat. When you played the Bridge House, you felt like a star.

Good luck, Terry, Rita, Glen and all the family
Love, Jackie Lynton

CAFE RACERS, DIRE STRAITS

The first time we heard of this band was in 1976 through a school friend of my son Terry. Richard Thake and Terry had been in the same class at St Bonaventure's School in Forest Gate and became mates. As always, you leave school and go your own ways, so Terry was surprised when his old friend came into the Bridge to tell him that he was looking after some mates who had just formed a band. So for the next few weeks I had to deal with Richard phoning every day and Terry keeping on about his mate's band.

At the time, we had started auditioning bands on Sunday morning. We were getting so many bands sending in demos and continually phoning that it was getting out of hand. We'd usually put a band on as a support before the main band. This sometimes caused agro, sound checks, room on the stage, etc.

So I booked Richard's band in on the Sunday morning. We usually had four bands during the two hours we were open. They played for half an hour, and were very good. One of the band members, Mark Knopfler, came over to see me and asked me what I thought. This was in the first year that I was at the Bridge House and all the bands were Heavy Rock (although I was later to change this with Iron Maiden which was New Wave Heavy Rock). I said to Mark that the band was too Bluesy and he knew the bands that were playing at the Bridge were Heavy. I understand he had been down to look at the venue a couple of times with Richard Thake, and his brother who was also in the band. Mark said to me, 'Give us a chance, we will play some different music.'

I could see he was ambitious. He told me he had a residency at the King's Head in North London and that the band had built the night up. So I gave him the next Tuesday.

On the night, Terry was to meet a lot more of his old school friends. Richard had worked his socks off to get a crowd along. I was hoping that the following the band had built up in Islington would come over to our pub, but no such luck. Although it was a nice night and I really liked their music, there were not enough people there to make it pay. But I had heard enough to realise that I preferred the type of sound they were playing to Heavy music.

So I think we can say that, although I don't believe they played again for me, it was Dire Straits that changed the Bridge House from a Heavy Metal joint to a Blues-type pub. This was, of course, prior to the New Wave of music and before we started charging at the door. When this happened, I decided to have a different band on every night.

I figured that, as the customers only had a certain amount of money to spend from their wages, if you always had the same type of band, they could only come one or two nights according to their taste. So by having different bands they would arrange to come to the Bridge instead of travelling miles to see their choice of band. It was a good idea, and it worked for a few years.

Twenty years later, I had a meeting with Richard Thake and Tony Ciniglio, the original bass player with both Cafe Racers and Dire Straits. Tony told me the original line-up was: Dave Pask (vocals, guitar), Bobby Miller (soon to join Supertramp) (drums), Rob Mills, Mark Knopfler and his brother David (guitar). Dave Pask and Mark had got together at Loughton College with Tony. Mark, who grew up in the North East, was living in Buckhurst Hill in Essex. An advert was placed in *Melody Maker* and the guys held the auditions in Richard Thake's mum's kitchen, and at one time Mark actually slept on Richard's living-room floor. One night, Dire Straits were on TV, and Richard mentioned this to his mother. By this time, 'Sultans of Swing' had made them famous and very rich, and his mum's reply was: 'Oh he's doing all right then. That bit of carpet must be worth a few bob now. I best save it for a rainy day.'

This is East End humour at its best. The East End can claim that all the local guys, mainly from Stratford E15, made Dire Straits the band they were to become. Mark's brother, Dave, and Tony C were to leave less than two years later.

ROBIN TROWER: THE PARAMOUNT, PROCOL HARUM, THE JAM (NOT PAUL WELLER), JUDE WITH FRANKIE MILLER, ROBIN TROWER BAND AND BLT!

My favourite instrument has always been lead guitar, and one of the first lead guitarists I met was Robin Trower, who was the first guitarist I watched in 1965. Also in 1965 I had been offered a large hall that was part of the Tarpots pub in Canvey Island. A boxing colleague had taken over the Tarpots when my brother John had been made the new manager of the Royal Oak in Canning Town by Courage the brewery.

Morrie Vickers asked me and my partner Dave Sammons, if we were interested; we had a look at the hall, which was licensed for 400 people, and said yes. Morrie knew I had a lot of experience, as I'd run the Bongo, a club in Barking Road, Canning Town. We knew that, for instant success, you needed local bands who had already built a following. We were dealing with MAM agency, the best in the country at the time, and they offered us a new band called the Who, who had started to make a name for themselves. We could have them for £100! I got them down to £75 (it was still too much). We were charging seven shillings and six pence (7/6 – 38p in today's money) so, even if we had a full house, we would still lose money, what with other expenses. We had boxing champ and former Olympic Gold Medal winner Terry Spinks and Jim Gaiger managing the security. They and their team never came cheap. MAM then suggested the Paramount who were a local band from Southend, which was 20 minutes from the Tarpots. They had a new single out that was getting some airplay, and it looked like it might chart. We settled on a fee of £30 and gave the local band a home gig. The band were delighted to come home to play in their own area. They pulled a fairly good crowd, so we gave them a few more gigs.

The line-up for this band was Robin Trower, Gary Brooker, BJ Wilson and Dix Derrick.

The Paramount got their hit single. The band broke up when Robin left to form the Jam. Gary and the band formed Procol Harum and had a massive hit with 'Whiter Shade of Pale' and also had several other good-selling singles and albums over a few years. Although Robin never played on 'Whiter Shade of Pale', he did play guitar on five of their albums, so they must have remained friends.

Robin lost his way a bit. After the Jam, he formed Jude with Frankie Miller (vocals), Jim Dewer (bass) and Clive Bunker (drums), but this band never happened. He then formed a funky-type band, the Robin Trower Band (that made its debut in Vienna), which included Reg Isadore on drums, and they had two hit albums.

By the time I had established the Bridge House as a 'great gig' (Rory Gallagher's words), Robin came back to see me, and asked for a gig, a low-key affair to get the record companies down to see his new band, BLT, who were looking for a new record contract. Robin had formed BLT with Jack Bruce (bass guitar, vocals). Robin and Jack were joined by Sly and the Family Stone drummer Bill Lordan. He remembered me and the Tarpots, so he came personally to ask for the gig, and we reminisced about the old days.

Robin is still gigging, producing and is very busy, based in the USA.

SASSAFRAS

We had been at the Bridge House for a few years and everything was going well but, whatever I do, I always want to go that one step further. I got to a point where I wanted to start promoting bigger bands at bigger gigs. My first venture in 1978 was at the Poplar Civic Theatre in Bow, a place that was well known to all the family. I had boxed there as an amateur; both me and my wife Rita had been to dances there in our youth; and my son Glen got married to Linda Bowers there, so what better place to start my promoting career? We tried to get some bigger bands than we were getting at the Bridge. One of the ideas I had was to put them on at Poplar, make friends with them and then get them to come and play some secret gigs at the Bridge. It was a nightmare trying to get established bands to play a new venue, as they all wait to see how it goes down with the first to play there. We could not get any major names as they would just price themselves out of it, so we were pleased in the end to get Sassafras, who were a good Rock band who had been there and done that. We also had another band plus Gerry Floyd, the number-one DJ in Britain from the Marquee (Wardour Street, W1).

Bob Sachs, who was my partner in this promoting enterprise, was running a nice gig in Brentwood called the Hermit Club (which is still going strong). I financed things and Bob and his partner did the setting up. We did the whole bit: posters, mail-outs, etc. and got a nice bar set up. The only people to turn up were my customers from the Bridge House, which was great, as instead of working I could mingle with the crowd and this made it a special night. When we got back to the Bridge, it had been fairly busy, so maybe sometimes you've got to be happy with what you've got.

It worked though. Sassafras played the Bridge House about a

month later on 70 per cent of the door takings. Taking what I paid them at the Poplar Civic Theatre as a baseline, this saved me £300. They were a nice band and a nice bunch of fellows, and I hope that they are still around in different bands, unless, of course, Sassafras are still playing together as a band. Ray Jones (one time of Smokestack) is certainly still performing from time to time in Wales. Musicians never give up, so you can bet the rest of the band are still around playing somewhere.

TOM ROBINSON

I was reluctant at first when asked to give the Tom Robinson Band a gig early in 1977, as we had heard all kinds of rumours about them being a gay band. I had asked Barry Hart to check them out and he told me that they were a good band. They had a residency at the Brecknock Castle in North London, and Barry had played there with his band a few times.

Their manager at the time was Colin Bell, and I trusted Colin because he had booked a few bands he was managing with us. So, when Barry gave them a good report, I let them have a gig and worried all day about whether I had made the right move, given the negative feelings about 'alternative sexuality' that can be quite forceful in working-class areas like Canning Town. I had imagined they would have a large gay audience, which I didn't think would mix very well with my regular customers. And that would spell trouble we did not want. It always starts off with a laugh and a joke, but then someone goes over the top and it's off.

I shouldn't have worried though, as the band were very good, and they wanted a residency. I said, 'I'll give you another gig next week and see how it goes; you will have to make yourself busy and get more fans in.'

This surprised Tom, but he was pleased and said he would try.

I told him to try to keep the number of gay fans down. He said, 'Well, *I'll* be here.'

At the time, I wasn't sure whether the gay tag was just a gimmick to be a bit different, as I had heard Tom was married and had children, but he was to prove me wrong when he started to sing 'Glad to be Gay', which our customers really enjoyed, with some of them even singing along with it. The BBC actually banned that song from being played on the radio but it was still a big hit. Funnily enough, 20 years on, he won a Sony Radio Award for some of his work for the BBC. That must have been one of Tom's sweetest moments.

An even sweeter one for him was becoming a father. So it seems he might have changed that side of his lifestyle slightly in the last couple of decades. In 1982, at a Gay Switchboard benefit, Tom saw the boyfriend he had always dreamed of across a crowded room. However, the dream lover was a woman. They moved from being friends, to become lovers, and then parents. The tabloids had a field day, with the *Sun* hollering: 'GLAD TO BE DAD'!

Most of his set was made up of original songs. Tom had a number of hits after 'Glad to be Gay', including '2.4.6.8 Motorway', which I think has great lyrics:

2,4,6,8
It's never too late,
To listen to my radio,
3,5,7,9
Little white lies.

Tom is still out there touring with his band and he's done some work for BBC Radio 5. He has just started work on the new BBC 6 Music Radio. We all wish him well.

Colin Bell went on to have a good career, managing the Tom

Robinson Band. Tom recalled, 'Colin Bell managed Tom Robinson Band from the outset in 1976. The band signed to Pink Floyd manager Steve O'Rourke in 1978 and Colin came along with us to work out of that office, he then managed Sector 27 from 1980 to 1981 before going on to work for Polygram and eventually becoming label manager of London Records.'

Recently Tom wrote to me about the Bridge House.

MEMORIES OF THE BRIDGE
Tom Robinson

Hi Terry

How the devil are you?

I certainly remember the warm friendly reception we got at the Bridge as an unknown band, though the combination of hitting my fifties and several misspent decades of drug abuse have robbed me of most of the brain and memory cells I once had …

The main things I seem to remember from the time are:

1) Being extremely grateful to have been given a gig at all at the time. As a little-known band on the London pub circuit with no record contract who'd only been in existence a few months, we needed all the bookings we could get. And being treated with a friendliness and respect as performers when we arrived, which was (and still is) all too rare among pub managers.

2) I remember being nervous about playing the East End where the band had no existing following and particularly because our set included 'Glad to be Gay', which was never exactly a guaranteed singalong crowd pleaser, especially back then before it had been in the Top 20.

3) Coming back to the venue in the evening, having done our sound check earlier in the day, and finding nowhere to park — the whole pub was surrounded by parked cars up on all the kerbs and pavements and everywhere. We wondered what else could be going on in the area that evening, then we walked in and the place was stuffed with people who'd come to see *us*!

We had a storming show, and by the end of 'Glad to be Gay' most people had just gone, 'Hey, brave stance, fair play to 'em.' And applause-wise the song was one of the high spots of the night. Ironically, I remember that night taught me exactly the same point the song itself was supposed to be making: don't pre-judge people or make ignorant assumptions about what you think they're going to be like. The Bridge House actually had one of the warmest, most responsive audiences TRB ever played to.

Hope that's some help and moderately accurate — i.e. that my dope-addled memory hasn't made me hallucinate the whole episode after all these years!

Best
Tom

THE TROGGS

I found out that the Troggs were available for gigs while talking to an agent one day, I guess in 1979.

We didn't have set fees for the bands that played for us, our policy was a percentage of the door takings, from 70 to 100 per cent and if the bigger bands wanted set fees we then knew they were probably not going to pull enough people to make it pay.

To try to break us over the percentage rule, we were given a copy of the famous tape of the Troggs' recording session, where the tape had been left running and they were ranting and raving at each other. We though it was very funny. The agent had said that they needed £200 or they would not play, so I gave in and signed the contract; after all, they had been major stars with many hit records.

The gig was scheduled for the Saturday evening of that dayand, in the afternoon, the guys came over to get the band's instruments and PA system in. I went down to let them in and they got all the stuff on stage. I told them, 'We don't open until 7pm, so I've got to lock the doors. When the band get here, give me a call and I'll let them in.'

They replied in their strange accents, 'But we *are* the band!'

I was shocked. Reg Presley and the famous Troggs were dressed like farmers who had just left the fields! And they were their own roadies! But when the time came for them to be on stage they were dressed in nice leather clothes.

I charged £1 on the door, and I really thought over 200 people would turn up. I was wrong, only 120 people paid so the band even ended up taking the profit on the bar; we worked for love that night.

A friend of mine, Eddie Richardson, came all the way from Durham to see them. Well, it was his release day. And I thought he came to see me!

It was a nice night and they played all their hits. But we lost money that night and I was to learn a lesson. This was a Rock pub and the Troggs were a cabaret band who had not moved on from the 60s. But they should worry! They and their songs are still going strong to this day.

LINDISFARNE

We got the call from this band in 1979 when they had just finished an album called *Kings and Queens* or *Jack of Clubs*, something to do with cards as I remember. They had a big tour set up and they wanted to judge how the songs sounded live in front of an audience. It was a great gig for us. We had to keep it quiet because they were a really big band at this time. On Saturday nights, we had a regular crowd that always turned up as well as the ones who came just to see the different bands playing.

The gig was going well when all of a sudden the singer, Ray Jackson, and another band member started arguing and then fighting. Everyone dived in to stop it. The singer jumped off stage and went to the dressing room, so the band carried on and played an instrumental. The singer came back and started singing but did not speak to anyone for the rest of the night. When the gig finished, the singer jumped off stage and went straight out of the door. I know why the argument started and who was right and what it was about, but I am sworn to secrecy, so I can't tell you. Ha ha! It was something to do with the band's next album being put out as a solo album. That meant that the band would get paid as session musicians and not be entitled to a split of the royalties and the vocalist Ray Jackson would get all the glory and the royalties too. It's only Rock'n'Roll but we like it!

NASHVILLE TEENS

The Nashville Teens had a sensational hit in the 60s with 'Tobacco Road' and had a great deal of success with their other songs too, so I was excited when I booked them at the Bridge in about 1978. We did all the advertising, local write-ups, etc. at a reasonable ticket price. We had extra staff laid on, all ready to go, but it ended up a really disastrous night and the pub was not even a quarter full. The band were good but, like the Troggs, they had become a cabaret band. True, it was their living, but when you're just playing for money that old vibe goes and you get the same worn-out jokes in between the songs. It was a good job that they saved 'Tobacco Road' until near the end of the set because nearly everyone left after they had played that great song. Pity; it's tough at the top.

IRON MAIDEN

I wanted to change the Bridge, but I wasn't anti-Heavy Metal. We had Iron Maiden play for us around 40 times and you can't get heavier than them. Garry Bushell named them New Wave Heavy Metal and this title stayed with them. What a good idea!

Iron Maiden learned how to play at the Bridge. Steve Harris was the leader and I had a Poplar phone number for him, very local, which was handy when we had a cancellation and they came and played for us.

They were a nice tight unit and pulled a really big crowd of followers, so I gave them a four-week residency in 1976. They really built up a big following and I gave them plenty of gigs over the next year or two but I still wanted to phase out the Heavy Metal at this time.

My brother-in-law, Joe Lucy, had lost his resident band, the Mission Bells, who had decided to call it a day about 1977. They were a girl vocal band singing mainly standards who had played for Joe for years. He rang and said he was in trouble, as, without music in a big pub like the Ruskin Arms, your takings hit rock bottom. I said, 'Well I've got this Heavy Metal band who pull a really good crowd of their own.'

I gave him their number. Joe was delighted after the first night and gave them a full-time residency playing three nights a week and every weekend, and again they pulled really good crowds.

In the meantime, Steve continued ringing for a gig, which I never gave him. He came in the pub one night, when we had a band on, but there were only a few customers in. Steve said angrily, 'Why won't you give us a gig? I can't understand you; you know we pull a good crowd and look how many you got tonight.

'We need to play here to get our name about and to get a record deal. You advertise in the *Melody Maker* and the *NME*. And this is a real gig!'

I phoned Joe the next morning and told him about my conversation with Steve. Joe told me that no way did he want them to go; end of story. It was awkward, as my brother-in-law needed them and he didn't charge on the door, so the customers saw Iron Maiden for free. At the time, we had started to charge on the door, 30p per night. It doesn't seem much now but it was the cost of a pint which is well over £2 now. Why would they pay to see them at the Bridge when they could see them down the road at the Ruskin in High Street North in East Ham for nothing?

The band went on to become one of the biggest and best bands in the world and I am honoured to have played my part.

It was not all plain sailing for Iron Maiden, plenty of group changes, and they had at least three different vocalists while playing for us. The first singer Denny came from Enfield. I believe he was idolised by the Maiden crowd, and only the band know why he left. Their next singer was a regular customer at the Bridge, Bruce Dickinson; he is on one of the inner-sleeve group pictures on the *Live – A Week At The Bridge E16* album, as all our regulars were. Iron Maiden also included a keyboard player to see if it would help them add the final touches to the making of this great band. Unfortunately, it didn't. At the end of this gig, the band had a big argument and the following week they arrived to play … without a keyboard player.

It was when RDB split that Dennis Stratton joined Maiden; he was very successful and they toured the world. I heard Dennis ended up leaving because their management wouldn't let any of the band members have any cash. Their money was paid direct into their bank accounts. I wonder why they would not let them have any readies; that's hard to work out. Dennis thought they were being treated like children. There was a ruck, so they replaced him.

Paul Di'Anno was another of Iron Maiden's singers for a while. When he left them he got a new band together and came down the Bridge to play. He is now managed by Lea Hart of the Roll-Ups.

I still see Steve, as he plays for my son Glen's West Ham celebrity football team and I see him at West Ham watching the Hammers. He's a lovely fellow, not changed by stardom, always with his children. I knew his wife, Lorraine, who he was courting while playing at the Bridge, and, although they are now not together, I still see her as well, at football matches.

At the time Iron Maiden were playing for Joe Lucy, Lorraine's best friend, another Lorraine, married Dennis Stratton, who was to became Iron Maiden's guitarist. Rita and me organised their wedding reception at the Bridge and later became godparents to their daughter who has grown up to become a lovely young lady. So, with all these connections, it's easy to see how some of our bands felt more like friends and family to us!

SAMSON

Paul Samson had his own band called Samson that he formed in the late 1970s with Chris Aylmer (bass) and Clive Burr (drums). Clive left, and after a while became part of Iron Maiden and Barry Graham, aka Thunderstick, took over drums with Samson. Barry wore a gimp mask on stage, and, as this was when the masked Cambridge Rapist filled the newspaper pages, unsurprisingly this made Barry a target for criticism.

The band's personnel was increased to four in 1979 when Bruce Bruce (Bruce Dickinson) joined as a vocalist, and they released the albums *Survivors*, *Head On* and *Shock Tactics*. In 1981, Thunderstick left, and Bruce Bruce changed his surname back to Dickinson and joined Iron Maiden.

Samson played a lot of gigs for us and were on the circuit for a long time, before Paul became the guitarist with Iron Maiden.

Nicky Moore was recruited as the replacement vocalist and Mel Gaynor took over on drums. When he left, Pete Jupp was brought in, and it was this line-up that released the *Before the Storm* and *Don't Get Mad Get Even* albums. These sold much better than their first three efforts, and this predictably lead to the band touring more countries and playing in front of bigger audiences than they had with Bruce and Thunderstick in their ranks, although by this point the New Wave of British Heavy Metal was in the process of petering out. Samson disappeared into Rock history in 1984.

Paul spent the following years in a range of solo and group projects, including a number of reformed line-ups of Samson. He had some success as a producer and as a Blues player, and spent a year in Chicago.

Sadly, in August 2002, Paul, who had been suffering with cancer, passed away at the age 49. He was recording a new Samson album with Nicky Moore at the time. Paul was a talented guitarist and it was probably a run of bad luck and dodgy decisions that stopped him achieving more than cult status.

U2

I suppose the band that has made it to the very top is U2 and arguably they were the most famous of the new bands to have started at the Bridge, although I know they played their first gigs in their home town in Ireland. The band was formed by their drummer, Larry Mullen, while still at school in Dublin, at Mount Temple Comprehensive, where they were all pupils.

Irish bands always got a little more encouragement from me. Is it the old Irish blood in this Cockney-born Londoner? No, it wasn't that; they had to come to a strange country to try to make it in the music business, which was almost impossible anyway, but they managed to do it. Well done, U2!

I remember very well the first night they played. Bono was only 18 at the time. It has been said in the press that their first gig in England was at the Hope and Anchor in Islington in December 1979. I absolutely challenge this statement because they were billed as 'The U2s'; their first gig in England as *U2* was at the Bridge House, Canning Town! I remember talking to Paul Hewson and David Howell Evans (as Bono and The Edge were known in those days), and discussing another Irish band I had given a start to: Bernie Torme, a really good guitarist. He gave it a go, but never made it with his own band, and he ended up joining the Ian Gillan Band. Of course, Rory Gallagher's name came up; he was a god in Ireland. In 1968, he had been voted the best guitarist in the world. Then his bass player, Gerry McAvoy, walked into the pub, and I introduced Gerry to Paul and David. It was at this time Bono told me it was their first gig and that they had another gig booked for the following week.

Although it was a nice tight band, they seemed nothing special. Bono's vocal range did not reach the highs and lows that most of the bands coming through were achieving. In fact, I have just heard his latest single and he has got a great voice but still cannot hit those high notes. But we had done our bit for the band, got their name in the music papers, playing a known gig. This helped them get more. They never did any business for us:

only 18 people paid to see them that night and the pub had a few guests. I paid for their PA system, Rita fed them, we had a few drinks and they were gone.

Around six months later, promoter John Curd, who was booking the Lyceum, wanted Wasted Youth to support them, which at the time was an insult. We said we would headline for the same money he was offering, but they would have to support *us*. We were already playing a joint headliner with Killing Joke, so to support another band would be a step down for Wasted. We had previously supported Jim Kerr's Simple Minds at the Lyceum. What they do to the support band is turn the PA down to half its power, turn off some of the monitors and pull plugs on the mixing desk, which makes the support band sound 'untogether' and less powerful. You also only get about a 10-minute sound check. I am not saying U2 or Jim Kerr would have done this, but once bitten …

Now U2 are one of the biggest bands in the world, we wished we'd done the support. But, at the time, it was the right decision.

Later on, we were on the same bill as U2 at the Futurama Festival in Leeds, which was filmed for TV. Siouxsie and the Banshees and Echo and the Bunnymen shared our dressing room; Human League's Phil Oakley was ligging and many more bands were there. This was an all-dayer, when the best bands go on last. Everyone in the crowd – and it was packed – were sitting on the floor. Wasted struck up and the audience were straight on their feet cheering and they didn't sit down again till we were finished. No other band got the reception Wasted did that night, including U2. But, once again, well done, U2!

U2's first recording was an EP called *U2.3*. There was talk that this was going to be a name change, and at that time U three is what the imitators of the band were called – there's probably U three hundred now!

In March 1983, when Bono was being interviewed in Newcastle, he signed a picture to go on a picture disc thanking me – you can hear him on the interview asking for the pen! A friend of mine asked him to sign. I was not there, so that was a nice idea. I've still got the recording somewhere. In the interview Bono talks about another band called Virgin Prunes, a really loud Punk band who were mates with U2. In fact, The Edge's brother was in the band.

I later wondered if U2 had started off with the Punk scene, as they did start to play while at school during the Punk era. But, when they played the Bridge House years later, the Punk scene was coming to an end and U2 certainly were not a Punk band then.

PUNK ROCK, NEW WAVE ... AND BEYOND

Punk started in earnest at the beginning of 1977. I think it can be thought of as the rebellion of youth, and the rebellion of non-playing wannabe musicians. Before Punk changed things, a few mates would get together and practise, rehearse and keep going until they were good enough to get a gig. Punks would get together and try to prove that they could *not* play – and they couldn't, and it showed.

This was the era of Rock Against Racism, which was strongly supported by the Tom Robinson Band who put stickers all over the Bridge House when they played for us.

At that time the music business did not know what to do with the new bands. Work was in short supply; kids were leaving school and were unable to get jobs. The National Front (the unpricked blister of the British National Party) was stalking like a bad smell all over the place and we had Bob Marley on *Top of the Pops* singing 'Stand Up For Your Rights'. And, guess what, Rod Stewart was number one with 'First Cut is the Deepest'. Tell this to the 'Oi' bands and the second-generation Skins who were appearing at that point and mostly carrying the old Stanley knife for protection.

One night, I caught a bloke called Andy with one. When I grabbed him, he said, 'Leave off, Tel! I'm a painter and decorator and I need it for my work.'

So he collected it at the end of the evening. But you have to laugh sometimes; when he got it back, he found that the blade was missing – how'd that happen?

While Punk was beginning to thrive, Stevie Wonder's 'Isn't She Lovely' was released, and, although it was inspired by the birth of his daughter, in Britain it was used as a perfectly timed tribute to the Queen, which she deserved.

1977 was also the year we lost the greatest Rock'n'Roller of all times, Elvis Presley; Maggie Thatcher was elected our first female Prime Minister; and we were further shocked when Malcolm McLaren was arrested on Jubilee Day.

When the Punk bands started to ring me for gigs, I gave them a chance; after all, it was something new and getting some press coverage and we all like to be into something new. The Sex Pistols' agency used to telephone me regularly trying to get them a gig. I wasn't keen, but eventually relented and said OK. I said we would like two 45-minute sets. 'No way' was the reply. They would only do one set of 15 to 20 minutes. They wanted all the door takings and a free PA system too. I wouldn't want to put my reply into print! They kept ringing and I kept saying no.

But I wanted to see what it was all about so we gave a few local bands a chance; they were terrible! Spitting, pogoing, pill popping and dressed in dirty torn clothes! But we kept the night going and, as they played more regularly, they got better musically.

As the year went on, we booked the Damned, who were the first Punk band with a record deal. Dave Robinson signed them to his new label Stiff Records and their first single was 'New Rose'. He put them in the studio and released an album, *Damned Damned*, within the week – yes, that quick! Most albums, from start to finish, would take up to a year to get released. Well, they wanted to beat the Sex Pistols and the other bands to a Punk release on vinyl. And they did.

Here, in no particular order, are some of the Punk and New Wave bands who played (or tried to!) at the Bridge.

SEX PISTOLS

'God Save the Queen', in my opinion, was a great record, perfectly timed, plenty of press, a great plan. The Pistols got signed to EMI then were sacked by them. After that they signed to Richard Branson's Virgin label. It was headline news, on the front page of nearly all of the papers.

The record was banned from air play, and, on Jubilee Day, Pistols manager Malcolm McLaren had cleverly hired a boat to perform the song because they could not get booked in any gig on that day ... and got arrested for his trouble!

Also on the boat that day was the head of Virgin Records, Mr Richard Branson, who, ironically 25 years later, for Her Majesty's Golden Jubilee, would be sitting with the Queen as, by that time, *Sir* Richard of course.

The Pistols' line-up at that time was Johnny Rotten (vocals), Glen Matlock (bass) (Glen Matlock played a lot of gigs for us after he left the Pistols), Paul Cook (drums) and Steve Jones (guitar). We won't mention Chris Spedding (although I just did).

THE WASPS

The Wasps were the first New Wave band we were impressed with – well, they were very well dressed for a Punk band. They still had the safety pins in their ears, noses and everywhere, but they had smart leather shirts and trousers. We started to give them gigs in 1976 and they were good. It was 1976 that we first started getting Punk, New Wave and Oi bands. The Business and the 4-Skins are a couple of names I remember. The 4-Skins were local boys who wanted to be taken seriously. They even came with me to my publishers, Martin and Coulter, to try to get a publishing deal. They went on to get a record and publishing deal with a different company and released a number of records. What a great name! I used to wonder why all the Skinheads turned up. They played for us a few times and there was never any trouble. The band, being locals, liked and respected our family and the Bridge, so Hoxton Tom (Tom McCourt of the 4-Skins) and all their mates put the word around to be on their best behaviour.

The big proof of this was when Vince Riordan and Gary Dickle, a few of the guys who were looking after Jimmy Pursey of Sham 69, got him to do a gig for us. The band pulled a lot of Skins from Tottenham, so it was the West Ham Skins v Tottenham Skins. It was a great night; the pub was packed but there was no trouble at all. They all enjoyed themselves and the feared punch-up didn't happen.

Fights only used to start when punters got bored with the night and the band. But I must say that, in those days, Canning Town Skins ruled the roost. I have got a great picture of some of our best-behaved Skins, which was taken in the bar at the Bridge for a newspaper: John Butler, Gary Dickle, Glen Murphy Jr, Vince Riordan and Kevin Hennessy. My grandson Glen was two years old at the time. Vince was the bass player in the Cockney Rejects and John and Gary minded a number of bands including Sham 69.

THE DAMNED

The Damned played quite a few gigs for us in 1977. They were getting a lot of punters who got to the gigs early and they did not have to pay to get in; all their gigs were packed and Stiff sold a lot of albums. They were a great bunch of guys, Rat Scabies (Chris Millar) (drums) (Johnny Rotten said that Rat was the drum roadie for the Pistols, but I don't believe that), Captain Sensible (Ray Burns) (guitar, vocals), Dave Vanian (vocals) and Brian James (bass). Rat Scabies and Captain Sensible also came to the Bridge with different bands. I remember the White Cats was one name Rat used for a band.

Captain Sensible left the Damned a few times. He went on to have a hit single with 'Happy Talk' and has worked constantly on a range of projects over the years. A few months after 'Happy Talk', he was back down the Bridge gigging. This went on for about a year and then he came back with the Damned.

The Damned always did a good gig for us. They had decided to leave their management team and do some gigs on their own. Rat Scabies said to me that the most money they ever got for a gig was when they played at the Bridge. There was never any trouble that we could not handle when they played so everyone was happy.

The Damned would have a row and split up, but they would all call me for info about what artists were available and they would book a gig. Sometimes, about a week later, I'd get another call saying they were back together again. You got used to it after a few years.

THE VIBRATORS

This band were around at the very start of the Punk movement. I gave them a few gigs in late 1976 because I liked their attitude and you could see that they were hungry for success. They started to get gigs elsewhere after we had advertised them, so we got them back to play a headliner. But their conduct had changed and they behaved really badly. After the gig, I gave them their money and thanked them for the gig.

This flash guy in the band said, 'What did you think? We were brilliant, weren't we?'

I replied, 'Well, I don't like Punk music, you're not good instrumentalists, and the spitting and pogoing is unruly. Remember I have to keep the peace.'

The mouthy bloke came back at me: 'What do you fucking know anyway?'

I told him, 'I know one thing: you won't be playing here again.'

One of the other band members told him to shut up and told me the gobby one was out of his head.

I agreed, saying, 'Just let him know he's out of here.'

A while later, I got a call from a band called Knox asking for a gig. The guy on the line said his previous band had been the Vibrators and he remembered the disagreement and assured me it wasn't him who had caused the problem. I gave them a gig. When they turned up, they *were* the Vibrators, they had just changed their name to get the gig! They had learned to play and were a lot better and very well behaved. Whether it was the same line-up I wouldn't know because the next week I got a call from the Vibrators asking for a gig. So I said, 'Fuck off! Don't take me for a idiot! If you'd said your name was Knox, I would have given you another gig; it would have been water under the Bridge.'

Their thinking was: we played as Knox and got the gig back, so let's front him (well, if fronting someone is making a phone call to them) and let him know we're the Vibrators. They certainly were not from the East End. They never played again for me. If a little word like 'sorry' had been said, I would have probably relented, as I know at times we all need a second chance.

UK SUBS

Charlie Harper's UK Subs were one of the best-loved Punk bands. Charlie's enthusiasm was infectious, and he must have been the oldest Punk around, probably 20 years older than the young upstarts.

They really worked their balls off, gigging three to four nights a week all over the country. One of the times they played for us was at the end of a 40-date tour of Britain, and they were knackered.

They played at breathtaking speed, some of their songs were only about minute long; no pause, straight into the next one. But the hard work caught up with them. The bass player Paul Slack nearly died on the tour and was replaced by his brother Steve but only until he was fit again. Steve had been the original bass player with the Subs. Eventually, though, their hard work was rewarded with record contracts and Top-20 hits in the charts as well as a tour in America.

CRASS AND JOHN LOADER

John Loader booked the night (and day) in 1980 with Crass. This wasn't a gig, it was a *happening*. They blocked off the stage and the dressing-room area in the afternoon, did the gig in the evening and we never saw them again. Even if I'd wanted to I couldn't have got in to see them. It wasn't the security men in my way, just barriers of flight cases, speakers and crates.

Crass went on to release many recordings and became cult icons.

John Loader had a studio in Woodford Green where we all recorded our music. He started it in his garage. We did 'Jab and Move', the Roll-Ups' single 'Blackmail' and the album *Low Dives for High Balls*. Wasted Youth's 'Jealousy' was also finished there. Gerry McAvoy and loads of others used John's place.

John started to distribute records from his own house, and then operated under the Southern Distribution banner, one of the main independent distributors. Following John's death, the distribution is being carried on by another old friend, from Jungle Records.

COCKNEY REJECTS

Canning Town's own, the Rejects were the subject of an hour-long television documentary about music and West Ham football hooligans, presented by Janet Street Porter, which was filmed at the Bridge House in 1980. We all thought it was a great night, but the Rejects didn't agree. It was the first gig they had done where they hadn't had a fight, and they felt frustrated, so after the gig they went up the West End and got rid of the frustration.

When the police interrupted their night out, they said, 'We are in a band and this is our encore!'

Naturally, the four blokes on the floor didn't feel like applauding them.

Although they liked a fight, the Rejects played quite a few gigs at the Bridge and never brought us any trouble. Of course, when I say *no* trouble, I don't mean when one or two punches are thrown, that's nothing. We had no trouble with the Rejects, but at most of their gigs trouble kicked off.

Later on, they went from being Skins to Heavy Metal and then changed back again. They had quite a bit of success in the record business. Remember their hit 'I'm Forever Blowing Bubbles'? (Strangely, that song is the most recorded song in the history of music.)

Wasted Youth drummer Andy Scott joined them for a while and, according to Jeff Turner and Garry Bushell in their book *Cockney Reject* (2005), Andy ended up getting a bashing just for being stoned. Well, of course, Wasted Youth were signed to Bridge House Records, my label, and our story is a bit different. Andy Scott at that time was, without doubt, the best young drummer in London; in fact, he was so good that, when Darren and Andy's elder brother Ken Scott formed Wasted Youth, they wanted him in the band (they had played together in a previous band called the Tickets). So, when

Andy left Cockney Rejects and joined Wasted Youth, the Rejects beat him up, because they did not want to lose the best drummer around at that time. But the bit of violence didn't work that time.

In their book, Jeff and Garry write that when they arrived at the Bridge they were told by my son Glen that they were barred. When Glen called me down, we had a chat, good old 'Towners' together, four of them and four of us. A couple of drinks and, without a punch being thrown, we sorted it out and they were allowed back in their 'office' (they made all their important meetings at the Bridge during the day, so it became known as their office).

I still see all the guys at boxing matches and Bridge House reunions. In fact, the guitarist Mick Geggus and I have had a few meetings and something really exciting may come out of it. So watch this space ...

GLORIA MUNDI

Gloria Mundi were a great band who really should have made it. A friend of mine from my boxing days, Jackie Bowers, came to the Bridge in 1978 to learn about the pub business and after some training started working on my nights off. I would give him a list of the bands that were available in case one we had booked dropped out. He soon picked the game up, so off I went on a cruise for three weeks with Rita and my kids. He had given Gloria Mundi a gig, liked them and sacked the regular Wednesday band to give them a residency. When I got home, I had the hump that he had got rid of my regular band but when I heard them I had to make him right; they were good and I continued to give them gigs when they wanted. They got on the main circuit, the Marquee, the Nashville, etc. The female singer Sunshine

Patteson was very punky, with good vocals, and the male singer was Eddie Maelor. For a time, they were a cabaret-type duo called Sunshine and Eddie, performing theatrical songs to backing tapes. I'd really like to know how their careers ended up.

THE REZILLOS

This band did well for themselves after coming down from Edinburgh. They were a modern New Wave band, completely moving away from Punk, although they were labelled as such, and they had a fast poppy type of sound. If my memory is right, this was in 1976. They were put in touch with us by another Scottish band called the Skids. Their singer Richard Jobson later became a well-known TV presenter.

The Rezillos managed to get a major deal and made some hit records, then, like the song, just faded away. But today they are back, playing gigs around London. Good luck to them.

TENPOLE TUDOR

This band played quite a few gigs for us in 1980. An unusual band, they were quite different from the normal, punky, theatrical, fast New Wave music. The line-up for the band was Eddie Tudor (vocals, sax), Bob Kington (guitar, vocals), Dick Crippen (bass, vocals) and Gary Long (drums, vocals).

Tenpole Tudor started out with a single called 'Real Fun' on a small independent label and were eventually signed by Stiff Records. The band appeared on the Sons of Stiff tour with Lena Lovich among others. They also recorded a couple of albums for Stiff. Tenpole's hit singles included 'Who Killed Bambi' and 'Swords of a Thousand Men'.

We had a secret gig one night with Depeche Mode. Bob, the guitarist in Tenpole Tudor, was escorting Kim Wilde who had

Greetings from
LONDON BOROUGH OF NEWHAM
CANNING TOWN

BRIDGE HOUSE

RECORDS

$33\frac{1}{3}$ rpm   STEREO

SIDE ONE   BHLP001A

LIVE!

1 Everybody's Gotta Have A Hero — ROLL UPS
   (L. Hart Jnr. — Arnakata)
2 It Hurts Me Too — S.A.L.T.
   (London — Jewel Music)
3 Hipshake — S.A.L.T.   Cambell/Connelly)
   (James/Moore
4 Move Over — FILTHY McNASTY
   (Janis Joplin — Carlin)

℗ 1978

LIVE

BRIDGE HOUSE
COURAGE

A WEEK AT THE BRIDGE E16

Top: Lea Hart, the multi-talented vocalist guitarist of the Roll-Ups.

Below: Bridge House pub logo becomes our first record label.

Top: Glen Murphy and Ray Winstone, who both boxed for Repton and both became successful actors.

Below: Tom Lucy, John Conteh, Ray Winstone, Glen Murphy, Terry Murphy, Jason Connery, Liz Hinkley. Front: Glen Murphy Jr with Trevor Brooking trophy during film-break making *Tank Malling*.

The band's 1st birthday L - R: Ian Stewart, Alexis Korner, Hughie Flint, Tom McGuinness, Stevie Smith, Paul Jones, Dave Kelly, Gary Fletcher, Mike Vickers, Manfred Mann, Paul Gillieron

Top left: Glen Murphy and Terry Murphy Jr, our pub managers.

Top right: Glen Murphy and cast perform *Jailhouse Rock* at the Bridge House.

Middle left: Blues Band first birthday party bash, includes Ian Stewart, Alexis Korner, Stevie Smith, Tom McGuinness, Paul Jones, Dave Kelly, Gary Fletcher, Manfred Mann, Hughie Flint and others.

Centre: Bridge regular and Manfred Mann band member Chris Thompson in fine voice, aided by the sultry vocals of Stevie Lange.

Left: Robbie McIntosh and Chris Thompson – Filthy McNasty.

Top left: Alexis Korner, Paul Jones, Gary Fletcher, at a Blues Band jam session.

Top right: Joe Brown, one of the world's best musicians, and late wife Vicky – Browns Home Brew.

Bottom left: Small Faces and Humble Pie frontman Steve Marriott with Colin McFaull and Steve Burgess aka Cock Sparrer after the Blind Drunk gig.

Bottom right: Reg Presley, lead singer of top Rock band the Troggs.

Top: Rory Gallagher truly was an amazing guitarist once voted the best in the world.

Below: Rod De'Ath, Rory Gallagher, Gerry McAvoy, Dave Edwards and Lou Martin – Ramrod debut at the Bridge.

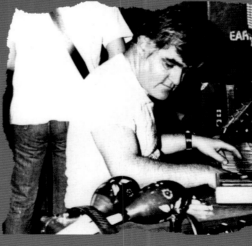

Top: Jammin at the Bridge are Chris
Thompson, Terry Wilson-Slessor, Stevie
Lange and Huey Lewis.

Middle left: Steve Harris and Dave Murray
– Iron Maiden.

Middle right: Iron Maiden at the
Bridge House.

Bottom right: Ian Stewart, on piano, the
sixth Rolling Stone.

Top: Nine Below Zero's harmonica supremo Mark Feltham, Modern Romance boys Dave Jaymes and Robbie Jaymes plus barmaid Sharon and Wasted Youth's Darren Murphy.

Bottom left: Vocalist Jess Lyn Dean and drummer John Rich of Punk band the Wasps.

Bottom right: Sunshine Patteson of Gloria Mundi, a great New Wave band that should have made it.

Top: The Misfits, Kelvin Blacklock and Midge Ure. Midge tasted success with New Wave bands Visage and Ultravox.

Middle: Bridge Skins – John Butler, Gary Dickle, Glen Murphy Jr, Vince Riordan and Kevin Hennessy.

Bottom: When the Geggus Brothers formed the Cockney Rejects they played the Bridge and built up their strong local following.

Top: Ian Page and Dave Cairns's Secret Affair put the Bridge House at the forefront of the Mod revival.

Middle: The Merton Parkas – Mick Talbot, Danny Talbot, Neil Hurrell and Simon Smith – were great live favourites with the Bridge House Mod crowd.

Bottom: Robert S Lee is the Mod on the *Mayday* album cover recorded live at the Bridge.

Top: Daughter Vanessa auditioning for me in the bar.

Middle: Here's me with Wasted Youth after a gig at the Electric Ballroom, plus a few friends.

Bottom: Last night at the Bridge House August 1982. Remus Down Boulevard re-form to wave goodbye … Dave Edwards, Mickey Harris, me, Steve Gough and Dennis Stratton.

Top: Me and Rita have time today to look back on some wonderful memories.

Middle: Boxer Terry Spinks is an Olympic champion and a good friend who is there for you.

Bottom: Iron Maiden's Steve Harris, lovely fellow, not changed by stardom.

Top: The Murphys, Vanessa, me, Glen and Rita at Bridge House reunion 2002.

Bottom: The Bridge House football team that included sons Terry Jr, Glen and Lloyd and nephew Paul Cole.

Top: Dennis Stratton.

Bottom: Jamming together: Gerry McAvoy, Paul Jones and Chris Thompson (also on front cover of book).

THE APRIL ALBUM

SUN   FILTHY McNASTY
MON   SPRINKLER
TUES   GERRY McAVOY JAM
WED   REMUS D. BOULEVARD
THURS   ROLL UPS *
FRI   JACKIE LYNTON
SAT   SALT

A WEEK AT THE BRIDGE E16

Top: British Rock band Crawler achieved USA success. Bridge House line-up: Geoff Whitehorn, Tony Brunagel, Terry Wilson-Slessor, John McFee and John Rabbit Bundrick.

Bottom: The Warm Jets – Paul Ballance, with ex-Cockney Rebels Paul Jeffreys and Milton Reame-James – became the first band to record a single 'Sticky Jack' on our Bridge House Records label.

Top: The spirit of the Bridge House was often captured in the legendary jamming sessions, at the heart of this one is Rod De'Ath, Stevie Lange, Tony Brunagel and Gerry McAvoy.

Bottom: Depeche Mode after a gig at the Bridge.

Top left: Me with our favourite barmaid Linsey.

Top right: Far more enjoyable this side of the bar, say me and Rita.

Bottom: Our other barmaid Jo Sylvester with Gerry McAvoy, myself, Brendan O'Neill, son Glen and the Bridge legend that is Jackie Lynton.

come to see the band. At the time, Kim was a big star, having had hit singles, but she was a nice, down-to-earth person and a pleasure to meet. After we were introduced, I tried to get her to do a gig but it wasn't practical.

Bob's sister Ramona Carlier fronted a band called the Mo-Dettes who played regularly for us. They had chart success with a single called 'White Mice'. They came from Forest Gate, so they were locals as well. Ramona was married to Madness drummer Daniel Woodgate (Woody) for five years. Daniel, who had been in a few other bands before Madness, then went Heavy Metal, with FAT.

The lead singer Eddie – or Edward Tudor Pole (touch of royalty!) – is now a very fine film and TV actor, who made his acting debut in the film *The Great Rock 'n' Roll Swindle* with the Sex Pistols. He went on to present the TV series *Crystal Maze*.

I have noticed that there is still a band called Tenpole Tudor doing the rounds, so I think it must be the same band, but maybe with a different line-up.

ANNIE LENNOX, TOURISTS, EURYTHMICS

I remember one new band we had playing that were just starting out in 1980; in fact, it was possibly their first gig. They were called the Tourists. On vocals was Annie Lennox. She was wearing a *really* short miniskirt and a blonde wig, which she changed from time to time; she had a different wig for each song, so it seemed. Annie always tried to be different, even over the course of one evening. She was great, very energetic.

Her manager, Tony Gordon, booked the first gig for the Eurythmics at the Bridge House. I can't recall that gig, but it is recorded in my calendar of the time as being supported by Howard Jones.

127

I was to meet Annie again much later in the Eurythmics. It was an end-of-tour party and they sang a few songs from a boxing ring that had been set up for a contest, the press versus record companies. My son Glen and I had trained Garry Bushell for the contest and we were in Garry's corner. He was supposed to be fighting John Blake of the *Evening Standard*, who went on to form his own successful publishing company. We got in the ring with Garry and his opponent got in with a Father Christmas robe on. They did the introductions, the bell rings and who is Garry's opponent? Lloyd Honeyghan, the world welterweight champion! I think he took a few liberties with Garry, knocking him to the floor a couple of times. But Garry was game, and he kept getting up.

Lloyd probably needn't have gone as heavy as he did. I pointed this out to his trainer George Francis, who had trained a lot of fighters including world champions John Conteh and Frank Bruno. As the trainer, George had to defend his boxer, but he knew that I had been a professional boxer, so I was a little surprised and angry with his excuses. We started shouting and hollering at each other, and it nearly came to blows. Number-two son Glen stepped in between us, and pushed us apart to calm down. Garry Bushell was also there and was a bit worried that he might have to help out. But, an hour or so later, with tempers cooled down again, we all had a drink together. We talked about having a return fight, but Garry said, 'Oh no!'

It was a good night, and as usual we had some famous friends there: Andy Fletcher of Depeche Mode came up and said hello, as did Paula Yates, who had been introduced to us by a friend of Glen's.

Garry wrote to me about the 'event' recently.

MEMORIES OF THE BRIDGE
Garry Bushell

Remember the Eurythmics challenged me to fight John Blake, cos he had the 'White Hot Club' in the *Mirror* and I was working on 'Bizarre' in the *Sun*.

They had a ring put up at their end-of-tour party, up Covent Garden way, in a club in the road parallel with Long Acre. I took the bout seriously. You and Glen trained me up for it. But on the night I was in the ring and we saw Blake still in a tuxedo. Then, all of a sudden, there's the *Rocky* music, and a mystery hooded figure entered with two massive black minders. I thought it was Bruno, so I wasn't bothered. Then he showed his face. Lloyd Honeyghan! I tried to shake his hand and he blanked me. The first round started, I went in playfully, going through the motions, and a red mist came down over him. Wallop! He put me on my back with three jabs to the chest. He was six weeks from a title fight and mean as f★★k.

I had him worried though. He thought he'd killed me!

You convinced me to go back in for round two. Someone must have got to him 'cos I managed to last the round and 'win' the fight – £100 for me and £5,000 for Help The Aged. It made all the papers. Lol.

RON WILSON, THE ELECTRICS, BILL HURLEY AND THE INMATES

There was this guy who was the image of Jimi Hendrix and imitated him perfectly; he made no secret of this because he was an extremely talented guitarist. I can't remember his name but I remember that he played guitar with his teeth, behind his neck and on his back. It was really exciting, just like Hendrix. We all thought he would make it, big time, and this was in 1978 before the current trend for tribute bands. When our first photographer Colin Rapp left us in 1978 to go to work in the Midlands, the bass player in this band, John Squires, became our resident snapper. In fact, a lot of the photos in this book were taken by him.

He had good management in Ron Wilson, who had been managing the Electrics and the Rocker of our times, Bill Hurley, Britain's Elvis Presley. Bill really gave it his all while playing for us; he had a lot of chart success and almost made it into the big time. Although he was born in the East End, he lived in the Islington area and is still around playing today. Keep your eyes open for him; it's bound to be a great gig.

Bill learned the art of singing by 'sitting in' with many of London's established and Dixieland jazz bands. He started his career in entertainment at the age of 16 and over the years he proved himself as an all-round vocalist, but particularly in Rhythm and Blues, Blues, Rock'n'Roll.

In the late 1970s, Bill teamed up with the Inmates. In 1980, they had Top-40 British chart success with the single 'The Walk' and their album *First Offence* got into the Top 50 in the US, both on the Radar record label. The Inmates built a big following in Europe, principally in Scandinavia where, in 1987, their album *The Inmates Meet The Beatles* made number one. They were also pretty successful in France, Spain and Holland.

Bill left the Inmates between 1982 and 1986. He recorded a well-received solo album *Double Agent* on Demon Records (Elvis Costello's label). He had two Top-40 UK hits as lead vocalist with JB Allstars on RCA Victor. With the Big Heat, Bill managed another British Top-40 single with 'Watch Me Catch Fire' on A&M Records, which was produced by Elvis Costello.

Bill made his second solo album, *Angel to Memphis*, in June 1996. It was released on indie label Last Call and went down well in Spain, France and Scandinavia.

Having supported musical performers like Tina Turner, the Stranglers, the Jam, Shane MacGowan, Joe Jackson, the Ramones, the Cure, Elvis Costello and the Blues Brothers, Bill has shown himself to be a talented all-rounder as far as Rock and Pop goes. His vocal range covers an amazing four octaves, from a deep, rich, silky dark-chocolate bass baritone rising to a velvety smooth poignant falsetto. In Europe, because of his raw, powerful and rasping tenor tones, music journalists have called him variously 'the white Otis Redding', 'the white Wilson Pickett' and 'the British Elvis Presley'. The likes of Shane MacGowan, Robert Plant, Joe Jackson, Jimmy Page and Elvis Costello have all credited Bill Hurley as one of Britain's greatest Rock/Pop vocalists. He certainly has been capable of some quality and unique sounds.

I saw Bill recently in Stratford, playing a great set. I also heard he is running a Blues jam every Sunday at the Standard in Walthamstow, check it out; see you there!

Ron Wilson who managed Bill Hurley and the Electrics in the early days became one of us, a publican with a nice pub in Enfield; I don't know if he carried on managing after taking the pub. Managing musicians and pubs is really hard work, and I hope he is doing OK.

WARM JETS

Paul Ballance was another talented front man, and we'd first met when he was fronting Dogwatch. He really did use to frighten everyone, including us in the pub! He would dress up in different costumes and some very weird faces. He really was terrifying. We were surprised when he left Dogwatch in 1977 but within a month he was back with the Warm Jets, named after Brian Eno's first solo album. (Ironically, we recorded a live album with Dogwatch with their new front man Roy Weard.)

Paul's new act was a complete change from Dogwatch. His first gig with Warm Jets was at the 100 Club supporting the Sex Pistols. It was also the Pistols' first gig and we think it is where Johnny Rotten got his stage act from, aping Paul Ballance.

Originally a four-piece band, after a year the Jets' line-up changed. Out went the rhythm section and in came a new drummer, Dave Cairns, who had played with Joe Jackson in Arms and Legs and two really top musicians, Paul Jeffreys (ex-Chartreuse) (bass) and Milton Reame-James (keyboards), who were previously in Bill Nelson's Red Noise and Be Bop Beluxe and were part of the original line-up of Steve Harley's Cockney Rebel. These three joined founder members Paul and a polish guitar player called Magic Hrybowitz, who had grown up in the same road in Poland as the late Pope John Paul II. After the Warm Jets had split up, Magic went on to play in the Carol Grimes Band.

Paul Ballance, Paul Jeffreys and Milton Reame-James came to see me in 1978 and asked if they could be considered for the next live album.

I said, 'Maybe. But the trouble with you guys is you are not compatible with any of the other bands.'

Paul Ballance as quick as ever said, 'You mean we are too original.'

'You could put it like that,' I said, and the argument went on and on.

They gave me some clear ideas about what they wanted to record and, from the tracks they played me, I liked 'Sticky Jack' the best.

I told them that I had booked the mobile recording unit for

the following week but we were booked up gig-wise for the whole week. Then Colin Barton came in. It was his mobile and he was to be the producer, so I put the situation to him. He said that he would be there all day, so why didn't we just record them in the bar during the day. I thought this was a really good idea.

I told the band that, if the recordings were good, I would put them on the next album. We had already made all the arrangement for the *Live – A Week At The Bridge E16* album, which was why Colin would be there with all the equipment a week later.

After we had recorded their tracks and listened back to them, we thought that they didn't sound too good because there was no live audience. The pub had a great ambience for live gigs but it was hard to block off the sound for the individual instruments. Milton, who was also co-producing the band with Colin Barton, said, 'Let's take them into a studio and get them right.'

We were using the Pathway Studio where we had edited the *Live – A Week At The Bridge E16* album. It was only an eight-track studio but it had a good sound. So we booked a day there and the band came out with the finished product.

Arthur Brown, who'd had a smash hit with 'Fire' in the 60s, and who owned the studio, was very supportive and gave us some good ideas. If you listen carefully, you can just about hear him shouting 'Fire' in the background. The tracks did not go out on an album but became our first single on Bridge House Records.

So our first single was by the Warm Jets (BHS01). Milton and Colin Barton produced the record, side one was 'Sticky Jack', written by Ballance/Hrybowitz; side two was 'Shell Shock', written by Jeffreys/Reame-James.

Paul Jeffreys and Milton Reame-James were banned by Cockney Rebel's management from playing gigs that didn't involve Cockney Rebel. In fact, they banned them from playing in any band, so we also could not advertise them. But Steve Harley liked the Bridge, and he came down to see his brother in his band many times.

Much later, in 1988, we were in for a real shock. Paul Jeffreys had just got married and was flying off to the USA with his American bride. Tragically, they had boarded the plane that had been targeted by terrorists and was carrying a bomb that exploded over Lockerbie. The Lockerbie disaster killed all 243 passengers plus 11 people on the ground.

Paul was a lovely easygoing fellow who will be sadly missed by those who knew him.

I still see Milton to this day; he has a lovely studio at his home in Surrey, and he has given Jeff Ellis and me carte blanche to use it. He is a kind man as well as a fine musician. I can still remember Milton walking into the Bridge one day and being totally speechless. One of his idols, Manfred Mann, passed the time of day with him, and he said to me after, 'Manfred was asking me questions about how I arrange songs and we chatted about keyboards!' It had really made Milton's day, being a piano player himself.

Milton and Paul Ballance recently had a business meeting and we will soon be working together on a new project, which Jeff Ellis will control our end. So, get ready to download tracks and albums on the internet.

At the moment, I am at my desk with this single 'Sticky Jack' and 'Shell Shock', and this copy is signed by the entire band. I have also just listened to Warm Jets on tape doing a radio interview pushing the single and their tour of Ireland. This would be in the summer of 1978, and Paul Jeffreys would have just over 10 years left of his life. Looking at the lyrics that Paul wrote, it seems he knew his life was going to be short.

1978 – THE INTERVIEW ON RADIO MEDWAY
WITH WARM JETS BY MIKE Q

Q: Magic, why did you record a live single?

Magic: Well, we are a live gigging band. Terry liked us and suggested a live session to see how it sounded. Colin Barton and Milton produced it. We had a meeting and it was decided that, if it went well, a single would be released. The rest of the session will be on the next *Bridge House Live* album.

Milton: The Bridge House is very important to us. It has developed into a major force in the record industry, so a recording by them gets the attention of the major record companies. The Bridge House is a real prestige gig and the quality of the bands playing there speaks for itself. It's not just a pub in the East End that puts bands on; people think of the East End as some rough, tough no-go area; well, it is maybe, but the Bridge House is certainly not. You have got major stars like Manfred Mann and Rory Gallagher who have played down there. I went in to see Terry one afternoon and Manfred Mann was rehearsing with his band. They were playing Hammersmith Odeon the next night. Chris Thompson had arranged it. He plays there all the time.

Q: Paul Ballance, what is, and where is, the Bridge House?

Paul B: A really famous gig, with its own record company in Canning Town with extremely expensive beer.

Paul J: Well, that's because they have bands there seven nights a week and, when some bands only pull 30 or 40 customers and the band get £40, they've got to pay their way somehow.

Q: Paul Jeffreys, you write all your own music?

Paul J: Yes, I get all my ideas for music while in the bath. Then it develops in a room close by (the toilet). The hook lines come in about five seconds. I can write a song in 30 minutes. If it turns out rubbish, we just move on. I know in eight seconds if it's any good.

Q: Is 'Sticky Jack' a filthy record?

Paul J: No, not at all. It is a cynical look at people who get away with murder. This is about a pimp who gets away with murder and 15 years later is presented with the OBE at a dinner with all the lords and ladies applauding him and singing 'For he's a jolly good fellow'. Then the scandal is revealed. I don't think anyone should get away with murder.

Q: Would you say success is more important than money at the present?

Paul J: With Warm Jets, yes, but I have just been through a court case where I sued the management of my previous band for £7,000. I lost that and a lot more, which I was not pleased about.

Q: Magic was saying that at a lot of your gigs you get Cockney Rebel fans turning up to see you.

Paul J: Well, that did happen at the start of the Warm Jets, but we have built our own fan club now because the music is altogether different from theirs. We have got the Jetettes, Vanessa and Karen from Gillingham in Kent, handling it for us. They do a very good job. We are getting about 400 people at our gigs around this area. We played in Germany and there was over 1,000 that had come to see us, so we are excited about the forthcoming tour of Ireland that we are going to do next week. Our tour manager Gary Packer is Irish. We are going to Southern Ireland, then Belfast. The next tour, we are going by ferry; I am not that keen on flying. A good friend of Johnny Branch arranged it for me and throughout they were minded by the IRA.

The Warm Jets' line-up didn't change for two years. They had management with Frank Samson, a publishing deal with Dick James, music and record deals with Robert Stigwood's RSO label and Elton John's Rocket Records. I don't think they were very successful. We couldn't help them any further, apart from giving them a gig, because they were tied to their own management who ran all aspects of their career. After the Warm Jets, the band members had a brief career going under the name of Electric Eels (not to be confused with proto-Punk band of the same name that was active between 1972 and 1975 in Cleveland, Ohio, USA, infamous for using Nazi imagery).

I think that this was probably to do with contractual obligations. The aliases they chose to go under were Red Leader

(Paul Ballance), Pablo Hallam (Paul Jeffreys), Mad Molecule (Milton Reame-James) and Methane Wernik (Maciek aka Magic Hrybowitz). I don't remember who the drummer was.

Both the Pauls were extremely creative and had a number of other bands that played at the Bridge. These were all jam sessions, set up as a bit of a mickey-take on all the jam sessions that were happening at the Bridge with major celebrities. The aim of these jam sessions was to have people play who were not stars at all, many of whom were not even musicians but they thought they could put on as much of a show as any old Rockers. The intention of these bands was to promote the more avant-garde styles of music along the lines of Paul Jeffreys's hero Captain Beef Heart and his Magic Band. The line-ups for these jams changed gig by gig along with the name. The name had to change regularly, otherwise most of the venues that they played in wouldn't let them on again if they knew it was the same outfit! My good friend Jeff Ellis was one of the instigators and also the DJ.

These sessions happened on Bridge House quiet nights and some of the names used were Atazoa, Reagan's Aids, Nasty Norman's Naked Feet and the Sperm Wails. The Sperm Wails were the most successful of the experiments and lasted a couple of years; they went a long way ... to Cardiff, in fact. The last of these experiments was called Wattle and Daub and they played at the Merlin's Cave, in Margery Street, Islington, when I took over in September 1982.

A while later, in 1980, in came two of Paul's pals informing me about this new band they had formed with Jake from the Brakes (a Bruce Springsteen look-alike) called the Pope, the name of Magic's friend from Poland (John Paul). The miracle never worked. However, we gave them some gigs, both supporting and headlining, but it never happened for them.

God bless Paul Jeffreys! I still maintain that Paul Ballance was a great front man. Money was always important, but so was fame.

MODERN ROMANCE

Modern Romance was not Rock, Punk or Mod psycho; it was in the middle and attracted a different audience and had a big fan base. This band was, I believe, the happiest to play the Bridge. They reinvented salsa music and went on to have a few Top-10 hits.

Their music was very dance orientated, and both Geoffrey Deane and David Jaymes really worked the audience, party hats, whistles, doing the Conga all round the pub, out in the street, all round the building. When they were doing this, me and the staff behind the bar would be standing there with nothing to do, as all the customers were doing the Conga! Thankfully, this only happened for one number and would last for around 10 minutes.

I first met Dave and Geoff when they came in looking for gigs for their band at the time, the Leyton Buzzards. As the Leyton Buzzards, although they came in under the banner of New Wave music, they were far from being Punks. Smartly dressed with longish hair, it was hard to pigeon-hole them. We gave them a few gigs. They could play, pulled a nice crowd and I thought they would be one of my regulars. They played for me, then split up. I could not believe it. A few months later, in they come. 'Tel, give us a gig. We've got a new band called Modern Romance.'

They got themselves a record deal and, within a few months, there they were on *Top of the Pops* with 'Everybody Salsa' and then 'Ay Ay Ay Ay Moosey', a Top-10 single. I was so pleased for them. I believe this was in 1981. But things did not go too well from then on.

They had a new manager, Steve Donohue, and new

girlfriends, one worked for *The Face* magazine and the other one became a good friend and an able barmaid at the Bridge. I gave Modern Romance a gig; I knew they would be OK. They were professional musicians and they'd been there before so we knew they would be well rehearsed.

Well, they went down like a sack of potatoes! This sometimes happens when bands are trying something new. They came over after the gig to get their money, and the first words from David's mouth were: 'All right, Terry. I know, I know.'

Geoff was equally subdued. In fact, they were both really gutted, and it seemed this was the end of the road.

I said, 'Well, it's been a disastrous night. Apart from the people with the band, everyone walked out. The only thing I can say is I will give you a four-week residency starting next week.'

They thought I was joking, but I told them, 'Your music is different from what we have got on other nights, so you rehearse a bit more and we will work at it.'

They were over the moon. By the next week they had changed some of the band. Dave's younger brother Andrew, who was only 16, came in.

The band did not happen overnight. But they really had to work at it. I continued to give them gigs over the coming year and they eventually got it together. As I said, they were the happiest band to play the Bridge. By this statement I mean, 'ha ha' happy, not a forced feeling. They were having hit songs when they came back to play. I was surprised and disappointed that they had replaced Geoff, who, with Dave, was a founder member of both Leyton Buzzards and Modern Romance. The new singer was good. He probably had a better voice and was younger and hungrier. I never found out the reason for the break-up, and I didn't ask. I knew by the look on Dave's face not to question him. I think he was as sad as I was.

We all stayed in touch. For a while Modern Romance had become a really big band who were very busy, so I did not see them.

Some time later, I was having a quiet drink at the Merlin's Cave in Islington, the new pub and venue I had taken on in 1982 after the Bridge House. It was about one in the morning when there was this banging on the door. I told Terry Junior to open it and in came Modern Romance. Along with their manager and a few friends, they were singing 'For He's a Jolly Good Fellow'. They had come to present me with a silver disc for 250,000 sales of their single. It was inscribed with the words 'For Believing From the Beginning'. I was amazed and delighted. It must have been over a year since I had last seen them, but they had not forgotten, even though I had.

I have seen Dave and Geoff over the years. Dave ended up in management, and, after a few health problems, which he conquered, he was managing Jah Wobble (Stepney's own John Wardle), an old friend who was the bass player in Johnny Rotten's Public Image, before forming the band named after him. Jah Wobble are still playing, and I saw an ad for the band a while ago.

Before I moved to the Merlin's Cave, I was sitting in the Bridge House one afternoon in 1982 and this guy came in wanting to record the song 'Lawrence of Arabia' with Wasted Youth.

'I'm a friend of Dave Jaymes from Modern Romance,' he said.

'They're a chart-topping band,' I told him. 'Why don't you ask them to do it?'

I thought the guy was just name-dropping and making himself busy. Wasted were on tour and too busy to do it at the time anyway.

The next day Dave Jaymes rang, and asked, 'Do you want me to record a song for you?'

I explained to him what had happened.

He said, 'If you want it, I will do it for you.'

He took the guy in the studio and fetched half of Modern Romance down to play on the record. It came out quite good, but we never released it. We may include it in the Bridge House collection that we plan to do soon. Fair play to Dave Jaymes, though, he wanted to do me a favour and he worked hard producing the song. This proved that not all stars forget their beginnings when they make it.

Geoff Deane has gone on to become a top scriptwriter for television. I saw him in Cannes a few years ago, and he hasn't changed. Number-two son Glen went to his wedding, but I was not invited because when he left Modern Romance I still gave the band gigs. I said, 'I didn't know there had been a change of lead singer. The new fellow must have been a great mimic.'

We laughed and poured another drink. Nice guys.

WASTED YOUTH

Enter the Dead Flowers. My son Darren had got a few friends together and formed the band in 1979 with Martin Joliffe (vocals), Darren (bass), Andy Scott (drums), and Lee Drury, Mick Atkins and Ken Scott (guitar). They had not rehearsed and now it was their first gig. A band had pulled out at the last moment so in they went. Quite a good crowd had turned up, all their mates, as they were all local boys. This gig is still remembered today; it's become one of those 'Do you remember?' nights. People spoke more about this night than when U2 or Dire Straits played. It was the first time at least four of the band had been on a stage. The vocalist, Martin, couldn't take all the heckling so after about six songs he jumped off stage, punched and kicked a bloke in the head and stormed out. But the band played on with Lee Drury on vocals. Lee did a really good job saving a disastrous evening. Twenty minutes later, Ken Scott took over, our real front man at last. Sadly, the Dead Flowers never played again, but we do have this night on tape to remember them by. Ken, of course, at this time was the lead singer/guitarist with the Tickets.

Darren and Martin shared a ground-floor flat in Forest Gate, and Ken had the flat above. They had all arranged to come down to the Bridge House at lunchtime to form their new band after the Dead Flowers gig. They were getting ready to go when a friend of Martin's knocked at the door. Martin said he would see Darren at the pub and left with his mate who had some forged prescriptions to go to the chemists. The chemist realised that the prescriptions were forgeries and locked all the doors until the police arrived. They both got arrested and ended up doing two and a half years.

While the chemist business was going on, Darren, Ken, Andy and Mick were waiting at the Bridge to discuss forming the group, named by Darren as Wasted Youth. (If Martin's friend hadn't called for him, he would have been the vocalist in the band and might have never gone to prison. On Martin's release, he became a bank robber and got another 14 years. After his release from the 14 years inside, he wasn't seen again by any of the guys. I hope he is OK.)

Darren called a meeting for the next day, but Ken, Andy and Mick Atkins were the only ones to turn up. Darren came to see me. He said, 'I've got a four-piece band together. Can I have a gig?'

After what had happened the previous night there could only be one answer: 'No.' But then I said, 'Get rehearsing, get a demo tape and I'll listen to it.' I agreed to let them know when I would give them a gig.

The next day, they turned up at the pub informing me that they had booked a studio but did not have the money to pay for it, or to get their instruments to the studio. Would I give them a lift? So we loaded my car up and went to the studio and unloaded. We had to make two trips. Well, Darren is my son after all.

Exciting news the next day, they had finished the recording ... would I come and pay for it?! It was estimated that the cost would be £50. They had run over and they wanted the master tape; it came to £90! Quite a few bob in the 70s. Well, when we heard it, it was truly unbelievably, very good.

I told him that, although the demo was good, he would have to get the band a gig and then I would come and see them. This of course caused a big argument between Darren, the band and me. I had let them rehearse in the cellar at the Bridge and they sounded terrible. Also, I was giving them a hard time, letting them know they were not going to get an easy passage. Because they knew me, I wanted to see if they had the determination and guts that would be needed if they were going to make it.

I never should have doubted them. Darren came in a few hours later and informed me that they would be playing the Theatre Royal in Stratford on Sunday night with the band In Camera. This was amazing. I could not believe they had got that gig in a real prestige theatre. That was my first surprise with Wasted Youth and there were going to be many more. Rita and I booked two front seats and off we went. They were great!

I booked the band for the next weeks. The first week, they half-filled the pub; by the next week, the pub was packed. After the demo was made, I gave them some money for clothes to play in. They went out separately and returned all in unusual black clothing. For their third gig, the pub was once again packed but this time the audience dressed exactly like the band. 'All-in-black Goth' had arrived.

I made the first Wasted Youth record and took it to publisher

Bill Martin of Martin and Coulter. Bill went mad. His first words were: 'This is better than the Troggs' "Wild Thing".'

The main track was an original song entitled 'Jealousy'. Within a month, it was on BBC *Round Table* and getting plenty of radio play. Even Noel Edmonds, on BBC Radio 2's Sunday lunchtime show, played it four weeks running. This was the start of Wasted Youth.

The band went from strength to strength. Every promoter wanted them. Tours were being planned and record companies were keen to sign them. One in particular, Tarquin Gotch of WEA, loved the record. He kept coming to see the band. He said to me, 'I am really unlucky. I always miss their single "Jealousy".'

I had to tell him that they didn't play it live. They said it was too slow and melodic for their live set. The truth was they *couldn't* play it live. They had gone into the studio and put it together. They started rehearsing it but it was too slow so for their live set they played an up-tempo funky version. This worked for them because the fans were still buying the record, although it was a different version. 'Jealousy' should have been a major hit record. Who's to blame? How can you say? Not having major distribution certainly didn't help. The publishers were pushing it but never got the radio plugger in. So I had to do it.

I was on the phone all day. This is how it works: you buy the *Radio Times*; find the producers of all the radio shows; make contact (the producers are always too busy to talk to you); find out who to send the record to (*always* get a name); send record with a biography; ring back three days later – 'Did you get the record? No? OK, I'll ring again tomorrow.' This goes on for a week.

After a week, you send another record then start again. 'Yes, we received the record. The producer listens to all the records on Thursdays.'

Another week goes by, another phone call: 'Sorry, he didn't have time to hear it, he will listen next week.'

Next week, phone call: 'Yes he likes it. He'll give it a radio play. He doesn't know when.'

Ring again next week: 'He didn't think it went down very well. He's not playing it again.'

Send a copy to the record library.

Remember, there were over 100 radio stations so it was a full-time job and so aggravating! If they really like it, they will play it a couple of times and get an audience reaction. If the response is good, you get on the play list, and, as we all do, if we like what we hear on the radio, we go and buy it. This is why respectable pluggers are worth their weight in gold. If the producer trusts the plugger and they have built up a good relationship, working together, anything is possible. But the plugger can't work a record he doesn't think is very good because the producer trusts his ear and, if he pulls a stroke, he will not get any other records played. This is why most pluggers only work two or three records per week. They get paid thousands, plus a percentage of record sales. For example, if they get it in the Top 50, they get a higher percentage that might be increased if it goes into Top 30 and so on.

We got Alan James of Rime Ents (at this time, he was President of Leyton Orient Football Club) to try to push 'Jealousy', and he loved the record. We offered him half of the publishing rights to it, because we couldn't afford his charges. He was up for it, but Elton John's company, the firm he worked for regularly, came in at the last moment and he had to pass on our record.

Jeff Griffin, a producer with Radio 1, helped us. We found out later he used to come to the Bridge to hear the bands.

He put us in contact with a certain Clive Black, who was a top man at Polydor. I made the meet, and they were up to sign Wasted Youth. The A&R person I was dealing with said, 'If you can come in under £80,000 for your advance, we have got a deal.'

They were going to repackage the singles with some new tracks and promote them. We worked out what we needed and I asked for £75,000. We shook hands and he told us that the contract would be ready in one week.

In the meantime, Wasted had been in their studios laying down some tracks and they were hating it. I called a meeting and told them about the deal. They said, 'We are not going to sell out. They want to make us a New Romantic band; the producer in the studio is useless.'

I told them, 'Listen! Get in there, do as you are told for a week. By then, the contract will be signed; we will have the advance, then we will get our own producer in.'

They went back. One of them was missing and two were out of their head (not my Darren). Equipment got broken and the producer and the staff ended up leaving the studio. This was shock number two from Wasted Youth.

Twenty years later, I am still waiting for the contract to arrive.

However, this episode didn't really harm the band's reputation. Other companies had heard that Polydor wanted to sign them, so their interest was aroused. Bridge House Records were also very interested. Wasted Youth's records were selling well. Throughout their career, they always sold 10,000 on each release. Their first album, *Wild and Wandering*, sold 10,000 in the first month! We were selling to all the independent distributors which got us into the alternative charts. But, if we could have got major distribution for the marketing and advertising, we would have made the main charts which would have at least trebled the sales. The major record companies knew this, and that's why they wanted to sign them.

As they got more well known, Wasted Youth would not change their musical ways. 'We're not going to sell out!' was their cry. But I told them they would probably have to if they wanted to sign to a major and get chart success. 'No way,' they always said, and in the end this was their downfall.

They stopped writing new songs, perhaps believing they were not good enough. Although this was never discussed and we never doubted their ability, they went into free fall. They were still gigging almost every night and continued to make good-selling records for us when their writing ceased. This was their strong point. It was only a matter of time but they had a very good three years before splitting up.

Twelve years after they split, a major distributor released all four albums on CD, 2,250 of each (10,000, the magic figure again), and sold them in one month.

Garry Bushell never ever gave Wasted Youth a good review but they played at the old YMCA building in Greengate Street, Plaistow (the latest of many incarnations of that place will be as a housing development), without a fee on one of his birthdays. After that gig, he had his birthday parties at the Bridge House. He would book the bands and get many star names to come. Stiff Little Fingers were one of the bands he got. His birthdays were always good nights. He had many locals friends like Cockney Rejects, Oi bands, the Business; nearly all New Wave bands and Punk. I think he was the original Oi man.

MARTIN HANNETT, PRODUCER OF WASTED YOUTH'S SINGLE, 'REBECCA'S ROOM'

Martin Hannett had recorded all the Manchester labels and made Joy Division a chart band. Tony Wilson, the manager of Factory Records, had mentioned to me that the sounds Martin got on his records were very original and this appealed to us. I had met Tony at a Wasted Youth gig in Nottingham; he was managing New Order which had been formed from the remaining members of Joy Division after the vocalist, Ian Curtis, had committed suicide.

Wasted Youth wanted Martin to produce their next single so I went along with them and arranged to book him. He was creating a great new sound with a very loud echo that seemed like it was coming out of a tunnel. Or it would have been, if he had finished it properly. For me, the sound crashed halfway through the tunnel!

On the day Martin came to London in 1981, we had set up a rehearsal studio in Islington at John Henry's studio because Martin had not seen the band play. We got there early on a Sunday evening. He arrived very late and said, 'What have you set this up for? I don't want to see the band.'

I couldn't believe this. I had left the pub, which was always busy when RDB played, and it had cost me a couple of hundred quid for the hire and equipment.

He said, 'OK, get them ready and, oh, have you got £50? I've no money on me and I've got to get something to eat.'

I gave him the money. He watched the band play two numbers then he left and didn't come back; no phone call, nothing! I didn't realise that he was heavily into the illegal stuff. I saw him the next morning at the recording studio. He never said a word until lunchtime when in he came for another £50 of his fee. I said, 'When the recording's finished, you get paid.'

Martin did a very bad rushed job on the single, got his money and was gone. We called in John Holliday to remix it before it could be released and we had to work hard to make the single a fairly decent hit.

The photo on the cover caused a lot of trouble, as a ghost-like figure seemed to appear in the background. The *News of the World* heard the story and came to my office with experts in photography to check it out. They took the negatives of the photo back to their laboratory but still could not find out why. We think it was a ghost. The photographer, Allison She, was so shocked she gave up taking pictures … well, for a while anyway.

Martin Hannett, who had worked with the likes of the Clash and later on with U2, spiralled into decline due to his heavy drinking and massive drug use, especially his love of heroin. His weight eventually doubled (to roughly 26 stone, or 364 pounds), and he died of heart failure in 1991. Ace Records have put out a tribute to him releasing all his singles in an album called *Zero*. This includes 'Rebecca's Room', his version of Wasted Youth's single, which is a different mix to our release. All these years later, it still sounds weird, but good. Very good. We have both versions on the Wasted Youth single collection, entitled *Memorialize*, so buy the collection and you can choose which you think is the best version.

NORMAN LOVETT

We invited Norman to come to the Bridge. An Essex lad, from Clacton, he had just started to think about becoming a comedian so we told him to get up before Wasted Youth played. They always pulled a really big crowd. He said, 'No. I am not getting on stage in front of all those people. Look at them, they'll lynch me! I will never get out of here alive.'

151

I said, 'The only way you're going to get out of here alive is by going on stage.'

He gasped, 'Oh, gaud! If I don't go on, you'll kill me and if I do go on they will.'

I told him, 'Norman, get out there and don't die a death.'

A big push on his back and there he was on stage at a Rock gig in front of hundreds of people, who, as he stumbled on, went deathly quiet. I remember it so clearly. He turned and looked at me, and I gave him the old clenched-fist 'Go on, my son!' He only had to do 10 minutes, but after 20 minutes he still would not come off stage. He was enjoying himself so much. I had to escort him off the stage.

'Oh, thanks, Tel,' he said, 'that was wonderful.'

I said, 'Do you want a drink?'

'What? I get paid for it as well?'

He was to become a regular on stage at the Bridge. He also did some gigs on tour with Wasted Youth and he got himself a record deal.

As I write, I've got the agreement that Norman gave me in front of me. He had asked me to check it for him. I told him I didn't think he should sign, but I don't know if he did or not. He really wanted to record on the Bridge House label. The track was called 'John Peel Sings the Blues Badly'. The label was Pipe Records and the signature at the back is Morgan Fisher, a well-known name in the music business. Item one reads: 'For the nominal sum of one pound (£1.00) receipt of which is hereby acknowledged and goods and valuables outlined below, etc.'

He did get a 10 per cent royalty on the first 5,000 sold (but he had to sell 5,000 to get a 10 per cent royalty!). Hardly Rock'n'Roll! I wonder if it ever got released and how many it sold.

Norman has gone on to become a fine comedy actor, having worked on stage, film, radio and TV (perhaps his best-known role was as the face of the computer 'Holly' in *Red Dwarf*); we continue to wish him well. I wonder what would have happened to him without that little push in the back I had to give him to get him on stage.

THE MOD REVIVAL

MODS MAYDAY '79

In my opinion, Secret Affair should have reached the heights of stardom, just as the Beatles had done in the early 1960s. They had a Top-20 hit with their first release 'Time for Action' in 1979, which was about six months after their first gig. The Beatles took over a year to get their first Top-20 record. This, however, shows that you have got to have more than just talent to make it to the top; determination is what success is all about, and Secret Affair lacked this. Yes, they were a really busy band, playing all the new venues, getting themselves known to a bigger audience, which you have to do, so that when your records come out you get good sales. But you must never forget your beginnings, all your pals and buddies who were there from day one.

When Secret Affair came into the Bridge to see me, I think with a demo tape, I saw right away they were Mods, all suited and booted. This was the same way that I had dressed many years before. I asked about their music, and they said they played soul and R&B. I gave them a support gig the same week, and, after that, I gave them a gig on the Monday and wrote on the poster 'Mods Monday'. A fair crowd turned up, nothing special, but encouraging. I then gave them a residency for the next four Mondays, with support from similar types of bands, but nobody mentioned Mods.

We were getting a lot more Vespas parked outside, and there were plenty of Skinheads around but there was no trouble. We were all from Canning Town, my family and the Mods' and the Skins' families, so I knew many of their parents; if they caused trouble, their fathers would give them a wallop for me. I am joking now, but this did actually happen on a few occasions. But we had a good crowd of customers who became friends. My sons and all my family's kids all had mates who had mates, and, if anyone caused trouble, they would get barred and have nowhere to go on these nights.

Of course, by early 1979 we had formed the record company, and we'd already released two live albums, *Live – A Week At The Bridge E16* and *Penfriend*, a live Dogwatch album, on our Bridge House label. As Mod Monday was doing pretty well, I decided to make another live album, knowing a bit about Mods, and remembering the 1960s. We waited for the May Day Bank Holiday Monday to do the recording. Ronnie Lane had a 16-track mobile recording Winnebago bus, so we hired that.

This was the maddest day ever. We had selected six bands – Small Hours, Begger, the Mods, Squire, Secret Affair and Merton Parkas (although the Merton Parkas would not appear on the finished album) – and planned that they would have four tracks each.

Squire were the luckiest band to be on the album. The Little Roosters were the band we had chosen, but, when they got to the pub, they got cold feet, even though they were good enough; Garrie Lammin, the lead singer, had been in Cock Sparrer, a Punk band that almost made it. Garrie left them and formed his own band. He had played a few gigs and started to get a Mod following; he dressed like a Mod. But on the day of the recording he decided not to be a Mod. So we replaced them with Squire who were one of the many bands waiting to try to see if they could play.

Squire, like Secret Affair, later signed to Arista, and had a hit record called 'Walking Down the King's Road'. These two bands had their own record label called Eye Spy (via Arista).

Small Hours were the happiest and best-behaved Mod band. They welcomed the chance they were given and took it with both hands. Neil Thompson (their vocalist) had an unusual voice, deep and gritty, great for the R&B songs. The only trouble we had with this band on the night of the recording was they turned up without their drums, but good man Seb Shelton of Secret Affair lent them his kit. As it turned out, this helped us out because we were running late and Secret Affair were on next. So it saved a bit of time as the drums took the most time to set up. Small Hours went on to sign both management and recording deals and played plenty of gigs, including many more for us.

Begger always went down well with the audience. Nigel Gregory had a good voice and played great harp. He always worked the crowd. The band also played many times throughout the following year for us. Nigel is still out there today rocking on.

The Mods really had a lot to live up to with their name. They used to get plenty of stick as they had the habit of upsetting the crowd. On another night, when they did a gig for us, they ended up being dragged from the stage and their instruments broken, so they weren't welcomed back.

We had wanted the Purple Hearts (originally the Sockets in 1977) on the *Mods* album but they elected to play the Music Machine (later renamed the Camden Palace) on the night we recorded the album. We had given them a few gigs. They were another local band, from Leytonstone or Walthamstow, I think.

I remember one night, when they were playing for us, they very nearly literally brought the house down! My son Lloyd went down to the cellar to change a barrel of beer, and came running back up to me saying the floor was collapsing. Garry Bushell, who was the feature's editor for *Sounds* magazine at the time, and was in the pub reviewing the band, was standing with me and I said to him, 'Come down and see what has happened.'

We went down to the cellar and the beams round the wall had split. Under them there were electrical and gas pipes. There were around 200 kids up in the bar jumping to the music. As the floor went down, the beams were splitting more. Fortunately, there were a few old doors in the cellar which we rammed under the joists. After we did this, I ran on stage and said, 'Unless you stop dancing, I will have to stop the gig!'

I told the band what had happened, but the kids in the audience took no notice at all. So there we were, me and my sons, grabbing hold of the dancers to stop them. I went on stage again, pleading with them. Was I glad when that evening was over! I would not let the band do any encores, much to the anger of the crowd. But what they did not realise was that, if the floor had gone, this would have broken the gas and the electricity pipes. The electric would have ignited the gas pipe and there would have been an almighty explosion and people would have died, including my family, Garry Bushell and me. But, if Garry had survived, I'm sure he would have given us a good review, which would have been a big change! (He certainly never ever gave Wasted Youth a good review. In fact, the only really good review he ever gave was for Chas & Dave. Oh yes, and Judge Dread, because he got him the gig anyway!)

On the Bank Holiday Monday, the bands started to arrive about 9am with their fans. The plan was to record the bands during the day and then we would let the audience in at 8pm and record all Secret Affair's gig.

By 11am, the whole of Stephenson Street (the road next to the pub) was packed with Vespas and cars plus the Winnebago. The police came round to see what was happening, so we had to let everyone in. It was a good job that it was a Bank Holiday as otherwise the cops would have closed us down.

We had no staff to serve the customers, but thank the Lord for a big family; all my five children, Rita and Glen's wife Linda mucked in, as well as Glastra, my six-year-old granddaughter, doing the washing up. I quickly got on the phone to try to round up the staff, but on Bank Holiday Monday getting anyone to come in was a big ask. We had 10 already booked for the evening, so none of them would come in. Anyway, a great family got us through. As one o'clock ticked round, there must have been at least 300 people in the pub, and we weren't even supposed to be open at that point!

Each band wanted to use their own equipment, so, after each band's recording, all their gear was removed to their vans and the next band brought their gear on stage. Then there were sound checks and of course the equipment had to be carried through the audience. The customers didn't want to move because they had front-row viewing and were worried about losing their places. This caused a few problems which I had to sort out. There was this group of about a dozen guys who would not move. I asked them nicely, but they would not move. So, with the help of my family, we pushed them out of the way, and what did we find in the middle? Three crates of my beer!

The little crowd claimed the discovered booze was nothing to do with them, saying, 'It was there when we came in.'

I knew that they had pinched them, but I let them off after they paid for the beer that had been drunk.

When we finally organised the staffing, we got some control over our pub. With the police coming round and making us tidy up the roads, we opened the back of the pub and asked everyone to put their scooters in the large garden. I couldn't believe it when a large amount of them said no; they wanted to get their drinks and sit on their scooters until the music started. They were waiting for the girl Mods to arrive to show off their machines. Around this time, none of the girls had scooters, unless they had boyfriends, so they all arrived by bus or train.

We announced that we were looking for the best scooter and rider to be on the front cover of the *Mods Mayday '79* album. So, in the early afternoon, myself, John Squires and John McGeady were going round taking pictures of the ones we liked. We took loads of pictures, and I wished we still had them all, but, as it happens, we have quite a few.

(Anyone who was in the audience that day may see themselves on the web or in the book, and, if you do, please let us know and we will try to follow it up. Perhaps we can even start a 'then and now' feature.)

The afternoon was really hotting up. The crowd had had a few hours' drinking, dancing and cheering the bands they were supporting, and there was a marvellous atmosphere.

All my sons were getting involved; and number-two son Glen

suggested that the scooter rider should be a girl, which would be more attractive on the front cover of the album.

I said, 'Well, let's have a look.'

Number-one son Terry said, 'Don't worry, Dad. Me, Lloyd and Darren have got the best-looking girls upstairs in the hall next to your office.'

'Oh, thanks!' I said.

Well, when I got upstairs, there was a full party of around 30 people, around 20 Mod girls and some of my boys' mates. They had the disco going, my private bar open and they were having a real rave-up. The girls had been invited upstairs to have their pictures taken and be interviewed for the front cover of the album. I heard a few expressions like: 'What a blinding way to chat up the girls', so I realised I'd really fallen for it, outwitted by my sons. Thinking about it now, I might even say 'clever sons'!

(The girls, of course, were perfectly safe with the lads upstairs. We lived on the top floor. The offices and kitchens were on the middle floor and there was another big room where the band had their dressing room. My Rita was always there, she would be up and down the stairs every five minutes looking after her family and the bar and feeding the customers, etc.)

It was a great day, which after 25 years still lives on.

When I had negotiated a deal on the *Mods Mayday '79* album, Charles Leverson, the head of Arista Records, signed the album from Bridge House Records. He then signed Secret Affair and Squire, two of the bands featured. The thing that really hooked him was the gig. We let Charles stand behind the bar and after the first number he was dancing like a teenager and drinking pints of beer.

With such a crowd packed in during the day, the sweat and

the body heat would rise to the ceiling and then would drip down, not only condensation but big blobs of nicotine as well. The first time I noticed this was on my shirt the morning after a busy gig. No wonder Charles and the crowd enjoyed themselves so much, nicotine in the beer! But is it a drug? Anyone we thought was taking drugs was out straight away, so, if 'nico-booze' did constitute 'substance abuse', we might have had an empty pub at times. Perhaps all the people I threw out were innocent after all. It might just have been the nicotine!

Mods Mayday '79 was our most successful album. But there was fall-out. We had recorded the bands all in one day and over the following week the bands had one day each at the mobile studio, which was parked next to the Rolling Stones, office at Shepperton Studios, to dub and remix their songs for the album. Over the week, one of the bands smashed up the Winnebago causing thousands of pounds of damage. We knew who did it, even though they denied it. In the end, we pleaded the old Fifth Amendment.

The engineer on the album was Ron Fawcus, who ran the mobile recording studio for Ronnie Lane, and he did a really good job for us. He was assisted by Barry Sage, who recorded and mixed the album. He also engineered the *Dogwatch Live* album for us.

Secret Affair were the only band that were untruthful with me. The deal I offered the bands to be on the album was that I should have the publishing rights to the songs, but only the ones they recorded. All the bands agreed and signed except Secret Affair. They said they would sign, but all that day they made excuses not to come to the office.

Ian McKenna, who was handling that side of the day, was very angry and said he thought they had no intention of signing, even though they had promised. When I confronted the band, they said they would not sign because they were looking for upfront money on a publishing deal. They said to me, 'You keep all the royalties from the album, we don't want anything.'

'What nice boys,' I thought.

But, unknown to us, they had just negotiated an £80,000 record deal. After the album was released, they got a really big deal with a major publishing company, Morrison and Leahy. They were a really good band with good songs, but within a year they were finished as a major act, but they are still playing now.

Years later, I wanted to release the live gig we had recorded that night. I got solicitors' letters threatening me with legal action and saying that Secret Affair had never received any royalties from the album, which Arista, their record company, released. I spoke to a good friend of mine, Frank Lea, at Trojan Records. He said he would like to release it and he did and gave them £8,000 for the rights plus a royalty.

The Merton Parkas came to see me. They had signed a contract with me for the recordings and asked me if they could come off the album because they had the chance to sign a major record deal, but the company, Beggar's Banquet, would not sign them unless they had exclusive rights to all their music. They were one of the best bands on the album, but I couldn't stop them getting a deal their whole future might depend on, so I let them go and took them off the album. They had an OK career with a couple of Top-20 hits. Mick Talbot, the keyboard player, ended up with Paul Weller and the Style Council. His brother Danny Talbot is still in the music business.

The fact that the Merton Parkas were not appearing on the album didn't matter too much, as we had plenty of tracks. We got it together, released the album and it was a big hit; we charted in the Top 75 in the *Music Week* charts. At that time it was the only live album in there.

But you can't beat the big guys. We were so pleased when we got the album deal, but, once we licensed the album to Arista, they just sat on it. They put Secret Affair and Squire in the studio to record new versions of the songs on the album and released them. They didn't get behind the album because they wanted to promote the Secret Affair and Squire singles, which both charted in the Top 20 and, of course, there were no royalties for Bridge House Records from the singles.

But the radio stations still played our live versions rather than the studio versions, which, of course, were the real thing. Well, John Peel did. He was great and played all our records.

TAPE FROM RADIO INTERVIEW, 10 AUGUST 1979

The BBC did an interview with us about the live recording. It began: Return of the Mods, revived by Terry Murphy at the Bridge House, Canning Town. The record playing was 'Time for Action', by Secret Affair for the *Mods Mayday '79* album.

Q: Terry, tell us about Mods Monday, that you have every week at the Bridge.

Terry: When *Quadrophenia* is released later this year the Mod revival will be massive. The bands and fans have been through the Punk thing, they are all looking for a change. They want to look smart and dance again. All that pogoing is out. It's about fashion, the new youth, the 16-plus-year-olds, are fed up looking at their big brothers. Punks are scruffy and the Punk blokes look at the 'Modettes' and

> they look more attractive, so there's a big change going on.
> This Mod revival is different from the originals. They still
> play a few of the Who numbers and there is still a Ska,
> Blue Beat feel. Still soul orientated, but in a one-hour set
> they are playing 75 per cent of their own original songs.
> It may be more of a London thing at the moment, but
> wait for *Quadrophenia*.

Line-up of the bands on the *Mods Mayday* '79 album:

Secret Affair
Ian Page (vocals, trumpet)
Dave Cairns (guitar, vocals)
Dennis Smith (bass, vocals)
Seb Shelton (drums)

Begger
Nigel Gregory (lead vocals, harp)
Jeff John (guitar, vocals)
Mark Williams (bass, vocals)
Mike Slocomb (drums)

Small Hours
Neil Thompson (vocals)
Carol Isaacs (organ, piano)
Almond Hand (guitar, vocals)
Kim Bradshaw (bass)
Dave Burke (drums)

The Mods
Mark Casson (lead vocal)
Alan Robson (guitar, vocals)
Dave Ross (bass, vocals)
Ian Guthrie (drums)

Squire
Tony Maynell (guitar, vocals)
Enzo Esposito (bass, vocals)
Steve Baker (guitar)
Ross di Landau (drums)

PHIL DANIELS AND *QUADROPHENIA*

We were in the middle of the Mods' revival when the film *Quadrophenia* came out, and I got a phone call from Phil Daniels, who played the main character, Jimmy Cooper (the name was derived from 'Mini Cooper', the car that, along with the Mods, symbolised 60s Britain), asking for a gig. That was wonderful. I said, 'How much money do you want?'

He told me, 'I don't want anything, just a gig.'

I asked, 'Do you want to go on Mods Monday?'

'No,' he replied, 'I'm not a Mod. I got a band together and just want to play; don't even mention my name. I am in the studio doing a record. The band's called Phil Daniels and the Cross.'

He didn't know that I knew that he was up for the co-lead with Hazel O'Connor in the film *Breaking Glass*. Our audiences had been rehearsing for the producers as extras for gig scenes for a long time and I had got to know them. (They sent big private buses to collect them.)

There was a good crowd for Phil, but he upset them straight away with the type of music he played. It was arty avant-garde, but he was absolutely the Mods' hero so they cheered him on.

After about five songs, a Mod jumped on stage with a parka coat and asked Phil to put it on, but he refused. Then a few more jumped up to make him put it on. Things were looking nasty. I ran over, pulled Phil to the side and said, 'Put it on for Christ's sake or there will be a riot if you don't.'

'No,' he said, 'I am not putting the parka on.'

A riot was close, and there were always a few looking for trouble, but I had an idea. I said to Phil, 'When I look up at you, just nod.'

I went down to the rowdy Mods and told them that Phil couldn't wear a parka because, ever since Jimmy, his character in *Quadrophenia*, drove over the cliff, he had nightmares that if he put on a parka he would be killed the same as Jimmy. I said, 'Ask him yourself.' I shouted at Phil, 'Isn't that right?'

Phil nodded like I told him to. I said to the Mods, 'You must never tell anyone about this or Phil will not be able to get any more work.'

The young Mods loved it. They cheered their heads off for the rest of the night and Phil was once again their hero. But he never came back and played for us again.

He made his comeback in Rock'n'Roll when Blur asked him to do the vocals on 'Park Life'. He did his bit in the studio in half an hour, went on tour and became big mates with them. At the end of his vocal bit he would thank his backing band Blur! Typical Phil Daniels.

I have seen Phil on a number of occasions at charity football matches when he plays for my son Glen's team. Phil is a great actor and, more than that, he's a fine, loyal man. Pity he supports Chelsea but we can't all be perfect.

MORE MUSIC (AND THINGS) PLEASE!

The Bridge House was both a starting place for new bands and also a place where established bands, or members of bands, could come and play without being hassled; they knew that they could relax and enjoy themselves. They also used to try out other instruments that they had not used before and, of course, they played different types of music from what they played with their main bands. An example of this was Charlie Watts, whose band was called Rocket 88. It was a jazz band with his own sound, although Charlie still played drums, as he always did, with the Rolling Stones. With Rocket 88, he used to play more lightly, with more of a jazzier Bluesy feel when he played the Bridge in 1980.

Gary Moore came down to a jam in 1981 and played the Blues all night. Afterwards, he said it was the best blow he had blown since he first started playing. Dennis Stratton had organised the jam and he also had Keith Emerson, one of the members of Emerson Lake and Palmer, playing. Dennis by this time had formed a new band called Lionheart.

Lionheart got themselves an American record deal and toured the USA. When they came to the Bridge, they were trying to get a deal in England. Funny sometimes how it works out; they had a deal in America but couldn't get a deal in their own country. It was a Heavy band, which were generally more popular in America than in Britain. Being an ex-Iron Maiden guitarist must have helped Dennis and he was on the *Live – A Week At The Bridge E16* album with Remus Down Boulevard. Of course, I'm jesting, although we did sell a lot of copies of the album in America and Europe.

FAD GADGET MEET DEPECHE MODE

Andy Fletcher, who played keyboards, had given me a demo with the name Composition of Sound, and John McGeady, my assistant, brought it to my notice. I got about 20 tapes like this every day, but I quite liked the name, so I played it in my office at the Bridge House. I would always have a few of my staff with me to get their opinion. Nobody liked it, except me, but I said, 'This is what we are looking for, something different.

Even though John didn't like it, I overruled him and told him to give them a gig. I thought it was different and adventurous, because anyone with the guts to send this type of music to a Rock pub must be brave and maybe have what it takes to make it.

The band had started to build a good following down in Rayleigh by 1980. They were from Basildon, not exactly local, but straight down the A13 isn't too far, and I thought it was near enough for them to bring a fair supporting crowd with them.

(When the band played their first gig for me, I am pretty sure that I had advertised it as Composition of Sound. I would put posters all around the pub with the forthcoming attractions, Saturday, Sunday and so on. If anyone has any old *Melody Maker*, *NME*, *Sounds* or *Face* music papers with listings of bands who played at the Bridge House, I'd be interested in getting them for the Bridge House website. I'm trying to get as many dated as possible, details of bands and names who played there, so, apart from checking if Compo of Sound were advertised, any info would be good for me.)

Before the band arrived at the Bridge, they informed us that they had changed their name to Depeche Mode, which is French for 'Fashion News' or 'Fashion Update' (not fast fashion as is commonly claimed) after a Parisian fashion magazine they had seen and liked the sound of the expression. I said, 'Good, I wish you luck with it.' I carried on talking to them, trying to get the feel of their ambition. Dave Gahan (lead vocals) told me that he was a regular at the Bridge House when Wasted Youth played and that they were one of his favourite bands. My son Darren, who was the bass player in Wasted Youth, lived with us above the pub, and luckily his band were having a rest that day. So I called him down to meet and watch the band, as he would be able to give me some ideas about them. I introduced him to Dave, who was very pleased to meet one of the members of his favourite band, who by this time were headliners all over England, Marquee, Lyceum, Rainbow, the Venue … everywhere.

The band had only brought about 20 fans with them, which was disappointing for us, as the pub was capable of packing in over 1,000 people, so you can imagine how empty it looked. But after the gig Darren said to me that he thought they were great, and I should get them to record for Bridge House Records. He said to me, 'Next time we play here, give them the support,' which I did. Darren also said he would put the word around when there were playing.

Playing live, Depeche sounded almost identical to the tape they had given us. This was my initiation to synths and drum machines. Although Nick Lowe of Wasted Youth used a synthesiser, this was the first time I'd come across a drum machine.

I spoke to the band after the gig, giving them their £15 fee. Dave said, 'We will definitely pull more of a crowd if you will give us another gig.'

Vince said, 'Yes, we have got a residence at Crocs in Rayleigh and they'll all come down.'

I said I liked the band and I would give them some support slots to build a crowd up.

The Bridge was their first gig in London. They had not been able to get any before so they were delighted when I said they could come back. We gave them a few support gigs but it still wasn't working out. Remember, the Bridge was a Rock pub, with loud drums and guitar riffs, so we had to build a new audience for them, and the nearest band we had to their style was Wasted Youth. Darren and Dave Gahan became friends, and Darren really helped them. Although they may not know this, Daren even gave free passes away at Wasted gigs so that their fans would come down to see Depeche Mode and he continued to bandy their name around when talking to the media. But I didn't know about the free tickets until much later. So, well done, Darren! He was a big help in building up the band, even though it cost me a nice few quid as well.

I set about building up Depeche, the crowd as well as the band. At the same time I wanted to sign them to Bridge House Records. They were pleased with my offer, so we organised a six-month period with support gigs. The idea was that they would get the experience of playing together and learning on stage how a song should be performed. Hopefully, the headline bands' supporters would like them and come down to see them the next time they played. Things were going well, and we were developing a nice audience for them. We always knew who the customers were for the support band because they would be there early, before 8pm. The main band would be on stage at 9.30 so their supporters would turn up during the support band's gig at around 8.45.

As I said earlier, I was always looking for something a bit different. And I noticed in the music press that Fad Gadget were doing the rounds and getting some rave reviews. I really wanted to book them, as I had seen them when they supported Wasted Youth at the Lyceum in the West End of London. I always kept an eye on the music press and one day I saw the name Frank Tovey. Well, a good friend from our working days in the fish market had the same name, and he was also a best friend of my brother-in-law Joe Lucy, who ran a pub gig at the Ruskin Arms in East Ham E6. So I rang Joe and got Frank's number.

I called Frank and asked about Frank Tovey.

He said, 'He's my son. Don't you remember? You played with him enough when you fetched your kids around my house in Stepney.'

I said, 'Yes, but why didn't you tell me that he had a band?' I asked him to get the agency to telephone me as I'd like to book them. I also gave him a coating for not telling me his son was in a band.

He said, 'You don't pay enough money!'

We laughed and I said, 'See you at the next funeral.'

(Sadly, this turned out to be very poignant, as Frank Tovey Jr died of a heart attack a couple of years ago. At the funeral I told Frank Sr what I had written, but he said, 'Leave it in. It will not fetch him back.' Frank and his wife Maureen are lovely people who I have known for over 50 years.)

The agent rang the next day and we booked Fad Gadget. Their manager, Daniel Miller, who I had heard of as a synth man when I was down at Rough Trade Distribution Company, had a couple of hits under different names with his own label, Mute Records. Fad Gadget were really up-and-coming, and an ideal band for Depeche Mode to support – young, trendy and hip.

I rang Dave Gahan's house and spoke to his mother, who was always very nice and friendly. Nothing was too much trouble for her and she would always write down what I said, so as not to make any mistakes. Dave was never in whenever I phoned, but he always got back within an hour or so. When I told him Fad Gadget were playing and they could support them, he screamed out with pleasure. He said Steve had mentioned it and thanked me for confirming it.

The night arrived, and it was going to be a good one. Although we never opened until 7pm, we would let in the band at 5pm so they could set up all their instruments, and, without fail, Andy Fletcher was always first to arrive. I think he was working in central London, and, after finishing work, came straight to the Bridge House. The rest of the guys came from Basildon, and the A13 was always busy that time of night, so they were always a little bit late. Not Andy … he would be banging on the back door, waking me up from my afternoon snooze.

What a showman my friend's son, Frankie Tovey Jr, turned out to be! During the gig, right at the front of the stage, Stinky Turner (lead singer with Cockney Rejects) was transfixed by the sight of Frank Tovey dressed as a Womble (Frank did the whole gig in the costume). The only problem of the night was the challenge of trying to calm Frank down. He was so active, even during the rehearsal, when there were no customers! He really put everything into it. When he came on the audience erupted. He was diving all over the place ... in the crowd, on the bar, smashing all the glasses. Standing at the back, I thought there was a riot happening and ran round to the backstage area to see it was just Frank. I was delighted to see everybody laughing and cheering.

It was also nice to see his brother, who was a really good boxer and was there with my son Glen and Ray Winstone, also members of the Repton Boxing Club. Stepney born and bred, or is it Bethnal Green? Whatever the case, they always looked out for one another.

The gig went off perfectly and, because of the good feeling to the evening, Depeche did not want to come off stage. They even got an encore and came back on, which is unheard of for the support act. Frank said to me, 'Let them go back on again, as many times as they like!'

I was also introduced to Daniel Miller from Mute Records that evening, and he said he was impressed with Depeche Mode. I told him we were going in the studio soon to get some tracks down, and he was very interested and asked me to send him a copy of the recording when they were finished.

Daniel, of course, loved Depeche Mode and offered them management.

I talked to Vince Clarke and Dave Gahan about the recording, and they said, 'Any time you're ready.'

They had promised to record on my label. I also spoke to them about publishing and they agreed to come and meet my publishers Martin and Coulter. They met me at the pub at 10am and I drove them to Kensington for the meeting. We had a good chat for an hour or so with Richard Gillinson and Bill Martin. Dave was encouraging Vince to sign a publishing deal there and then, but Vince, being the main songwriter, had given his word that he would not sign until he had further talks with another publishing company he had spoken to. This was wise of Vince, as it's always better to have one against the other; you always get a better deal that way. But I was sad to have lost out on the deal. No one at the time knew how big they were going to be, and Vince was to write many a hit song and make millions, but, if they had signed, I would now be a much more well-to-do man and the Bridge House never would have closed.

We never did get Depeche in the studio, as we were very busy at the pub. The record company was releasing two albums and four singles, and Wasted Youth were on a European tour so things were very hectic. Daniel Miller spoke to the band and got them in the studio. Because of Bridge House Records, he did it as a one-off, with no contract exchanged. So he was very fair to me.

Daniel confirmed that the band had told him they had promised to record for me and there was not a problem. After hearing this direct from Daniel, I thought, 'Well, there's no rush to get them in the studio. I'll give them a few more gigs to tighten them up and get them a more confident approach to playing their music.'

So it was a really big blow when I found out that a guy called Stevo had booked the studio I used in Forest Gate, John Bassett's studio, and recorded Depeche for his New Romantic label! I had given Stevo a Thursday night for new bands. He was a DJ and I would put on bands in between him playing records, Soft Cell being one of them. (Marc Almond, who along with Dave Ball was Soft Cell, later complained in the press, saying that they had been obliged to sit on the steps of the Bridge House all day waiting for the doors to open.) Stevo had booked John Bassett's in Forest Gate, and recorded a compilation album which included Depeche Mode's first recording, which should have been mine. I had planned to make another compilation after the big success I had had with the *Mods Mayday '79* album, and I had arranged with John Bassett to record Depeche Mode. John was shocked when he found out it wasn't me working with them because I had made the arrangements with him. I could have made a fuss about it and blocked the album, but I just thought, 'Another lesson learned.'

The album sold really well and launched Stevo's record company Some Bizarre, so another success story from the Bridge House. But one which I could have done without.

I had missed out on Depeche Mode's first recording but I still had the task of building them up to be a headliner, which didn't take long, thanks to Darren and our help. The Fad Gadget support gig did wonders for the band and, after we gave them a couple more supports, they were ready. Depeche played for us regularly throughout 1981.

Daniel got them in the studio, even though he had not signed a recording contract with them, and they were still expecting to sign to my label. Their first single with Mute Records, 'New Life', reached number 11 in the UK charts. Mute signed them and they have had a great career, selling out at every gig. They played all over the world in the 80s.

One evening in 1982, I was speaking to a *Melody Maker* reporter, who was at the pub reviewing one of the bands, and it was a quiet night, not many customers. He said to me, 'Lost money tonight?'

I said, 'Yes, it's getting a bit too regular. I am thinking of moving on, the record company is busy. I might channel my energy more into that side of the business and leave the pub.'

Of course, by the next week, in the paper, I was shutting down the Bridge House over falling sales. 'THIS GIG WILL BE SORELY MISSED' was a typical headline in the *Melody Maker* and some of the other papers.

Soon after, I got a phone call from Depeche's agent saying that the band wanted to do a secret gig at the Bridge. I said, 'Great.'

He said, 'They are on tour, and have Saturday free.'

The Saturday was Charles and Diana's wedding day so I missed the wedding to see Depeche Mode one last time at the Bridge. A secret gig? At 12 o'clock, crowds began to arrive, but, of course, we had to keep them outside. Come five o'clock when Depeche were doing their sound check, the pub was full. They were climbing through windows, through the toilets at the back – no way could we keep them out. So the band let them stay for the sound check, providing they left after that and made an orderly queue. Dave had made the speech and, from my point of view, we had to get the punters out so they could pay to get back in! Sounds funny, doesn't it. I just thought the band wanted their money for the work they were putting in.

Anyway, they all obeyed Dave's instructions and left the pub. By seven o'clock, when we opened the doors, the place was surrounded. Over 1,000 paid to get in the pub, and, when they were in, we opened all the doors so the crowd outside could hear the music. Needless to say, it was a sensational gig.

At the end, I went into the dressing room with the door takings and Dave said, 'We want you to keep it and keep the pub open, it's a great gig.' And he gave me the bundle of money back.

If I can remember correctly, it was over £1,000. We were licensed for 560 people, so there must have been double that, so it would have been nearer £2,000. There was a lot of jibbers who had got there early before we opened up and got in for free. Trust me, I was not complaining when they told me to keep it.

As Depeche were growing in popularity, the New Romantics, as they were being called, were emerging. I tried hard to get Spandau Ballet, but they would only play non-established venues. Boy George's manager, Tony Gordon (who I have only recently found out also managed our very own Cockney Rejects at that time), phoned and booked Boy George in for his first gig. He came to visit me at the Bridge later and asked me what I thought might be the next new sound. I told him, 'You're watching it!' Wasted Youth were playing.

In June 1988, Depeche Mode's sell-out world tour ended with a 75,000 capacity gig at the Rose Bowl, California. In the 90s, they had a singles tour. The band played 64 dates in 18 countries for 650,000 fans.

In the last few years, they have all been fit and well and working with new material. They have children to look after, a new album and a new tour all arranged. Good luck to 'Modepeche', that's the name I used for them when they had secret gigs, so everyone knew it was them.

I was then, and am still now, over the moon about the success Depeche has had over the years. It proved to me that I was right to trust my judgement. The only time I have seen them since was on the TV. Vince came down to the Bridge House to watch Alison Moyet when she sang with the Little Roosters, and we had a nice chat. I have seen Fletch a couple of times, the last time at Frank Tovey's funeral. It was great to hear Fad Gadget supported Depeche in 2001. I bet they had a good laugh about it.

Steve Fisher, of SCV London, a friend of mine and one of the most high-profile distributors in the UK music industry, wrote a kind of 'Bridge House Memoir' a while back and remembered an offer to support Fad Gadget:

MEMORIES OF THE BRIDGE
Steve Fisher

Depeche Mode's big break
I think Wasted Youth must have been on tour, as I was hanging about in the office with Terry before opening up. We got into conversation about Depeche Mode who were headlining that night, and then about Fad Gadget who were headlining later that month, one of us, or both of us, thought we should see if Depeche wanted the support gig.

Being the boy, I got sent down to ask. I can remember it like it was yesterday, getting up on stage while the band were setting up and having a chat. I asked them if they fancied the gig. Three members played it very cool and shrugged. Vince, meanwhile, grinned like a Cheshire cat and replied something very close to 'Bloody hell, yeah!!' At which point I spotted out of the corner of my eye the other guys clenching fists in a subdued celebratory fashion.

When the gig came about, Frank Tovey (Fad Gadget) did it dressed, I think, as a Womble. Right at the front of the stage for the whole gig was one Stinky Turner (lead singer with Cockney Rejects), who stood totally transfixed by this sight.

Steve also had an interesting memory of a visit from one of the greatest guitarists ever to come out of Britain:

MEMORIES OF THE BRIDGE

Jeff Beck forgot he was the guitarist
Jeff Beck came down one night to get up with a band called UPP. He'd just played guitar and produced an album for them. UPP were nearly unique for a Rock band in that they had no guitar player, just drums, bass and keyboards.

Jeff arrived, looked at the stage and muttered, 'Oh fuck, I forgot I was their guitarist.' I offered to drive home and get my Strat and an amp for him but he declined the offer, deciding to just have a beer or five instead. He spent the gig right dead centre of the audience, headbanging for want of a better description; a very cool chap.

Steve told me, 'If you want any more, my memory of those days is still pretty complete. Ask me what happened last year and I wouldn't have a clue – I couldn't believe the reunion was nearly three years ago. I truly thought it was last summer – but get me back to my teens and it's all still there.'

I know what he means, perhaps you do too.

VINCE CLARKE, ALISON MOYET, THE LITTLE ROOSTERS

Thinking about Depeche now, I remember that, when Vince Clarke left the band, I thought that they would fail. At the time, Vince was the sole writer of the songs in the band and their strong point. He was the original founder member and the force behind the band. When they turned up without him, they introduced the new guy, Alan Wilder. It was his first gig with the band at the Bridge. They introduced some of Martin Gore's songs which were good, but the originals always sounded the best to me. So, although I worried, Martin became the most prolific writer in the band and I'm glad we were wrong.

I had got wind that Vince was leaving the band when he turned up at the Bridge House one Sunday night, when the Little Roosters were playing. They had a girl singer called Alison Moyet (her real first names were Genevieve Alison Jane), although they used to call her 'Alf'. Vince and I sat and had a drink together. He said that Alison was from Basildon and he had popped in to see her. We spoke about her powerful voice and I told him she had got her own band together and that I'd have given her a couple of gigs. I am only guessing, but I think he was checking her out for his new band. He knew what was going on with Depeche, although he never said. He must have already given notice that he was leaving. But it was not for me to ask so I didn't.

Alison's band were terrible, so she did right by teaming up with Vince.

The Little Roosters were going to be on the *Mods Mayday '79* album. Before that, the Roosters' guitarist/singer Garrie Lammin had been in a Punk band called Cock Sparrer. He's still performing. We had recorded the band with Alison singing a couple of songs, with Garrie being the lead singer, but nothing was done with it at the time of the recording.

Garrie had signed to Cliff Cooper Management and Orange Music Publishing. His manager was trying to get a record deal off the back of the album, which never happened. A few years later, Garrie came to see me to see if I wanted to release this album. Of course I said yes. Alison was on vocals with Yazoo, who were in the charts. We got the album together, a nice bright

MORE MUSIC (AND THINGS) PLEASE!

sleeve, called it *To Whom It May Concern* and released it. I think we only pressed 1,000.

Within a few weeks, a threatening solicitor's letter arrived from top lawyer James Wyllie's company, Harbottle and Lewis, stopping us from selling the album. We spoke on the phone and I arranged an appointment to see the lawyers, taking with me all the artwork, metalwork, labels, etc. I said, 'Drop the writ and here is all the material. Forget it, or I will challenge it in court and carry on selling the albums.'

But that's how some people turn out. We helped Alison and she sued us.

I spoke to Cliff Cooper who said Alison had signed a piece of paper and he did not want to get involved. I believe, if I had wanted to take it further, I would have won the case. So, what stopped me? Well, I couldn't sell the records anyway, as nobody wanted them. But I did sell a few at the start and maybe got the outlay back.

I've got the record in front of me, which I got at a car boot sale. I wrote the letter on the back cover. Barry Mizen mixed and produced the album. He was in the band and was a fine musician. Well done!

I have recently listened to it again and I can see from Alison's point of view why she tried to stop it being released; it was a bad vocal performance. I wonder if she joined the band just to exercise her voice, because, as Chris Thompson always said, 'Go for it, always try to hit a higher note each time you sing, then when you're recording you know what range you can get away with.'

Alison really went for it, almost screaming, even though she knew the gig was being recorded. Was she trying to impress? Only she would know and perhaps that's why the record was banned. Alison once said, 'Instead of thinking, "That's a nice tune", you start thinking, "Is it the right pace, is it the right tempo?" That is the death knell for artists.'

That makes her seem like someone who might want to try things out rather than just think about them. She does have a lovely voice and has proved herself through her music over the years. I thought 'Only You', the single on Mute Records, was a classic. I still enjoy listening to it all these years later.

Vince Clarke went on to form Erasure with Andy Bell. It makes you wonder why they don't get back together, all of them, now and again, for old times' sake; Depeche, Yazoo, Erasure, what a sound they would make. Unless of course, they have 'musical differences' (the classic answer) which means they hate each other and don't even talk. My guess is we might find out one day.

THE PRETENDERS

I got my son Darren an audition with this band. Their management company had been to the Bridge House to watch Wasted Youth and they suggested that Darren should join their band. He refused. Billy Idol came to see them at the Bridge House and said, 'I want this band to tour with me as the "Billy Idol band".' This would have meant Ken Scott being the lead guitarist and doing backing vocals. The other people with Billy Idol were from Sigue Sigue Sputnik.

I said, 'I will contact you tomorrow.'

The next morning, after telling Darren about the news, he said, 'I am a founder member of Wasted Youth. I will never play in another band, ever.' And he has kept his word.

Foolish? Perhaps. But Darren went on to run his own record company, producing many bands. He is also the managing director of Vinyl Pressings Ltd, a record-pressing plant that the family own.

IN CAMERA

Dave Scinto's In Camera was the band that Wasted Youth supported on their first gig. Since then, Dave has gone on to write West End plays and major films, e.g. *Gangster No. 1*, etc. His latest film is *Sexy Beast*, starring Ray Winstone, a Bridge House regular. Ray used to come down the Bridge House after training with my son Glen at West Ham Boxing Club, and he would often help out behind the bar.

In Camera played for us at the Bridge and later signed with 4AD Records, part of Beggars Banquet.

MEMORIES OF THE BRIDGE
Ray Winstone, 2007

Old Uncle Tel, the advice he gave me over the years has always been the best. I've known him all my life, and he has always been there for me. He and my dad were friends from their younger boxing days, so, needless to say, like all sons of boxers, I wanted to be like my old man and I started a boxing career, eventually winning national titles and boxing for my country, and doing pretty good.

Then, after training one day, I went to the Bridge (for a lemonade of course!). 'What's the trouble?' Uncle Tel said – he could always tell when something was up.

I plucked up the courage and said, 'I've been offered the chance to go to drama school – what do you think?'

He said, 'I thought you were gonna turn pro as a fighter. You're certainly good enough.'

'Well, that's the problem,' I said, 'I just don't know what to do, turn pro or try this acting lark.'

Was I surprised when he said, 'Forget about all this boxing and get stuck into the acting. Boxing is the hardest game in the world, and you don't get your brains knocked out while you're acting. But don't forget: work just as hard at it, you don't get anything for nothing in this life!'

And so I went off to drama school leaving my boxing days behind me.

It's funny how things happen. I've managed to make a living in the acting game, and, guess what, Uncle Tel was right again – when you're acting, the punches don't hurt, though some of the critics do.

We all still remain loyal friends after all these years, so, thanks again, Uncle Tel. And don't forget, if this book turns into a film and there's some punching to do, I've kept my eye in, and can still do three rounds … but perhaps not as a middleweight!

PETER PERRETT AND THE ONLY ONES

Peter was the producer of Wasted Youth's single 'I'll Remember You', and we got very friendly with him. He played and did the vocals for the Only Ones, who were signed to CBS and had a few hit songs. Wasted asked me if Peter could produce their next single. I was a bit worried, as he had a big reputation for leading 'the true Rock'n'Roll lifestyle'. We met and I persuaded him to do a gig for me. He had straightened himself and the rest of the band out. They had a tour planned so I asked him to produce Wasted's next single. He was pleased, as he said that was the direction he wanted to move into. We booked a studio in Notting Hill and had the all-night session, which was a lot cheaper. I could also be there during the recording after we had closed the pub that night. They were due to start recording at 10.30pm. I got there at 12 o'clock, but nobody was there.

I eventually found them in a club in Bayswater Road. I start shouting and hollering: 'Studio time is working out at £50 per hour and you're all here drinking!?'

They told me Peter the producer had not turned up. He got there around 2am, telling me he had overslept!

The five days we had booked turned into eight, but we had a great single with 'I'll Remember You'. So all was forgiven. You can never plan time in the studio. To get the acoustics right can take ages and drums can be a nightmare. The whole kit has to be miked up, but there's the old saying, 'The earlier you start, the earlier you finish.'

I got the Only Ones to play for us on New Year's Eve 1980. The gig was a real sensation. There were a lot of new faces at the Bridge that night, a really good crowd that would not let the band off the stage. They had four encores and only got off the stage because I turned the lights out. We all ended up drinking until about 4am, a great night.

After this gig, Wasted Youth supported the Only Ones on a 24-date British tour. Having a similar style to the Only Ones, Wasted built up a larger following during the course of the tour, which is always good for record sales, and of course that is why you pay to get a support gig on any major tour.

BLIND DRUNK WITH STEVE MARRIOTT

The good thing about the Bridge House was that you never knew who would walk through the door. One night in walked an old friend, Laurie O'Leary, with East End, Rock/Pop legend former Small Faces front man Steve Marriott. I had known Laurie for many years. He was into music and had run

187

a good Rock club in the West End called the Speakeasy a few years earlier. I did not know that he also managed Steve, who had just returned from the States where he had been very successful forming Humble Pie with Beckenham boy Peter Frampton, member of band Herd. His return from America was very low key and he just wanted to play some music for fun. Steve told me he had got a few friends together, calling their band Blind Drunk. They all had different names; he was called Matt Vinyl (vocals guitar), Red Wine, and so on. The other members of the group were Ronnie Lane (vocals, bass), Mick Green (guitar), Jim Leverton (bass and vocals), Mick Weaver (keyboards) and Dave Hynes (drums and backing vocals). Other incarnations of Blind Drunk would include (in 1982) Mickey Finn (guitar), Zoot Money (keyboards) and Mel Collins (sax).

Steve said he wanted a small residency, and I gave him every Thursday for the following four weeks. We advertised the gig as Blind Drunk with Matt Vinyl, etc. and it soon got round that it was Steve Marriott.

One night, the pub was really packed. Steve had set the band up, done a sound check and gone to have something to eat. The intercom rang me upstairs: 'There are two gentlemen who want to see you urgently.'

They would not say what for or who they were, so down I went. They introduced themselves as police, and said, 'Mr Murphy, we have here a warrant for the arrest of Steve Marriott, on fraud charges.'

By this time, the pub was heaving with around 800 people in. I said, 'I'm sorry, but he's not here.' I told them, if they could leave their number, I would make sure he got it and rang them the next day. As the posters round the pub were advertising Matt Vinyl, I thought I could get away with a bit of bluff.

'We know he's here,' they said. 'We're not leaving without him.'

I said, 'There are 800 people here waiting to see him play. There'll be a riot if he doesn't.'

But they didn't care. They had their job to do. I told them to have a drink at the bar and I would see if I could contact him. I phoned Laurie who had left his home and was on his way to the gig. I jumped in the car and must have visited every eating place within five miles of the Bridge, but to no avail. But when I returned to the pub who pulls up behind me? Steve Marriott! I smuggled him in the back way and upstairs to my office. I said, 'We'll wait for Laurie to get here.'

'Fuck 'em!' Steve said emphatically. 'I'm not worried about them.'

'Steve, they've got a warrant for your arrest! They'll bang you up in a cell.'

I went downstairs and spoke to the two coppers. I told them Steve had to do this gig and asked them if they would stay in the guests' area and interview him after the gig. When Laurie arrived, I introduced the coppers, and they agreed to wait until the end of the gig, which was sensational. Steve's friends Chas & Dave, Joe Brown, Ronnie Lane (also formally with the Faces of course), Gerry McAvoy and Jackie Lynton were there as well; what a night! Even the cops enjoyed it.

It turned out that, before Steve went to America, he had opened a recording studio with a partner who had the full run of the place. It seemed all the equipment had vanished, allegedly stolen before it had been paid for. Fortunately, Steve could prove he was in America at the time. He had to go to court but was exonerated, so we were able to look forward to the next week, which again was a really good night but this time also aggravating!

When the band arrived, I went to greet them. They had

already set up for their sound check and started to rehearse. All of a sudden this rather largely built fellow jumped up on stage and started to hassle Steve. He was trying to sell him some drugs and he wasn't going to take no for an answer. We evicted him but he kept coming back. The third time he tried turned out to be unlucky for him. I got him outside and he never came back. Nasty business but someone had to do it.

Laurie had warned me not to give Steve his earnings for the night until everyone had gone home. If he had cash in his hand, he would give it away. We worked on a percentage of the door takings, our deals were generally 50 per cent or 60/40. Either way we were so pleased to get Steve, we gave him 90 per cent, about £1,200. The percentage came through for the night's work and I decided to give £400 to Steve's wife, who was always with him, to make sure that they went home with some money. She said, 'Thank you,' and put it in her bag.

The gig had only just finished and Steve was in the dressing room chilling out with his wife and the rest of the band. My wife Rita always supplied the bands with an abundance of different types of food and all the drinks they wanted, so it was always at least 30 minutes before we settled the earnings for the night. I was standing behind the bar, when Steve came over, shouting and hollering. 'I got a grand last week, how comes you've given that money to my wife? You know I got to have the money to pay the band.'

'Here's your money,' I said and gave him his £800.

'Fuck me, Tel! I'm sorry,' he said with surprise. 'I thought that was all we got. You told my wife not to give it to me, so I panicked. The boys are waiting for their cut.'

I followed him into the dressing room.

He said, 'Here's the money, take it all. I don't want anything.'

MORE MUSIC (AND THINGS) PLEASE!

As he turned, he gave me a little sly wink, a kiss on the cheek and he was gone. 'See you next week, Tel.'

I had been approached by Ralph Meade who asked me if I would like some of the bands on video. We agreed a fee and I asked him to come along the following week and film Blind Drunk. This was 1978, and the general public at that time had not heard of videos, so it was another first for the pub. The only trouble was that he filmed them on a reel of tape, not video cassettes, so we have them on film but cannot watch them! And the fellow has moved away, otherwise we could have used his equipment. It would be nice to see them some 25 years later playing the Bridge, and we have not given up! We are still trying to get them converted to film or on DVD. Just today, Brian Belton, the editor of this book, has found a couple of addresses and we have had enquiries from the USA. Colin Rapp, our original photographer, has found a studio there, and a customer from Brazil, Ricardo Lira, has made contact after seeing our problem on the forum on our website. Never give up!!

Steve carried on playing. We got him a few gigs. Ronnie Lane fetched his mobile studio down and they recorded their next gig at the Bridge House.

Poor old Steve had a terrible end. He went to bed out of it, after too much 'smoking', and a fire started at his home. He jumped up in the dark, felt round for the door, opened it but found himself in a wardrobe. The fumes took over and he died. He was only 44. God bless you, Stevie Marriott!

Laurie O'Leary, who wrote *Ronnie Kray: A Man Among Men*, wrote to me a while ago.

191

MEMORIES OF THE BRIDGE
Laurie O'Leary

The Bridge House was firmly positioned among the cobbled-stoned streets of East London's tough docklands while Canning Town is a name that conjures up images of men comparable to Desperate Dan, rough, tough and respected! Many famous names in the world of boxing were produced from the area, among them was Olympic champion Terry Spinks, a golden boy of boxing, who is still feted today. Another of West Ham's favourite sons was Terry Murphy, who also became a champion.

Terry Murphy, along with his wife Rita, ran the Bridge House, a pub used by the regulars, supping their usual pints and exchanging elaborate local stories of the times that were a-changing. Inspired by a younger son who wanted to become a musician, Terry soon became aware that a host of local groups were looking for a place to play. Terry decided to try it for just one night; 'Live at The Bridge House' was born and was so successful that it was extended until every night was a live-group night. The Bridge House became a venue where everyone in the music business would visit, because with Terry and his sporting sons in attendance it was a safe place to play. Groups, managers, record labels and producers, all looking for the mass of talent being discovered playing at the pub. It was justifiably a magnet to the business.

In the mid-1970s I was managing Steve Marriott from the Small Faces group. Steve had been working in America, but wanted to return to London. 'Get a few pub gigs in

London, mate, like the Bridge House,' he said. 'Yeh, Lol, that would be perfect for me!'

Steve called the band Blind Drunk. Amongst others, it featured Ronnie Lane, Joe Brown, Sam Brown, Jim Leverton and Zoot Money. The poster read: 'Almost Live at The Bridge House'.

The evening of the gig proved to be one of adventure if nothing else. A call from Terry to me at home went something like this: 'Lol, can you come down right away? Steve Marriott is wanted by the old bill! They are looking for him so I've hid him in the back room. Something about fraud.'

Explaining that I would be there in a few minutes, I drove the short distance to Canning Town from my home in Bethnal Green. On arriving, I went into the pub to be met by Terry.

'He's in there, mate,' he said, showing me into a small room in the back of the pub.

Stevie was looking very scared. His face was a picture of horror, his eyes wide in amazement. 'What's it all about, Lol?' he asked. 'Sort it out, mate! We've got a gig to do tonight and it's packed out there. And I've got something in me pocket they shouldn't see too!'

This of course meant Steve had a 'medicinal fag'. I met the police officers who explained that a firm wanted payment for some studio equipment Steve had hired. It was of a civil not criminal nature. In reality, the police shouldn't have been there. Thankfully, they left after a drink with me and a 'Hello' to Steve and the band.

Terry was relieved the gig wasn't affected. It was an

amazing evening to experience; real down-to-earth music and musicians thoroughly enjoying themselves. More than that, a residency was born for Steve and his mates that very night. The bonus was the night had been recorded on Ronnie Lane's mobile studio.

It is noted that, when a group called Terry a few times for a gig and said their name was Police, Terry didn't tell them, but he wouldn't book them in Canning Town with a name like Police; it just didn't seem right for the area! But Terry was wise to be selective. U2, Dire Straits, Iron Maiden, Squeeze, Q-Tips, Tom Robinson, A Flock of Seagulls, Rory Gallagher, Remus Down Boulevard, Mick Jagger, Keith Richards, Huey Lewis, Eric Clapton, Charlie Watts, Chas & Dave and a host of others even more famous all have history of appearances both playing or watching their mates in this biggest and best venue of all London pubs.

Terry Murphy must have been very proud to have added another dimension to Canning Town. It will forever be known for its history as a Rock-business venue. I should know about this, having managed the famous Speakeasy club for almost 10 years from 1968. Like Terry Murphy, I booked the groups into the club, promoted and publicised the people appearing there. The Beatles, Rolling Stones, Led Zeppelin, Eric Clapton, Bob Marley and the Wailers, Elton John, the Impressions, Neil Young, Three Dog Night, Jimi Hendrix, Jim Morrison, and so on, all appeared in the Speakeasy club in one way or other. Like the Bridge House, this club is also part of Rock music history.

God bless, Terry, to you and Rita.

Regards, Laurie O'Leary

MORE MUSIC (AND THINGS) PLEASE!

RONNIE LANE

Ronald 'Leafy' Lane has also passed away. He died in Trinidad, Colorado, in 1997. He was only 51. It's sad; he and Steve were so young. Ronnie and Steve had been school friends and together they formed the Small Faces in the early 60s. They were a massive success. Remember 'Itchy Coo Park'? That was Little Ilford Park in Manor Park E12, not far from where the boys grew up, and a short bus ride from the Bridge.

After the Blind Drunk gig, I got talking music to Ronnie Lane. He told me he would get a band together and do a few gigs. I booked him straight away. It was good for the pub to have musicians who had been there and done it. Our audiences had good memories, remembering the first time round and the new young bands could learn so much more just watching and listening. They always got a chance to talk to the more experienced guys after they had finished playing, and pick up helpful tips, etc.

Ronnie played a few times for us but by that time he had multiple sclerosis. He turned up to play on a Saturday night, when there was a really good crowd in, and he just collapsed in the dressing room. Ronnie's brother Stan was with him. We phoned an ambulance and off he went to hospital.

But it was Saturday night, 8.30pm, and we had a half-full pub that had paid on the door to watch Ronnie Lane. A couple of the band were still there but did not want to play without their front man.

I said, 'Stay here and we will see what musicians come in.'

First through the door was Gerry McAvoy (bass guitar, Rory Gallagher Band); next in Mickey Harris (drummer, RDB), then Garrie Lammin (Cock Sparrer) and Dave Edwards (vocalist/guitarist RDB). I got them all up on stage and a great night was had by all.

To any of the customers who weren't happy, I told the staff to give them a pint (of water, ha ha!). There were no takers and nobody went home. This sounds simple but wasn't and isn't. We used to have different audiences for many types of music. They had turned up for Ronnie's type of music. Gerry and the others, who were really Rock and 12-bar Blues players, had to adapt to R&B songs and music, but they managed easily because they were very good musicians.

Ronnie later moved to America where he was a bit of a guinea pig for this new treatment, when they injected him with snake venom. But it may have done a little good, as he lived a while longer.

When Ronnie died, Rod Stewart got a load of stars together and did a gig for him. It was a shame they didn't do it before he died, as the money might have made his life a little more comfortable, but it was a nice gesture from Rod that raised Ronnie's profile and helped his family.

KEITH MOON

Another sad story. Our friend Bill Curbishley, the Who manager, came down to the Bridge House to see me and asked me if I would look after drummer Keith Moon. He told me Keith was in a bad way and unless he could get him straightened out he would not be able to do the tour that was planned just a month later. Bill said I would have to stay with him 24 hours a day. He told me, 'Get him in the gym training and get him fit in both mind and body.'

I said to Bill, 'I'm sorry, but it would be impossible for me to leave the Bridge.'

We were so busy. I also had Wasted Youth on tour and our second album was due for release. I could see Bill was desperate so I told him not to worry and that I had the right man for the job. I immediately contacted a friend called Eddie Burkett.

Eddie, a former amateur boxer at the famous Fairbarn House club and West Ham, was for many years the trainer at West Ham Boxing Club. When the Peacock Gym opened in Silvertown, he was their first trainer, and he is still there today, training the elderly every Thursday. A few years ago he was awarded an MBE (or CBE) for his work with the kids. He must be 70 or so now, but still runs marathons for charities. A lovely man and a really good dedicated keep-fit expert from Canning Town.

Eddie came round early the next morning and I outlined the plan of action.

I phoned Bill's office and left a message for him to ring me. I did this a few times throughout the day but got no response. On the news that night, it was reported that Keith Moon had died; we were all devastated. Just a day too late, Eddie was sure he would have saved him.

That's Rock'n'Roll. When it hits you, it hurts.

JOE BROWN

Joe Brown came to the Bridge one night when Steve Marriott was playing with his newly named band Blind Drunk. Joe got up and played and sang some songs. After the gig, we were having a few drinks. I asked him, 'Is this the first time you have been at the Bridge House?'

His reply: 'You must be joking! See all them wires round the ceiling, I put them in when I was an apprentice electrician over 20 years ago.'

Joe was born in Swarby, Lincolnshire, but he lived most of his life in Canning Town and that is where he learned to play the guitar. He bought his first guitar off a local man, Georgie Dance, who used to play in the pub. He lived at the Sultan pub, in Grange Road, E13, which was owned by his uncle. An old mate of mine, Lennie Bristow, lived in the same road. Lennie used to have jellied-eel stalls and Joe worked for him for a while as a youngster. I said to Joe, 'I used to watch you pull the stall from the Abbey Arms to Poplar, a good two miles there and then back again.'

He replied, 'Well, why didn't you give me a push?!'

The area around the Sultan, Hermit and Grange Road, also produced two great comedy writers. Johnny Speight wrote the fantastically successful *Till Death Us Do Part* and invented the immortal Alf Garnett. Marty Feldman wrote the classic radio programme *Round the Horn* with Barry Took and of course became a comedy actor in his own right.

Joe's a great character, always laughing. I asked him to do a few gigs for us, and he agreed. His wife was in the band with him and they were great together. He seemed to have a different instrument for every song. I've got a good picture of him and his wife on stage. It was quite sad when you look at it because she died shortly afterwards. Later, their daughter, Sam, performed at the Bridge, doing backing vocals with Chris Thompson. She was only about 16, learning the business. I am glad to see father and daughter are still gigging. I saw them both on TV a while ago. One weekend, Sam was on with the Jools Holland Band on BBC 2.

Jools was a member of Squeeze who played for us in their early days. It was 1973 when Jools, then only 15, was introduced to Glenn Tilbrook and Chris Difford, and together they formed Squeeze, so he must have been in the line-up when they played at the Bridge. I was told by the manageress of the Only Ones, Peter Perrett's band, that her brother Harry Kakoulli was in the band then. He was the first member of Squeeze to go solo.

IAN STEWART

Ian Stewart was the piano player for the Rolling Stones and founder of the band. Despite being dropped from the group just before they made it big, Stu was the sixth Rolling Stone, their ever-present pianist and road manager right up until his unexpected and untimely death in 1985. He was recognised as the sixth Stone by the Rock'n'Roll Hall of Fame, which inducted him posthumously in 1989. It was Stu that booked Charlie Watts's band, Rocket 88, into the Bridge and, as far as I knew, he managed them. Stu was a great guy. He got Mick Jagger and Keith Richards to come to the Bridge to support Rocket 88. I spoke to Mick, who said he really didn't like this kind of music. He did get into the crowd, and watched and listened for a while, but then came back to us at the bar.

I believe it was at Paul Jones's first birthday of the Blues Band, which turned into an almighty jam session, that I first met Ian Stewart. He had played piano during the jam session so I knew he was somebody. I could hear he was a brilliant pianist. There were so many faces there that night, you tend to forget the rest of the band. We knew it was a birthday and Rita had made a beautiful cake with loads of other food, like she always did. Even the customers at the end would be catered for; she's a wonderful woman. She is still the same now with the family and friends and next door's dog and cats, the squirrels, the birds, the dustman, even the foxes turn up sometimes to see what's on the menu. (She has just looked over my shoulder and seen what I have written. She has informed me I've got to get my own dinner!)

Anyway, on this night at the Bridge, Ian came up to the bar where we were having a few drinks after the gig had finished. He introduced himself, thanked me for the gig, then said, 'I'm looking after a band called Rocket 88. It's a jazz band with a difference.'

I said, 'We've never had a jazz band down here before. I don't think it will go down very well, unless, of course, the band has got a following.'

'We've done a few gigs,' he assured me. 'And the crowds have been good.'

'OK.' I said. 'We'll give it a try. Let me know who's in the band and we'll advertise it.'

We exchanged phone numbers then got back to our drinking.

Later on, I was having a drink with Hughie Flint and asked him who Ian Stewart was.

'He's known as the sixth Stone,' Hughie replied.

'*The Rolling Stones?*' I asked, a bit surprised.

'Yes.'

I questioned him a bit more. 'Do you know anything about a band called Rocket 88?'

'Yes. That's Charlie Watts's band. He plays in that when the Rolling Stones are off the road.'

I was standing there amazed. Looking for more information, I enquired, 'Who else is in the band?

'Oh,' Hughie said casually, 'Jack Bruce, Eric Clapton, Zoot Money. There's always too many to play.'

Taken aback, I said, 'Excuse me, Hughie, I must find Ian.'

I searched high and low but he was gone.

The next morning, I looked for the bit of paper Ian had written his number on. As usual I couldn't find it. So a day or so later I was delighted to get the call from him.

'As it happens, I have got next Saturday free,' I said.

'No, that's too quick,' he said. 'They're rehearsing some new numbers.'

It was a bit complicated but we sorted a date out that suited us both. I gave a sigh of relief. It very rare to get major stars in your pub. In the West End, there's a bigger chance but, out in the East End, in those days, it was rarer than a Maggie Thatcher apology.

Sadly, Ian Stewart died of a heart attack at the much too tender age of 47.

CHARLIE WATTS AND ROCKET 88

The first gig was not as packed as we had thought it would be. It might have been a very good crowd, knowledgeable, as all jazz fans are, but a Rolling Stone at the Bridge! I was surprised when none of the Rock crowd turned up. It just shows you, people only watch what they are into. We began to think that, even once you get established, it's the music, not the names, that fills a pub or any gig for that matter. We'd first noticed this when Chris Thompson came down for the first time. He started off OK, but after a few months it was really packed, two nights a week. Like Chris, Charlie was to play many times for us and pull a good crowd.

One night, when he was getting ready to play, Ian came over to have a drink with me and said Mick and Keith were coming down to see Charlie's band tonight. I didn't get too excited, as we had had this before. Chris Thompson and Stevie Lange had been working with Elton John on an album and he had promised to see Chris at the Bridge. He phoned and said, 'I'm at Aldgate East. I've changed my mind, and I'm so near the West End, I've got to see a pal.'

Another time Glen Matlock was playing. He'd been in the studio the night before with Iggy Pop and David Bowie. Glen told me Iggy and David were coming to the Bridge that night. The band had just finished their set when I took a phone call asking what time Glen's band the Spectres were starting. I told the young lady that he had just finished. She asked, 'Can someone talk to him?'

I said, 'Yes. Who is it?

The voice said, 'Tell him it's Iggy.'

Glen told me they were on their way. If I had known this when the girl rang up, I would have told them to come to the pub, that Glen was just starting his set. I would have let them play no matter what time it was. What a jam that would have been! Ex-Sex Pistol Glen, Iggy and David. I refused to answer the phone any more in the evenings after that.

But on this night, about 10 minutes after I'd been talking to Ian, the doors burst open and in came two of the biggest fellows you have ever seen, followed by two beautiful blondes of model stature. It might have been Jerry Hall, his future wife, but I didn't ask. Then Mick Jagger and Keith Richards entered. It was just like a film set! The minders in first to check the place out, then the girls, then the stars.

And nobody noticed!

Well, the band were playing and I was the only person who knew that they were coming. Keith went backstage with a minder and the girls. I called Mick over to the bar where I was standing with Ian, who introduced me and I bought him a drink. We got chatting about music, and I asked him if he liked Charlie's music. He was honest, saying, 'No. I think it's really boring. We only came down to give him our support.'

He asked me what it was like running a pub in the East End.

I said, 'It's great, as long as you stay sober during hours and obey the law.'

We laughed, and he said, 'Different to what I've heard. The drinking you and Charlie have been doing.'

We were both laughing and he started to dance. I put my hand on his shoulder and told him, 'One of the laws we have to obey is "no dancing allowed", so please stop.'

He couldn't believe that, with the music and dancing licence we had, which was costing about £600 a year then (it's about £10,000 now), customers were not allowed to dance, and I explained, 'The only dancing allowed is on stage.'

'I'm not going on there!' he said and carried on dancing.

We had a laugh and another round of drinks. After the drink,

Mick said he wanted to go to hear and watch the band. He went down to the bottom hall and leaned against the wall and listened.

Hardly anyone recognised him. A couple of people even came up and said, 'I see Mick Jagger's brother is here tonight.'

When the gig finished, I tried my best to get them to do a number or two. No way! But in the dressing room we had an upright piano that my cousin John Davies had given me when he left the Essex pub. Mick started playing it. Charlie picked up the guitarist's guitar. They only fiddled with one number but I can at least say three of the Rolling Stones played the same night at the Bridge, and it was four with Ian!

Mick invited us all out to the Venue in Victoria. Charlie said, 'No. Me and Terry are staying here having a drink.'

I was up for going with Mick but I couldn't let my new pal Charlie down.

Charlie told Mick, 'I'll see you later.' Then he said to me, 'There's no way I'm going. They won't be home till nine o'clock in the morning and then they'll still be looking for somewhere else to go.'

They all stayed at the Bridge until 1am then off they went to the Venue, taking one of my barmaids with them. She was full-time at the pub but she didn't return for two days. On her return, she told me she went to this lovely big house on the Embankment and enjoyed herself for a couple of days. She said, 'There was a crowd of us, partying.'

I didn't enquire any further!

Charlie and I had another hour together, then off he went home. Charlie Watts was always the first member of the band to arrive, and he got friendly with my son, Lloyd, who used to let him in and keep Charlie company. After his chauffeur dropped him off, Charlie would unload his drums and set them up himself, not a roadie in sight. His chauffeur would return and wait until Charlie was ready to leave. I think that once a person becomes a star the thing they enjoy most is the chance to be ordinary now and again, even if it is only for a few hours. This is where 'chill-out' Charlie was a wonderfully ordinary star whose company it was a pleasure to be in.

In fact, after 50 years of service at the Savoy, the doorman there was asked who of the great and the good was the nicest person he had met while tending that legendary port of the rich and famous, and, without hesitation, he replied, 'Charlie Watts.'

CHAS & DAVE AND NOT FORGETTING MICK

Chas, Dave and the often neglected drummer, Mick, came to the Bridge to play for me when my cousin John Davies left the Essex pub in Silvertown Way and moved to another pub in Wanstead. While at the Essex, they were doing really good business for him. He had them on Friday, Saturday and Sunday every week, as a residency. They had been there a couple of years and heard that I was recording and putting records out, as well as managing bands. So John fetched them to the Bridge House and introduced them to me. Over the previous year, he had said a number of times that I should come and see them, although I never did because I felt that it would have affected his trade if I took them and, truly, as they had been playing there so long, for no charge on the door, I wondered if customers would now pay to see them at the Bridge.

John asked me if I was interested in managing them, but I said, 'No.' I was very busy and did not want to go down that route. I said, 'When you move to the new pub, I will give them a few gigs here.' And I did.

They played many times for us and were sensational. At the time, I didn't think they were Rockers, but after talking and listening to them I knew different. They had all been in Rock bands in the early 60s and they really could rock.

MORE MUSIC (AND THINGS) PLEASE!

About a year later, the band told me that they had recorded an album and that Bob England was going to manage them. I was pleased for them. Their album became a number-one hit and stayed in the charts for ages, making them and their management company big profits. Another missed opportunity for me! But Bob did a really good job – fate is fate.

Another coincidence with Chas & Dave was that my brother Mick, who at that time was managing the Cock Tavern, in High Street North, East Ham, used to have a regular band called Fred 'n Dell. Our cousin John had asked Mick to find him a band, so Mick lent him Fred 'n Dell for a short period, giving them a rest from the Cock customers. They were great, pulling a good crowd for John at the Essex. After a month or so, Mick said to John, 'I've got to have them back at the Cock.'

John said he'd had to have a band or he'd have no customers, and Mick told him that he'd heard about this duo Chas & Dave, in Bethnal Green, and they both went to see them. John liked them and took Chas & Dave to the Essex Arms. Mick got his Fred 'n Dell back and Chas & Dave (and Mick) went on to stardom.

We made a record later with Fred and it sold really well. Chas & Dave recorded a live double album at the Bridge House. They booked two nights; the place was packed on both nights and did they work their socks off! They rocked, they rolled, they fell over with exhaustion. Three hours each night, without a break! Real pros … the three of them.

Chas & Dave got their rewards though. The album was a really big seller and they got another record, the highest-paid band to play at the Bridge! One hundred per cent of the door takings.

I still see them. They played the Albert Hall a little while ago. I was there and saw them backstage and all three of them looked great. For all of us, the boozing days are over. We sat there drinking Perrier water and had a laugh. At the Bridge, it used to be booze until sometimes three or four in the morning. But, as they say, 'It's no good getting old, if you don't get wise.'

PAUL YOUNG

Paul first played for us in a group called the Streetband in 1979. He then went on to form the Q-Tips and asked us for some gigs to get the band known, so he could get a record deal. I told him it would take at least six months. The band agreed to give it their best shot, and most of them were already known to me from when they played in a band called Screemer. I was very friendly with Matt Irving, Dave Flett, Bernie Clark, Steve Bolton, Laurie Latham and Mark Pinder.

At the time, Dave Flett was Manfred Mann's guitarist, there was talk that the hit song 'Davy's on the Road Again' was dedicated to him and the antics he got up to while on the road with the Manfreds. It became a number-one hit record in the UK and the USA. I can vouch for the drinking days, nearly as good as me and Matt Irving.

From the original band Screemer, Zaine Griff, Matt, Mark and Dave Flett formed a band called Special Branch. Later, Vampire Batt was formed by Steve Bolton, Bernie Clark, Matt Irving, Mark Pinner and Laurie Latham. Laurie was to become a top record producer. Nearly all these guys joined Paul Young and after that they could be seen playing with Jools Holland on his TV show.

Paul quickly got a record deal. Even in the 70s a good voice got you through the door first. He was with the Q-Tips when they released an album in 1980. The line-up was Paul (vocals), Ian (the Rev) (keyboards), Barry Watts (drums), Mick Pearl (bass), Tony Hughes (trumpet), Steve Farr (baritone sax, backing vocals) and Stewart Blandarmer (alto sax, backing vocals). This is not the band I remember, apart from the Rev (Ian) who was the guiding force behind this band and the band I got to know. A lot of them were also in the Streetband that played for us a few times. At the time they were playing for us, Chas & Dave were regulars and were quite annoyed when Streetband brought out their hit single 'Toast', as they said it was a rip-off of 'Rabbit Rabbit', Chas & Dave's hit single.

The intended A side 'Hold On' wasn't great. A DJ somewhere found 'Toast' on the B side and began giving it air time. Soon this ditty about the wonders of eating toast was a Top-20 hit, peaking at number 18. The drummer with Streetband was Vince Chaulk, who had been the 'man with the sticks' in Mr Big, who had got a Top-5 hit in 1977 with 'Romeo'.

In the year after 'Toast', Streetband released another four singles and two albums without success. Just before the end of the 70s, they split and Paul Young and Mick Pearl formed the Q-Tips. The Q-Tips had a great reputation for their live shows but no commercial success. They split in the summer of 1982 and Paul decided to go solo. The rest, as they say, is history.

(This type of infighting that happened between Chas & Dave and Streetband is very common. If we, the ordinary people, hear a punchline of a song on the radio, we hum it and sing it without thinking. Musicians are no different. They hear a chord or a riff, they rearrange it and use it, sometimes without even realising they have done it. Former Beatle George Harrison had a number-one hit with 'My Sweet Lord', which was a rip-off of 'He's So Fine', composed by Ronald Mack and performed by the Chiffons. This dispute ended up in court. Bright Tunes, who owned the copyright to 'He's So Fine', received $587,000 when a judge ruled that Harrison 'subconsciously plagiarised' the song.)

Paul Young, even in his early days had trouble with his voice.

We booked the residency with Q-Tips and got to work building the band. After a month and just four appearances, we had a really good crowd of customers. At least 200 to 250 were turning up.

Then it happened! On the day of a gig, Paul's manager rang to tell us Paul couldn't do the gig because of a bad throat. From our point of view as promoters of the gig, this was the worst possible scenario. It's too late to stop the customers coming and when they turn up and find out that he's not playing they go home, even though we always had a back-up band to fill in.

But, of course, it was disastrous for Paul being the vocalist and trying to make it into the big time. This throat trouble was to happen on a few occasions. Paul had to cut down on some of the gigs, as he was playing at least three times a week. However, we were pleased when he stopped doing the other gigs and carried on playing the Bridge.

At the end of their six-month period, the Bridge would be packed to the rafters and we were delighted when he moved on to the major venues and became a star.

He is still gigging today and he sounds better than ever. My son Glen has met him a few times since the old days and they were recently on holiday together. Good luck, Paul!

SCREAMING LORD SUTCH

We had the pleasure of Screaming Lord Sutch at the Bridge House. I first met him when we gave him a gig at the Bongo, a club I owned in Barking Road, Canning Town, which my brother John used to manage. Sutch had only just started then but he caused havoc nevertheless.

He came early on a Saturday afternoon, the day of the gig, wearing a leopardskin cloak and a mask. John took him over to Rathbone Street Market (just across the road) and he spent a couple of hours running round frightening all the girls.

Someone called the police and they tried to arrest him. John intervened and told them it was a publicity stunt, but the cops still said, 'We'll have to arrest him.'

While this was happening, Sutch ran up the road where his brother Jim was waiting to collect him in the car. Jim had to put his foot down but they got away. They all met John at the club later and he had sorted it out. This was Lord Sutch, a complete nutcase!

That was in 1960. When I got him back in 1980, I thought he might have changed; but of course not! He was just as bad. During his act at the Bridge House, he lit this long pole after he had dipped it in petrol and ran around the bar chasing customers. He set one girl's dress alight and another girl's hair caught fire. Luckily, we had a fire blanket at hand and my son Glen smothered the flames (good training for his future work on *London's Burning*!). It was also lucky we knew the two girls who were members of local band Minnie Ralores, and a visit to the hairdressers and new dresses, plus a month of gigs, sorted it out.

Screaming Lord Sutch of the Monster Raving Loony Party, who stood for Parliament at every general election over the last few campaigns, committed suicide in 1999. Such a pity. He always lived on the edge. Things got bad and sadly taking his own life was his way out.

THE BRAKES

The Brakes were a really good band. They were all very experienced players, having performed with other bands. And, even as they formed this band, Bob Renny was still playing in Lonnie Donegan's band.

The Brakes' nickname was the 'Gants Hill Noise', as they lived in that part of West Essex. Their music was fast non-stop Rock, and they can be compared to many other bands; they were like Tom Petty, the Byrds, even the Beatles. The singer, Joe Fadil, was the image of Bruce Springsteen facially, although he was smaller in stature, and his energy on stage was formidable.

While playing at the Bridge, they got their record deal with Magnet and their first album was almost a hit. If a major had released it, with the marketing and promotions, it would have made it. Magnet were a good company but, in 1979, the organisation was still in its infancy, and they were relatively new at the marketing and distribution side of the business. But I am also sure that a major would have changed the title name which was 'For Why You Kicka My Donkey?'! But there's a great cover of Dylan's 'Like a Rolling Stone' on it. Their single off the album was 'The Way I See It', and the drummer, John Brown, was praised for his progressive play. It should have got more radio time, but that's how it goes.

The dual vocalist was Keith Wilson, who later fronted his own band. Today, Joe has his own tribute band – guess who? Yes, 'The Boss'! Joe's version of 'Born in the USA' is unbelievable.

Joe and Bob would always turn up for the Blues jams and have a blow. Joe joined Paul Ballance and Paul Jeffreys's new band after Warm Jets changed their style and line-up. The band were called the Pope, but alas their prayers were not answered. Today, Paul Ballance is a born-again Christian who devotes all his spare time to working with the Church and has recently formed a record company for new bands. He plays his music on Sundays, that's his gig nowadays. You have to work at getting gigs these days, eh?! Good luck, Paul!

MAGNET RECORDS

Michael Levy, the owner of Magnet Records, used to come to the Bridge regularly. He did well for a lad from Stoke Newington, and he is now Baron Levy, although he is the guy who was recently questioned about bungs for honours. Chris

Rea said of Levy, 'He is extremely tough, one of the hardest bastards I have ever met, but I would leave my children with him rather than anyone else.'

Music producer Pete Waterman said that Levy was 'the greatest salesman I have ever met. He would be able to sell sand to the Arabs.'

When Magnet was sold and merged into Eastwest Records in Britain, Levy started M&G Records (after Michael and his wife Gilda) supported by Polygram, which was taken into the main Polydor Records label in 1997.

Following the sale of Magnet Records, Levy got involved in fundraising for Jewish and Israeli causes, and between 1988 and 1994 he raised £60m for Jewish Care (he is now President of this organisation). Yep, Hackney Downs Grammar School did a good job with Micky boy.

PARK AVENUE, THE PARK

This band did quite a few gigs for me and I thought they had the chance to make it into the big league. Everything was done to the highest order. Firstly, they had a guy behind them who knew what had to be done, Martin Levett. He managed and promoted the band with fliers, posters, ads and continuous phone calls. He really worked for them. I suspect he also financed them; well, it is the manager's job.

They had two front singers, Michael St James and Beverley Jay, and, if I remember correctly, they were a seven-piece band. They also had a very good guitarist in Alan Reveille. This was more of a show than a Rock gig. They were not a Rock band. The singers were nicely dressed and there was a lot of harmony in the vocals, although they were both lead vocals on their individual songs. I don't know if they ever got a major deal, but they used to put out cassettes of their live work and a 7" single was released in 1983 called 'The Singer', although I don't remember how it did. They also recorded a live set at the Bridge once.

They never really won over the Bridge House regulars, who were more into Rock and Blues. However, they did build a nice following and, if it wasn't for the fact that they played for us at the end of the Bridge's heyday, they probably would have ended up making a live album for Bridge House Records. I would have been up for that.

On our last Christmas at the Bridge in 1982, I got a Christmas card from Martin Levett and the band. They had read in the *Melody Maker* that I was thinking about closing the Bridge and they offered their services to try to keep the pub open. They finished the letter by saying they had enjoyed their stay at the Bridge House.

I gave them a few more gigs for this kind thought. I hope it helped them.

HOWARD JONES

Howard became a regular at the Bridge House doing support slots. When John McGeady told me Howard came from High Wycombe, I thought, 'Bit of a waste of time. There'll be nobody here to watch,' but then I thought, 'High Wycombe!' I had spent many a day in my younger years during the war, when we lived there with my aunt Nora and uncle Bill Gates. (In fact, some of the family think there's a connection with the Microsoft multi-billionaire, as their grandfather left his family here in England in the early 1900s and went to Australia; he later moved to the USA and after that they had more no news from him ... be nice, wouldn't it?) There were six Gates and six Murphy children, plus the parents and other aunts and cousins who came from the Smoke, all living in the same house. Never a dull moment!

I really did think of all this before telling John I'd give Howard a support gig. There was only him and his brother in the band so they would not take up too much time and space. I was pleasantly surprised when they arrived. They turned up with a coachload of fans, I think about 30, so this was a good start. And what a good performer, a really hardworking talented musician. We gave him quite a few support gigs, before some headliners, and he would fetch his coachload for every gig. If I remember correctly, I think it was his brother who dressed up in chains or something like that, and was used as a prop.

When we left the Bridge, we continued to give Howard gigs at Merlin's Cave and I was delighted when I saw he had made it with some hit records and major tours. Well done, Howard! Anyone with real talent generally has more than one chance to make it. But who knows? If I had not been evacuated to High Wycombe in the war, I would not have given Howard a gig and he might never have been discovered.

I read an article only this week and it said that Howard and Ringo Starr were flying around America in their own jet plane, and it seems they are working together, which is great, isn't it.

BILLY BRAGG

In the final year that we were at the Bridge House, Glen's acting career used to take him away for work and, when he was chosen to appear in a play, *Oba Futervarda*, in Stratford with a four-week run, we had to fill his Tuesday theatre night, which he had been producing and acting in. At the same time, we were overrun with tapes from hopeful bands and had to have regular tape-playing sessions, so we decided to combine the two and came up with the talent contest night, and one of the finalists was an unknown singer called Billy Bragg.

Billy told us that he had been to the pub a few times before but, being a solo artist, he hadn't asked for a gig because we were band orientated. He had seen the advert for the contest in the *NME* and decided to enter. When he told us he was a local boy from Barking, we put him up the front of the playing list.

For the contest, we would put the tapes out over the PA. The bands would come to the pub to hear their tapes and we had a jury of well-known musicians to judge them.

We finally got down to 12 tapes and booked the bands to play live, three bands a night, and the winner of each night went through to the final. Billy Bragg was the winner of the semi-final. Eventually, the four finalists played and I had never seen anyone so happy as Billy Bragg, but he lost in the final, coming second.

As this was in our last year at the Bridge House, the next time I saw Billy was after we had moved to Merlin's Cave. We had stayed in touch and, when we booked Roy Wood, the bearded wonder of Wizard and the Move, as the headline act for the launch of the new venue, we gave Billy the support.

This was going to be a big night. Roy Wood, we thought, was still a big name. We booked him from an agency owned by an old friend, Kenny Lynch. Well, Roy Wood arrived, all the agency people were there and Wood stayed for about 20 minutes. He informed his agent that he wasn't going to do the gig and left.

We were in a real state. We had advertised a big name to try to get the new venue off the ground. Now we had egg on our faces and Billy was there waiting patiently. I walked over and said, 'Sorry, Bill. The gig's been cancelled and we're not opening the theatre tonight.'

Billy really went into one: 'Leave off! Let me play. I got management and record companies coming to see me. This is my big chance.'

I felt really sorry but it was just not economical to open. We'd have staff in an empty hall costing us money when we would not be taking any.

But then Billy came back, nearly in tears, pleading with me to play. 'I don't want no money, nothing. Just let me play.'

I relented. This was a local boy trying to make it. I had to give him his chance.

He went on stage at 8pm and played without a break for three hours. He had the audience shouting and screaming. This, I believe, was the making of Billy Bragg. He was sensational. That night, he signed a management contract and a little later a recording contract.

When Roy Wood swallowed it, we left all the doors open while Billy was on stage so the punters knew they did not have to pay and, of course, once they heard Billy, they stayed. So we did take a few quid. And Billy Bragg got what he wanted and some money to go home with.

Today, he is a big star. However, while writing this book, I continued to contact his company, who kept saying, 'Yes, Billy would love to write a page for your book.'

I have been waiting three years and I am still waiting. It seems some people have short memories.

And not forgetting ...

WILLY FINLAYSON

Yet another good singer/guitarist, Willy Finlayson played for us many times and was also discovered by Manfred Mann who auditioned him at the Bridge, and signed him up to join his band. He continues to perform and has a fantastic voice. Willy's influence was the Blues, but he can make any Rock song sound good with his soul-singer style. His major musical markers are Ray Charles, Donny Hathaway and Robbie Robertson of the Band.

Willy was born close to Edinburgh and was a gifted footballer.

At 17 he had trials for Falkirk and spent a month with Newcastle United. But he was just 13 when he started performing, singing with musicians much older than himself in Scottish band the Dukes. Willy has been settled in London for over 20 years. In the 70s, he sang and played with Bees Make Honey and Meal Ticket, and in the early 80s he recorded with Manfred Mann's Earth Band on the *Chance* album.

DENNY NEWMAN

Denny Newman, a best pal of producer Colin Barton (both from Brentwood), also played for us. He started writing songs and Manfred Mann released one of them on an album. Next thing he was the guitarist in Manfred's band. Denny is still playing with his own Denny Newman Band.

Have you noticed how Manfred Mann's name keeps coming up? But it's not too hard to work out why when you remember Chris Thompson, his lead vocalist and guitarist, was playing twice a week at the Bridge House. Chris just passed the word on and Manfred would come down when he was looking for new band members.

Manfred's original vocalist, Paul Jones, was also playing for us. When Manfred was looking for someone to replace Chris, who wanted to leave and go to America with his new band, I said to Manfred, 'What about Paul? He's still got a great voice.'

He looked at me and said, 'No. You keep him!'

ERIC BELL AND MITCH MITCHELL

Eric Bell, who played plenty of gigs for us, was Thin Lizzy's original guitarist and, from my point of view, one of the best. When you listen to him playing on some of the classics like 'Whisky in the Jar', it is hard to fault him.

I recently heard a John Lennon interview and he mentioned that Mitch Mitchell had played in his band at Hyde Park, when Mick Jagger had the gig there.

Mitch Mitchell, from the Jimi Hendrix band, also played many times at the Bridge. He's a great drummer. He has recently been 'using the brushes' with Keith Emerson; it's a natural move. The bands that they are in become successful, then break up. All the guys have still got to make a living, so they form their own bands. Starting again. They do what they do best and play music.

Gary Moore played a great set here in a jam session. He also formed his own band and played the Thin Lizzy all-time favourite 'The Boys are Back in Town'.

It's a pity Phil Lynott never survived. Another Rock'n'Roll disaster. But if he had lived, who knows? All these guys would have stayed with him and might never have come to the Bridge House, with new bands.

DUMPY'S RUSTY NUTS

Dumpy's Rusty Nuts are another good fun band who started at the Bridge House. The first time I met them they were the road crew for the Blues Band. Paul Jones introduced me to Dumpy (and he was) and we started chatting. He told me he was thinking of forming a band. He said, 'We're all frustrated Rock stars, that's why we started our own PA-rental company. We set everything up and look after the bands, so we're not just roadies.' (A little dig at me for calling them the road crew.) He said they were rehearsing their band and would be ready soon.

I said, 'Well, you have got your own PA system so that will save a few quid.'

He rang me back about four weeks later and I gave him a gig. They were really good and played for us many times.

THE BLOW MONKEYS

The Blow Monkeys, who went on to chart success, played many support gigs with Roy Weard's Last Post, before they headlined here. They had a Top-20 chart hit with 'It Don't Have to be This Way'. Roy had been the front man in Dogwatch, with the Blow Monkeys' manager John Trelawny, who played the flugelhorn and euphonium (I know!) plus the violin, trumpet and vocals. Need I say he was the leader of Dogwatch? Roy later joined Manfred Mann as a road manager and sounds man.

POWER PACK AND SNAFU

Bobby Harrison was a great favourite at the Bridge before I took over. The customers were always asking me to get him back. He had gone on to have some success with his band Snafu, so I was delighted when someone introduced me to him. He had come to see one of the bands playing. I asked him what he was doing and he told me that he did not have a band at that time. I asked him to get a jam together, but he said he had been out of the scene for a while and lost touch with people.

'Leave it to me,' I said and within a week I had contacted all his old playing partners.

Some told me politely to 'buzz off', and some weren't so nice, but we soon had plenty of his mates together. I phoned him and he said he would be delighted to have a romp.

'Oi, oi,' I said. 'None of that here!'

'Wait and see!' he said, and, on the night, well, I have never seen so many lovely girls … well, ladies really.

The jam was a great night. There weren't that many people but at least I buried the ghost of Power Pack, who had become legends playing four nights a week at the Bridge House for almost four years before I took over the pub, and I'm sure Bobby had a good night. He used to play with the Isadore brothers who were also his best mates and great musicians. They always turned up for him.

BERNIE TORME

Bernie came from Ireland with a big reputation as a good guitarist, and visited me to ask for a gig. After he had formed a band, we gave him an audition and liked him, so we decided to give him all the help he needed. He played a few times and we introduced him to Gerry McAvoy who gave him some interesting things to work on. This was good for Bernie who, like almost every Irish musician who ever lived, was a Rory Gallagher fan.

Bernie gave it a try for about a year in his own band, without any major success. He was then offered the chance to join Ian Gillan's band. Ian had just left Deep Purple, where he had been the lead vocalist, to form his own band Gillan. He was a great front man. He already had a major record deal and a big tour of Europe was planned. So, in the middle of summer 1979, Bernie folded his band and joined Ian in the studio. The album they recorded went really well and was a good seller.

Bernie has played guitar for Ozzy Osbourne's 'Blizzard of Oz', Atomic Rooster and Dee Snider's Desperado, and has fronted his own line-ups Electric Gypsies and Torme. He now has a new band not long off the launching pad, Guy McCoy Torme.

ELKIE BROOKS AND VINEGAR JOE

Vinegar Joe played the Bridge. The band included Robert Palmer (guitar, vocals), Pete Gage (guitars, piano), Steve York (bass, harmonica) and Elkie Brooks (vocals). Gage, Elkie's first husband, came down and told me about the band; he was involved with our publishers, Martin and Coulter, and I think he may have fronted his own band at one time.

RED DOOR RECORDS

Terry Hewitt and son, who later started Red Door Records in Woolwich, used to promote gigs. We both had some success when we started the picture disc series of interviews with major stars in the mid-80s, but we fell out over record production. We were trying to build up the pressing plant we had bought and were too busy sometimes to press the picture discs. Needless to say, deadlines were missed, rows started and friendships ended; a real pity.

Terry was a good photographer and took many good shots of Wasted Youth. His photos have been used on many album covers including some for Bridge House Records. He was very good at setting up the proofs and doing the artwork.

THE NEVER NEVER BAND

Neil Brewer (bass and vocals), Dane (he never used his surname but it was Jeffires) (guitar), Paul Fulford (keyboards) and Bryan Fitzpatrick (drums). They formed this band after playing in the Druids. They still played 'Painted Clouds', the only Druid song in their set, but their Reggae-type style never pulled a crowd, even though we gave them a residency. I admired them because they were trying something different from the norm. I did ask them to drop the title of one of their songs, which was called 'Taking Pills'. They still play it, without mentioning the title, but this was 1979 and New Wave was on its way: Psychedelic, New Romantics and Mods.

RONNIE GOLDEN (AKA TONY DE MEUR)

Ronnie Golden was always good value. He played for us as with the Fabulous Poodles, a pre-New Wave band formed in 1975, and sold more records in the United States in 1979 than the Clash. Known for quirky stage antics (such as exploding ukuleles), Ronnie appeared as a solo artist at the Merlin's Cave. In June 2001, I read in the *NME* that he was compering a gig.

The Clark Gable look-alike Bobby Valentino (violin) looked great. He now has two gold records, one from Tom Petty & the Heartbreakers, 'Pack up the Plantation', and one from Billy Bragg, *Talking with the Taxman about Poetry*. He is still a session muso and recently toured with Big Country and Mark Knopfler. These days Bobby is with a band called Los Pistoleros, which also includes BJ Cole and Martin Belmont. It's an Americana-style band and they recently released a CD called *Trigger-happy*, which has had its share of radio play. Bobby occasionally works as a Clark Gable look-alike and has been in many TV ads and played the great man in the film *RKO 281*. Once an artist, always an artist.

Our American friends

JOAN JETT

Joan Jett was introduced to us by her American producer Kenny Laguna in 1981. She came down and played a really raunchy set, pulled a nice crowd and came back and repeated the performance a few weeks later. She was over here recording an album, and she gave me a preview tape of it. Kenny got really into the pub scene at the Bridge getting me offers from America for our record product. He also produced an album for the Roll-Ups when Bill Curbishley signed them up.

THE TRAIN

The Train, an American band that played for us, were a real Heavy Rock band that turned up straight from the airport, no transport, carrying all their instruments and belongings; there were about eight of them, no money, nowhere to go and starving hungry. How they found us I will never know.

But they played a great set, wined and dined at the Bridge, and stayed a couple of days, sleeping on the stage. I gave them another gig and paid them the money upfront to help them out. They were touring Britain, and I wondered if they would forfeit the new engagement. I was not all that confident so I had a replacement band ready to step in, but, credit to them, they were hungry and tired but they played another great set, stayed the night and off they went. This was real American Rock'n'Roll. I hope these guys went on to bigger and better things. They deserved it.

HUEY LEWIS

Clover was the band that featured Huey Lewis, as the lead vocalist and harmonica player. They were not really suited for the Bridge, playing a kind of Country music. Huey used to come down and jam when Chris Thompson was playing. We would chat a lot while Chris was playing the first set. I would not let him pay for any drinks, as I realised he had no money anyway. When Rita fetched the food down, we always made sure he was looked after.

One night, he said, 'Terry, you are the boss and I am going to call you that.'

I said, 'Call me Terry.'

'No,' he said, 'you're the boss and I will never forget you.'

(I wonder now he is rich and famous if he remembers me. I'll find out one day.)

One day while we were talking, Huey told me he had a gig at the Nashville Rooms in Hammersmith and he really needed to pull a good crowd as a record company were coming down and they had done some big promotion with the music press. The next morning we hired a coach and filled it up. My son Lloyd was driving. Huey was really pleased and grateful to see us. When he came on the stage he pointed at me and said, 'You're the boss.'

Clover didn't work out for him. He went back to the States and formed Huey Lewis and the News and has had many hits. He is now a movie star, having featured in Gwyneth Paltrow's film called *Duets* and in *American Psycho*, and many others

LENA LOVICH

Lena's 'Lucky Numbers' was the most requested record in New York City in 1979–80. She was very quaint and had a smart punky look with a very catchy voice, which she used for her rendition of 'Lucky Numbers' as part of her set at the Bridge House a few months before. It was a very up-tempo sound with screaming in part of the act.

STRAY CATS

After the New Romantics, we moved on to the next big thing, which was Rockabilly, a faster-played version of the original Rock'n'Roll music of the 50s – Bill Haley, Little Richard, Gene Vincent and Elvis, and our own Tommy Steele, Marty Wilde and Joe Brown. We designated Wednesday nights for this. It went well, although very rowdily. This New Wave Rockabilly was a mixture of the old and the new Punk Rock which was fading out. I came in one night and the ceiling was red and, on a first look, I thought it was blood! My son Terry, who was in charge that night, quickly assured me that it was just part of a band's show and there had not been any trouble.

One day we got a phone call from an agency telling me all about this band called the Stray Cats who had just arrived from

America and were looking for gigs. They already had record deals. The Stray Cats' line-up was Brian Setzer (vocals), Slim Jim Phantom (AKA Tommy Lee) (small drum kit, snare, hi hat, bass drum) and Lee Rocker (upright bass).

We booked them for the Wednesday and they were really good, a three-piece with the old upright bass. They could really move. They had a few verbal rows with the audience, which I chose to ignore thinking, 'Flash Americans, trying to impress!' In fact, I liked them so much that I booked them for the next Saturday night, which was vacant, as I'd had a pull-out.

But then that week's *Melody Maker* came out and it had an article about fights every time the Stray Cats played. I had read that there was a gang out to get them and I thought, 'It's not going to happen at my place!'

The Saturday came and first to arrive were Hells Angels, who the band had hired for security. Having the Angels with them, the band were being outrageously flash, and actually picking trouble with the customers. The Hells Angels did not help, as they couldn't make their employers appear in the wrong (they couldn't have a go at the band who was paying them) so it was a horrible night. I had booked the Cats through their agent for a residency for the next three weeks but told them to forget about coming back to the Bridge. I said, 'You're sacked!'

They really went into one, the singer being the main culprit. He insulted me, and wanted to fight me. So I said, 'Come on, outside.'

He was a boy to me. I would have been about 46 years old and he was probably 20. We went outside to the garden, but the Hells Angels came to his rescue by stopping me from hitting him. I would have just slapped him, and put him in his place.

The drummer, Slim Jim (AKA Tommy Lee), ended up

marrying *Baywatch* star Pamela Anderson. He was all right; it was just the singer really.

The band did well in the UK, then they went back to America, had some hit records and are still around today. Perhaps the singer has grown up at last.

GIRL BANDS

We had many girl groups play at the Bridge, from Punk to Heavy Metal: Sadista Sisters, Amazulu, Tour de Force, Girls School, Diana Wood and the Avengers, the Alsatians, Minnie Ralores, Gymslips, Jane Berek (the Page Three girls came down), Linda Lewis, Androids of Mu, Carol Grimes, Dolly Mixture, Pin-Ups, Kim Lesley and the Spotons, Jo Ann Kelly, Shattered Dolls, Honey Bane and Top Hat all played the Bridge.

SADISTA SISTERS

The Sadista Sisters were a four-piece girl band that we first saw was at the Kings Head in Islington, where Rita and I had gone to see a play. It was our night off from the pub and we wanted to get away from music, but the girls were on first, before the play, so it was more music. I quite liked the band and Rita thought they were unusual; we were always on the lookout for something a bit different.

The promoter had told them that I was in the audience, so we went backstage and agreed to give them a gig at the Bridge, which they were really pleased about.

When the gig came round, it was good but never pulled a crowd. Some of their songs were – for want of a better expression – near the bone. The band had done OK for themselves, getting on the main gigging list and some TV but, to make it big, you have got to have the hit record. If you don't, you just fade away.

AMAZULU

Amazulu were made up of about eight girls. They were exciting, having a fast Reggae sound. They got themselves a record deal and had a few hit singles. They came back and played for us when they had made it, which is always nice, and it was a busy night. When they first played for us, as with all young people, they were always arguing and shouting at each other; consequently, they didn't last very long together. They came back as a six-piece, but this didn't work either. A few months later, they were only four of them, then they would pop up with a solo single. But that's the music biz.

They are still making a living playing today.

TOUR DE FORCE

This was a band I thought would make it. They got a deal and released a single that made the charts. They had a chart record and made a number of albums. After they did a few support gigs for us, we headlined them and gave them a run of gigs, and they managed to pull a fair crowd in the end.

I guess the problem they had was that their music was just too melodic. Although it bordered on the Heavy side, back in those days, there was no in-between; you were either a Rock band with more vocals or Heavy Rock with the long solos and riffs.

GIRLS SCHOOL

Kim McAuliffe (guitar), Enid Williams (bass), Kelly Johnson (lead guitar) and Denise Dufort (drums) were always good value; a Heavy, New Wave type of band, they made a refreshing change from our other Heavy long-haired brigade. They first played for us as Painted Lady (no Kelly Johnson at that time and Deidre Cartwright on drums). I still have a picture they gave me to advertise their gigs.

After a successful solo career, Toyah Willcox joined them in a new band called Strange Girl. These days they are back touring as Girls School.

DIANA WOOD AND THE AVENGERS, THE ALSATIANS

Diana Wood, a great sax player, fronted this avant-garde-type band, doing their best to be a bit different. Alan Draper was a good songwriter, and I think we published some of his work. I remember one song he brought to me, it was called, 'See You Around', written by Draper and Stockley. He also wrote songs for Top Hat 79, another band Draper was involved with. He wrote 'Our Man in Marrakesh', 'Teen Romance', co-wrote 'Sweet Yesterday' with Stockley and 'Social Insecurity'.

MINNIE RALORES

Minnie was outrageous, a really good trier. Minnie and the other two girls in the band, Sue Scott and Hope, wrote one of their favourites, 'I'm No Monster'. It was Minnie's hair Screaming Lord Sutch set on fire when she helped him out with his set. Alan Draper also wrote 'Crazy', for Minnie Ralores.

My son, Darren, bought Sue Scott's bass guitar, which was his first of many musical instrument he acquired.

GYMSLIPS

Rachel, Paula and (I'm guessing) Kim were a three-piece band who were really good. They toured with the Undertones. I remember there were some problems with the band. They took the place of TV Smith who had done a couple of gigs but were replaced by the Dolly Mixture, musical differences being the cause. The Dollys took their chance and went down a storm.

After this, they were due to sign to Paul Weller's label. They came back to the Bridge and Rachel said to me that they liked playing gigs there a lot better than the larger venues.

The first time they played, they supported 21 Guns. The evening was billed as a Reggae evening, but who the Reggae band was, I don't know, as we rarely had this type of music in the home of Rock.

JANE BEREK

A French act, Jane came with a big reputation. She was very good but never pulled a crowd. I remember original Page Three girls Nina Carter and Jilly Johnson came down to see her play. They then formed a duo themselves, and they were asking all kinds of questions about how long the set runs for, etc. They were preparing themselves to start gigging and Jane was showing them the ropes. However, they never asked us for a gig. I think their presence was a bit too 'wobbly' for our stage!

LINDA LEWIS

Linda was a big star when she came to the Bridge and jammed a few numbers with Remus Down Boulevard. Her family had the Red House pub in Barking Road, about a 10-minute walk east from the Bridge House. It was her brother, Keith, who played bass for RDB when Steve Gough electrocuted himself.

ANDROIDS OF MU

What a name! An all-female Punk band formed by a couple of the backing singers from the Here & Now. They played an energetic, rage-fuelled feminist/sci-fi set, including such gems as '(I don't want to be a) Boring Housewife'. They didn't have much in the way of technical ability but made up for this with their originality and songwriting talent, which had all the necessary trademarks of Punk. They had a Reggae/Blues style and an infectious sense of humour.

CAROL GRIMES

Carol Grimes and the Crocodiles would later become the Carol Grimes Band. Carol had a great vocal sound and was a big favourite at the Bridge. Maciek (Magic), the guitarist with Warm Jets, later joined the band.

DOLLY MIXTURE

Another great name! They were a New Wave band formed in the last part of the 1970s by Debsey Wykes (bass and vocals), Rachel Bor (guitar) and Hester Smith (drums). Legend has it that they got involved in the music business as they were girlfriends of some of the members of the Damned, but they were quickly acknowledged in their own right as one of the most talented New Wave acts. They made it into the Top 40 singing backing vocals for Captain Sensible's hit 'Wot', but, as a band, they never broke through. I can't remember them playing; I must have been on my night off. What a sweet band by all accounts!

PIN-UPS

This was another all-girl group, but the name has since been taken by a very Punk-orientated band who didn't start until the mid-1990s.

KIM LESLEY AND THE SPOTONS
They never let us down – a good, hardworking 12-piece/three-girl band.

JO ANN KELLY
Sister of Dave Kelly, the Blues Band's guitarist and vocalist. Jo and Dave had a band together for a while before forming their own individual bands. Sadly, Jo Ann died too young in 1990 at the age of 46. Paul Jones said of her that she was 'unquestionably the queen of British Country Blues singers'.

SHATTERED DOLLS
This Glam Punk band included Jaki Florek (vocals) who later joined Sharon & the Slobz and Adams Family. The Dolls made 'Lipstick Killers' (1980) which got to number 20 in the indie charts and was Mike Read's Single of the Week on his Radio 1 Saturday show. The Dolls gigged regularly, including a UK tour with Gary Glitter before breaking up in 1982.

HONEY BANE
Honey Bane (Donna Tracy Boylan) was a Londoner born in 1964. At the age of 14, Honey formed the Punk band the Fatal Microbes, who released a split 12" record with anarcho-Punk band Poison Girls in 1978. Her first single was 'Violence Grows'. Fatal Microbes split after about a year and Honey started to work with Essex-based anarcho-Punk activist band Crass, after a stay in a juvenile detention facility and while on the run from the Social Services.

1980 was an eventful year for Honey: providing lead vocals for Donna and the Kebabs; Crass released the EP *You Can be You*; she sang vocals for post-Punk band Killing Joke on 'What's the Matter' at the Venue club in London, later included on the album

Killing Joke – Live At The Venue LP; and she met Sham 69 vocalist Jimmy Pursey, who started to manage her. She was signed to EMI/Zonophone Records for a five-year contract. 'Turn Me On Turn Me Off' was released in 1981 and got to Number 30 in the British charts and Honey got to appear on *Top of the Pops*. That single marked a musical departure for Honey – no longer an overtly Punk Rocker, she had become distinctly New Wave.

Honey released more singles, but without any chart success. She appeared in a play opposite Richard Jobson of the Skids at London's Arts Theatre during 1982 and the following year she played Holly in *Scrubbers*, a Mai Zetterling-directed British film about the lives of young women in a girls' borstal, alongside such fine actors as Amanda York, Kathy Burke, Pam St Clement, Robbie Coltrane and Miriam Margolyes.

Honey became a pin-up model for erotic magazines for the rest of the 1980s. In the 1990s, she fronted Dog's Tooth Violet that saw themselves as a melodic alternative metal band. In 2006, she released a two-track 7" single entitled 'Down Thing'/'Got Me All Wrong'.

Honey now lives in Florida, USA, and is a grandmother.

THE POETS

JOHN COOPER CLARKE

John played for us a few times. Although he was called a poet, I would say he was a musical poet with a comic edge. He came from Liverpool with a bad reputation for drug abuse, but the producer Martin Hannett told me he had really cleaned up and asked me to give him a chance – although it seemed Martin, who had come down from Manchester to produce the Wasted Youth single 'Rebecca's Room', had problems of his own in that line, and he acquired an almost legendary reputation for Rock'n'Roll excess; he finally died of heart failure in 1991 at the age of 42.

John soldiered on and is still gigging today. Life's funny sometimes.

PATRICK FITZGERALD

Patrick was another to come through the poetry type of music. He came to us, like John Cooper Clarke, as an already established artist. It was very nice to book him because he was a school friend of my sons. The school was St Bonaventure's in Upton Lane, Forest Gate, which I had also gone to. In 1949, I became the first Great Britain schoolboy boxing champion from the school (a little plug for me, for a change).

Patrick was a very aggressive Punk poet and on stage he provided a lively night's entertainment. A few times he had to leave by the back door, but such is fame, and he wanted to be controversial. We booked him because he was a local; and it was nice to see one of our own make it.

Patrick had an EP out in the 70s called *Safety Pin Stuck in My Heart*. An album by the same name is available with 31 tracks. Some of them are particularly evocative of life around Canning Town and Rock'n'Roll, for instance, 'Work Rest Play Reggae', 'The Bingo Crowd' and 'All My Friends Are Dead Now'.

UNSUNG HEROES OF THE BRIDGE HOUSE

For me, the heroes of the Bridge House were the bands who just would not give up. Some got record deals that did not work out, while some never even got a deal, spending 20 years of their life gigging all over the country, summer and winter, in the back of transit vans, hoping for that magic something that would transform their lives.

Every song they wrote was going to be the one that would make it. I have got thousands of demo tapes that had been sent to me. They are little treasures. The hard work that went into making them is immeasurable. When listening to them, I often start to wonder about the talented bands that never managed to break through. Of course, they may have formed other bands or joined others. I hope some of them did. You can be a really talented musician or a great singer, but you have got to get the breaks and have that thing called 'luck' on your side.

Once we received a tape in the post, we would start getting

the phone calls asking for a gig. Basically, if we liked the tape, we would give the band an audition gig.

On one quiet night, we had a band get together (not really an audition more of a 'try-out'). They arrived for the audition looking good. The front man was over six foot tall, well dressed in leathers, really looking the part.

After the first band finished, I gave them a shout five minutes later. Ten minutes later I gave them another shout. 'What's happening?'

'Sorry. We're not ready. Another five minutes.'

I told them to forget it, they're out of time.

'Oh please! We're ready.'

On they go! The band starts to play. The singer is gripping the mike as if it's stopping him from falling. He misses the cue. They start again. Three times this happens. One more time the band start. The singer starts, stops, starts crying his eyes out. 'I'm sorry. I just can't do it.'

He was frozen to the spot. He didn't even jump off stage, just stood there crying.

I ran over, grabbed his arm, pulled him off stage, took him in a corner, gave him a brandy and said, 'Don't worry, this happens a lot.'

Of course, it didn't; in fact, it was the first and only time it ever happened, but I was consoling him. I felt really sorry for him and the rest of the band. I told the next band to go on and told them if they wanted another go an hour later it was OK. He started to cry again. They stayed in the dressing room all night. At the end of the night, the pub was empty. I told them, 'Get up and do just one number without the singer.' They started to play. After about a minute up he jumps and he was really great. This fellow, who I will not name, is today one of the top acts in the world.

We've had bands that can't play but had good singers and good bands with awful singers. We've had good and bad bands with no singers. Many people have asked me why, with so much talent around, I never created a band. I could have and, at different times, I had, say, the vocalist from one band asking me to get him into another band, as he felt that the band he was with wasn't going to make it. Maybe the songs that they were playing didn't suit his vocal style or he didn't get on with the drummer or bass player. These two might have run the band and/or had formed it in the first place and as such they can't be chucked out. So, when another band came to me looking for a singer, I would pass the names on, but not before the singer had told his band that he was leaving. Then I would attempt to find another vocalist for the band that had lost its singer.

It would have been easy for me to watch about 20 bands and pick five or six members to form a new 'super' band. They might have been great musicians, writers and singers but they would have to live and work together and it is very hard to get guys or girls with big egos to listen to each other. Within a week, they could be killing each other. It takes a long while for a band to gel together, but, when they do and if the talent is there, you've got a successful band on your hands.

I believe that we always treated the artists in the best of ways. We never cheated them out of the genuine percentage of the door and the word gets round; Chris Thompson opened the door; Gerry McAvoy got Rory Gallagher to come to the Bridge; Gerry McAvoy's Jams were also a major move forward. When RDB were touring with Status Quo, they wore our new T-shirts with the Bridge House blasted across the front. We even had our own matches made with the Bridge House on the labels. We advertised in all the music papers – *Melody Maker*, *NME*, *Sounds*, *The Face*, the 'Ad Lib' column, written by John Blake in the *Evening Standard*, and we got our records played on the radio. The first play we got was of our *Live – A Week At The Bridge E16* album, RDB's 'Only For You' with Dennis Stratton on vocals. He sang a good number but Dave Edwards was a great singer, although they always shared the songs in their set.

Wasted Youth were also getting big radio plays on Radio 1 with John Peel and Radio 2 with Dave Edmonds, as well as all the independents throughout the country. The colleges and universities always asked for records and put them on their playlists. It all helped.

CONCLUSION

The Preface to this book gives you an idea of the type of problems we had to endure on a daily basis at the Bridge House. You are a publican first and foremost and you have to ensure that, as we used to say, 'The ship's ready to sail', meaning that the pub is clean and tidy, the pipes and optics are all clean, the beer is at the appropriate temperature, your cellar is stocked up and the pub is well staffed.

So get the doors open and be ready to take money! It's no good having a pub full of customers if you haven't got the staff to serve them and take their money. Equally, it is a big downer when you think you're going to be busy, you lay on plenty of staff and not many customers turn up, which has happened to us when we least expected it. You have still got to pay the staff whether you're busy or not. This is where having a big family comes in handy. If you're busy, call them down; if quiet, give them the night off, so the family only get paid when they work.

The licensing laws were really strict in the days when the Bridge House was in its prime as a music venue, so we had to be careful when having a bit of afters (drinking after the permitted licensed hours), which we did every night. We were lucky at the Bridge, as we were on a quiet road with no houses or neighbours to worry about. If the police did come in, I would say that I was giving the band a free drink because they had been working all night. Providing they never actually saw you taking money for the drinks, the police could not charge you and, if they came in the early hours, either the van had broken down or the band had been repairing their equipment. The police knew what was going on, but we never ever called them out, as we always handled our own troubles, and they never had to keep coming round answering 999 calls. So really they just forgot about us; out of sight, out of mind.

In reality, we did have some really good afters, three or four in the morning nearly every night whenever Gerry McAvoy, Matt Irving, Dave Flett, Chas, Dave and Mick, Rory Gallagher or Charlie Watts were in town. There were many others, but if I mention them all I will never get this page finished!

A different band every night also meant new faces and new drinking pals. However, having many late nights meant that we had to have a good back-up team to make sure the pub was up and running in the morning. And we were lucky enough to have one. I inherited the cellar man, Dave, from my brother John, and my aunt Maggie O'Neil's sister, Rose, and her friend were the cleaners. Being family, Rose had her own key to let herself and her mate in, so as not to disturb us.

The pub was not all that busy at lunchtimes, and we would just have one barmaid on. My wife Rita, as always, was there to provide the food and do everything she was not meant to do. I used to say, 'That's their job, let them do it.'

She used to say, 'By the time I tell them what to do, I can have it finished myself.'

She always led by example, my dear wife Rita.

So, after breakfast, with everything under control, I would go straight to the office to book as many bands as possible. The adverts had to be in, at the latest, on Fridays for publication the following Thursday in the *NME* and *Melody Maker*. The free gig lists were even earlier. The 'Ad Lib' page in the *Evening Standard* was a daily print, so that was very important, and they needed 48 hours' notice. This was a free ad entry, as was *The Face* and all the local papers. We usually paid out about £100 per week in advertising costs to get into the music magazines. If you advertised the up-and-coming bands, then the major bands wanted to play. Everyone in the record business reads these journals and, if they keep seeing the same names, they assume they must be good enough to be asked back. This would make the PR men come to see them.

The benefit of advertising for us was that you would get a few write-ups for the pub and the bands. This would make the gig that bit more important. The large amount of interest we were getting from the press and record execs was one of the reasons I started the record and publishing companies in 1978. I have always enjoyed a new challenge and this was the year we recorded and released the *Live – A Week At The Bridge E16* album. It was not an easy project. I had to see lawyers and accountants to get the limited company up and running, as well as contracts for the bands to sign. Thankfully, Bernard Brown from our publishers Martin and Coulter got the contracts together for me. I was delighted to give them to the bands who took them away to read. Needless to say, I didn't get them back for months, the main excuse was, 'Sorry, Terry. When I was reading it I spilled my beer over it. Can I have a new one?' The next most common pretext was, 'Yes I read it, Terry, and I passed it on to the rest of the band.' I would ask who had got it and, of course, they couldn't remember.

There were six bands totalling 31 artists involved with *Live – A Week At The Bridge E16*, plus managers, roadies and helpful friends. I printed 100 copies. The contract was very fair, with no options for new recordings. Chris Thompson had protected his flock of musos. He had read it first and included the clauses to protect the bands. But in those days contracts frightened the artists. The main reason for this was that they were all hoping the album was going to be a smash hit and they wanted to be free in case they were offered a major recording deal. Chris Thompson was already signed to a major company, as he was the lead singer in Manfred Mann's Earth Band, and he signed, so they should have followed their leader. I was however delighted with the finished product, which showed a profit over the years. At least I got my outlay back and, if anyone has got a copy now, they're worth £50 each. When this book comes out, they will probably be worth a lot more, so hold on to them tightly.

WHERE DID IT ALL GO RIGHT?

Well, it certainly went right for six years, but, by the end of 1981, all the bands that were making it on to the next step of the ladder to 'stardom' did not have to put all the hard work in that the Rock bands had done in previous years. The Rock bands in the early 70s had to tour the country in the back of vans, playing anywhere that would have them, working for peanuts. This is how they learned their trade, not just learning to play together, but also understanding how songs were arranged, how to use their vocals to the best of their ability, when to hit the high and low notes. Many times, they would just turn up in a town and go round looking for a gig to play. What they did required unsurpassable guts and belief in themselves and this is what kept them going when they were hungry or cold and wet on the winter nights or boiling hot in the summer in the back of a busted-up old van. The golden pot was the few quid they had to save for their diesel or petrol, food came next. Sometimes, knowing all this, I decided to make a difference.

So along came places like our Bridge House. We would book them through agencies, lay the sound systems on for them, agree a fee, give them drinks and plenty of food after the gig. We'd also advertise them in all the music papers, giving them the chance to get record companies down to see them. This, for the good old Rocker, was heaven.

For example, we would pick out a band we thought had it all and work on that band for as long as it took. Sometimes it would take two years before they reached their peak and maybe still no record-company interest. This would not worry us because by this time they would have built up a big following, so they got well paid and we would sell plenty of beer; we were all happy!

Unfortunately for the Rockers around this time, Punk had just run its course and all the New Wave bands were coming through. It was so much easier for them, mainly because they did not have to have all the heavy equipment: no drums, a small machine instead, synthesisers in place of keyboards. In fact, all the equipment would fit in a car boot and the band in the car seats. By this time, pubs like the Bridge would lay on a house PA system, so, when they started, they did not even need roadies, all they had to do was plug in their drum machine and synth and they were off. Most of these bands never even had a guitar player.

Please do not think I am biased in any way. Not being a musician, I used to watch all the bands and enjoy every minute, whether it would be Heavy Metal, Punk, Rock, New

Romantics, whatever. When watching, I knew the amount of work they had to put into every song, and so I'd listen for a mistake that they would make, a bum note, singing/playing out of tune, things like that. I sometimes mentioned this at the end of a gig. By my doing this, they thought I knew all about the music business but I just guessed most of the time. But this kept them on their toes and they knew they couldn't cut any corners while the old fraud was around.

At the end of 1981, our biggest success that year was Depeche Mode. They had played for us for less than one year, and were heading for the really big time. I was so pleased for them. As a New Wave band, they did have it a lot easier than the older Rock bands, but they still had to put in untold hours of work rehearsing, writing and arranging new songs; you don't get anything for nothing in whatever you do in life.

This was also Wasted Youth's best year, with non-stop touring all over the world, although they were having trouble with new songs, mainly because they were too busy to rehearse and arrange them. By that time, they were too well known to play the Bridge House, so the only way they could play for their loyal fans would be secret gigs.

It was also in 1981 that we had Rory Gallagher play for us in an advertised gig. Sensational. Bridge House Records released four albums and six singles! We were all so busy that the venue itself began to fade; remember we were having 14 bands a week playing, two per night, with auditions at lunchtime on Sundays. There were also Glen's plays, talent contests and battle of the bands – something had to give!

And the main thing that gave was our regular bands – and they were irreplaceable; Depeche Mode, Wasted Youth, Filthy McNasty, the Roll-Ups, Remus Down Boulevard, Chas & Dave, Stan Webb's Chicken Shack, Blind Drunk, Tony McPhee and the

CONCLUSION

Groundhogs to name just a few. They were now successful and on a bigger stage; and you could not find bands to take the place of such quality acts who had worked for us for years.

I said earlier that the new bands didn't have to play for a year or so to build up themselves and an audience for us. Well, sometimes they literally would not even have to do a gig. Some even made their demo tape in their bedrooms and took it to a record company who would sign them up on the strength of the demo. They would then get them to do one or two gigs to see what they *looked like*, not how they *sounded* on stage.

For me, that was unbelievable and marked the end of an era. We were still getting the bands coming through who would make it; they would play once or twice for me and the next time I would see them would be on *Top of the Pops*; Soft Cell are a prime example.

Our audiences were built on seeing a band at the start of their career, liking them, getting behind them, being there for every gig, wherever they played, letting them know what songs were going down well or badly; and they would tell them. This was called 'feeding of the audience'. In a sense, the audience and the band were involved in the same project. And it certainly did the trick for a load of my regular bands, whether they were Heavy West Coast Rock, Mods, Punks, Oi bands, Skins, harmony bands or Blues bands.

By the early 80s, this was happening less and less. Currently, you cannot see a band once and like them. You might say, 'Yes they were all right.' Which would mean you would go and see them again. And I think togetherness is a great word, a great thing. You might get it from being a football supporter, a boxing fan, following speedway, etc. but what all people have in common is they want this 'togetherness', the togetherness when you are watching your band or your team, and sharing the feeling with everyone watching with you. It is a feeling that is hard to replicate and we feel better for it; it makes us feel more alive. Even when you lose, you're all in it together, and you know how each other feels. It's mass empathy; an antidote to the loneliness that sadly seems endemic in the modern world – the biggest killer on the planet.

So, with all this in mind, I was still working hard all day. I was sorting the record company as well as managing Wasted Youth, and a few other bands. Previously my big buzz had been going downstairs at 9pm to see one of my bands; the old butterflies in the stomach. But, at that time, I was going to see bands I didn't even know and, because of this, I didn't know any of the punters either, as only a few of the regular diehards would come to see the new bands. They knew they wouldn't be back next week, so why bother?

The word went round: 'The old pub's a bit quiet, might close.'

Depeche Mode by 1982 were one of the biggest bands around, and they booked the secret gig to help us out. Next, Chas & Dave make the call. Chris Thompson, Rory Gallagher, Remus Down Boulevard, Blind Drunk, Salt, Jackie Lynton (he got paid), Park Avenue, Wasted Youth (my band) and there were others as well. An agent phoned and said they would play for expenses only – £1000. They played, the agent got nothing and the band got paid by me, bashed over the head, ha ha!

But this was just not me. If I do a day's work, I want paying for it, and the band are no different from me; it's hard work. So they get paid.

I also thought that I needed a change and a rest. I had taken up playing golf again and was starting to enjoy being lazy. They say seven years is long enough at any one venue, and nearly all my regular bands had gone on to have success. By that time I had very successful record and publishing companies, so I was doing OK.

CONCLUSION

One day, my son Glen came in and said, 'I got you a house to move into.'

I said, 'Buy it.' And four weeks later we moved in.

So now I wasn't even going to the pub in the week, and was only there from Thursday to Sunday. The rest of the week me and my son Lloyd played golf at Bellus Park. (In one year, Lloyd got down from a 12 handicap to 4. I started at 28 and in the same time … stayed at 28! There's progress! My mate Terry Harris has persevered with me and I'm down to 18 – only 20 years on!)

In July 1982, a couple of old boxing pals came in for a drink, Dennis O'Callaghan and Roy 'Pretty Boy' Shaw. I had sparred quite a bit with Roy during our boxing days, who at that time was a welterweight (10st 7lbs). Today he is a big, fit healthy heavyweight (14st). Dennis was a really useful featherweight (9st) from Dagenham.

Dennis and Roy were partners in a pub in Shoreditch, and Dennis had a deal for me. He said, 'Don't get out the game, I own the Merlin's Cave in Islington. It could be a lovely music venue. Have a look.'

A few days later I did just that, and Dennis was right; it was a good-size pub, with a big hall alongside.

Dennis had a manager in there at this time and his plan was for me to double his takings, and he would then sell the pub and the building which he owned. He said, if I could do that, I would get 20 per cent of the sale price. (Coincidentally, one of Dennis's drinking partners, whom I met during our negotiations, was the father of Vince Clarke (Depeche Mode and Erasure), and Vince was supposed to do a gig for us at the Merlin's Cave. Posters were put up all over the pub, but he never showed up.)

I called Courage Brewery and put my notice in. I found them a customer who bunged me for putting a good word in;

well, my mate Johnny Whincup found the punter, so we all ended up happy.

I left the Bridge House in August 1982 and moved to the Merlin's Cave in Islington, a free house, in September 1982. I got all me old mates (bands) back playing for me. Within a year, I had *trebled* the takings, and Merlin's Cave was sold within the next year. Pity it only lasted a year.

During my time at the Merlin's Cave, the band and I agreed to break up Wasted Youth. At this time they all needed a break as they had continued to play all over the UK for three years and we felt they should look for pastures new.

Darren has not played in any bands since Wasted Youth finished in 1983, but he has stayed in music with his own label and pressing plant which he ran with his brother Terry. Our record-pressing plant in Stratford E15 closed in 2003.

The Bridge House was razed to the ground in 2002 to make way for a flyover and the extension of the A13. After we left, it became a nightclub, then a hotel.

These days, I play golf twice a week and run my website www.theBridgehouseE16.com with Jeff Ellis, my good friend from the Bridge House days. We are keeping the old Bridge House alive, never to be forgotten.

EPILOGUE BY STEVE HARRIS

The following was written on Sunday, 18 January 2004 while Steve was in Sao Paolo, Brazil, on Iron Maiden's Dance Of Death World tour.

Ah, the Bridge House! Now most Iron Maiden fans will know and think of the Ruskin Arms as the most important pub in Maiden's early career, but, in some ways, a pub called the Bridge House was just as important and influential, as it was here that Maiden played many of its earliest gigs, even before we ever played the Ruskin. In fact, even before Maiden was formed in 1975, I played the Bridge House in two other bands. I played there for the first time in 1973 in my very first band, Gypsy's Kiss. We were a Hard Rock band formed from schoolmates and other friends, and we only played the Bridge House three times, and did only two gigs at another East London pub called the Cart and Horses before we folded after just five gigs together. Musical differences of course! And then I joined a band called Smiler, a Rock Blues band, and did quite a few gigs around London with them, including a few at the Bridge House in 1974 before leaving to form Maiden in 1975 (not 1976 as most people believe!).

The Bridge House was very important to Maiden's early life. Having played there in two previous bands, it was a goal of ours to play there on a regular basis. It was an important place for us and other local bands and friends. It was a buzzing place at the time in the local Rock community and became an important gathering place for us to make our plans while checking out other bands who were ever present on the happening Rock scene of the time. I remember from my diaries that we were paid £15 for our first gig (not each, for the whole band!) but this was the going rate at the time for a Monday night and some pubs even charged bands to play.

The guv'nor of the Bridge House when Maiden played there was Terry Murphy, a big affable ex-boxer who took no nonsense and therefore we hardly ever saw any trouble in the place. It was a hard but safe place to go (unlike many other pubs) and had an exciting atmosphere. The Bridge was a strange place in some ways, stuck right next to the Canning Town flyover with an unusual configuration for a Rock venue as it was split into two levels with the bar running along the middle of the pub on the upper level opposite the stage and very close to it, so that, when you were on the stage, which was very wide, but not at all deep, you felt like you could almost lean over and shake Terry's hand at the bar! Of course, the gap was bigger than that but, even when the place was jam-packed, there were still only a few rows deep of crowd between the stage and bar. I always remember Terry leaning on the bar when not serving, watching the band and ringing the bell for last orders like a town crier! God knows how he could hear the customers, he must have had ear plugs in, but he didn't complain too much about the noise level!

Terry used to let us get changed into our stage gear in a cellar downstairs, just off to our left of the stage, and was generally very helpful, except at one point when we had to take a break from live performances to replace yet another member of the band who had left for the usual 'musical differences' reasons. It took a while to find a replacement and rehearse him in, and, when I approached Terry for a gig at the Bridge House again, I was told that we would have to go through the process of starting again on a Monday or Tuesday night which were his audition nights usually. We would have to graduate up to a Thursday again and would only get a Friday- or Saturday-night spot if he had a cancellation. While this was probably fair enough, we had a very large following and I remember having a moan at him because, as I pointed out, we could pull more people on a Monday night than some of his bands could pull on a weekend. But obviously that was to his advantage so he remained adamant and stood his ground, so we ended up playing the Ruskin Arms on weekends instead! We were a bit put out and regarded it as his loss and told him so. That was the only time we ever had cross words.

The Ruskin was run by another ex-boxer and a relation of Terry's called Joe Lucy. In fact, Terry's son Glen was also a young up-and-coming boxer at the time we played the Bridge House and I remember him coming into the pub with his kit after training while we were setting up our gear getting ready to perform. Glen was also a very nice affable lad, who later went on to become an actor known for playing a key part in regular TV series *London's Burning*. Glen became a star and a few years later formed a celebrity and ex-West Ham Football XI to play charity matches which I was invited to play in many times. So, I have still kept in touch with Terry and Glen over the years and they have still remained the very nice down-to-earth people I knew from all those years ago. Terry really helped Maiden at a very hard and important stage of our career and kept the Rock scene alive in East London for a long time and I thank him heartily for it.

Cheers, Terry!

Steve Harris

DISCOGRAPHY

BRIDGE HOUSE RECORDS
Bridge House singles

BHS 1.	Warm Jets	Sticky Jack★/Shell Shock
BHS 2.	Rebel	Rocka Shocka★/ Drift Away★
BHS 3.	Tickets	I'll Be Your Pin-Up★/ Guess I'll Have To Sit Alone★
BHS 4.	Gerry McAvoy	Streetalk★/Many Rivers To Cross
BHS 5.	Wasted Youth	Jealousy★/Baby★
BHS 6.	Roll-Ups	Blackmail★/Hold On★
BHS 7.	Crunch	2 B B-Side The See Side
BHS 8.	Crack	Silly Fellow
BHS 9.	Repton Boxing Club	Jab And Move★/ The Hook★

BHS 10.   Wasted Youth   I Remember You★/
                                 My Friends Are Dead★

BHS 11.   Johnny Holliday   You Are The Power/
                                 Dub Power

BHS 12.   Wasted Youth   Rebecca's Room★/Things★
BHS 13.   Wasted Youth   Wildlife★/Games★
BHS 14.   Wasted Youth   Reach Out★/Gone
                                 Midnight★

BHF bee1. Wasted Youth   Do The Caveman★
VC.001.   Darken   This World★/Stormy
                                 Weather

VC.002.   Chris Thompson   Strangers In Paradise/
                                 See You In Paradise

Bridge House albums

BHLP.001 Various Artists   *Live – A Week At The
                                 Bridge E16*
BHLP.002 Dogwatch   *Penfriends*
BHLP.003 Various Artists   *Mods Mayday '79*
BHLP.004 Roll-Ups   *Low Dives For High Balls*
BHLP.005 Gerry McAvoy   *Bassics*
BHLP.006 Wasted Youth   *Wild And Wondering*
BHLP.007 Wasted Youth   *Beginning Of The End*
BHLP.008 Wasted Youth   *Inner Depth*
BH.009   Wasted Youth   *Memorialize* (singles
                                 collection)★

WY100   Wasted Youth   *Live*
BHCD.009 Wasted Youth   *Memorialize* (singles
                                 collection)★

DISCOGRAPHY

Bridge House DVD

BH DVD.01

*Survivors. Wasted Youth Live
at the Bridge House
1980/81★*

★ licensed to Bridge House Publishing

Most of the Bridge House record collection is now
available on CD.

INDEX

INDEX

INDEX